DATE DUE

FREEDOM AND DESTINY

FREEDOM
AND
DESTINY

by

Rollo May

W · W · NORTON & COMPANY

New York · London

Copyright © 1981 by Rollo May. Published simultaneously in Canada by George J. McLeod
Limited, Toronto. Printed in the United States of America. All Rights Reserved. *First Edition*

Library of Congress Cataloging in Publication Data
May, Rollo.
    Freedom and destiny.

    Includes index.
    1. Autonomy (Psychology)   2. Liberty.
3. Fate and fatalism.   I. Title.
BF575.A88M39   1981   158'.1   81–4009
ISBN 0–393–01477–0   AACR2

W. W. Norton & Company, Inc. 500 Fifth Avenue, New York, N.Y. 10110
W. W. Norton & Company Ltd. 37 Great Russell Street, London WC1B 3NU

1 2 3 4 5 6 7 8 9 0

Contents

III

IV

V

VI

Two: Mistaken Paths to Freedom

VII

VIII

Three: Characteristics of Freedom

IX

Four: The Fruits of Freedom

XIII

Foreword

This morning a friend and I canoed out on a perfectly still and silent New Hampshire lake. The only ripple on the water's surface came from a great blue heron as it languidly took off from a patch of water lilies and headed for some secret spot farther into the swamp, undisturbed even by canoes. Amid this serenity, which seemed to cloak the lake and forests and mountains with a preternatural harmony and peace, my friend surprised me with the remark that today was Independence Day.

Whatever noisy celebrations were going on seemed far, far away from this quiet world. But being in New England, one could not keep from one's mind the images of lanterns being hung in the belfry of Old North Church, Bunker Hill, and the shots, fired by New England farmers, destined to be heard round the world.

Political freedom is to be cherished indeed. But there is no political freedom that is not indissolubly bound to the inner personal freedom of the individuals who make up that nation, no liberty of a nation of conformists, no free nation made up of robots. This book seeks to illuminate this inner personal freedom underlying political liberty. When I mention political liberty in the following pages, it will be generally as illustration.

This personal freedom to think and feel and speak authentically and to be conscious of so doing is the quality that distinguishes us as human. Always in paradox with one's destiny, this freedom is the foundation of human values such as love, courage, honesty. Freedom is how we relate to our destiny, and destiny is significant only because we have freedom. In the struggle of our freedom against and with destiny, our creativity and our civilizations themselves are born.

Rollo May

July 1981
Holderness, New Hampshire

One

The Crisis of Freedom

I

The Present Crisis of Freedom

*The true end of Man . . . is the highest and most harmonious develop-
ment of his powers to a complete and consistent whole. Freedom is the
first and indispensable condition which the possibility of such a development presupposes.*

—KARL WILHELM VON HUMBOLDT

"Freedom's just another word for nothin' left to lose."
—K. KRISTOFFERSON AND F. FOSTER, *"Me & Bobby McGee"*

It is a startling fact that freedom has been considered,
throughout human history, so precious that hundreds of thousands of human beings have willingly died for it. This love of
freedom is seen not only in venerated persons like Giordano
Bruno, who died at the stake for his freedom of belief, and Galileo, who whispered to himself in the face of the Inquisition that
the earth *does* move around the sun, but it is also true for hosts of
people whose names are forever unsung and unknown. Freedom
must have some profound meaning, some basic relation to the
"core" of being human, to be the object of such devotion.

Many people still assume that they and their countrymen
should be ready to die for freedom. This feeling typically takes
the form of patriotism. Other persons who would not agree that
political freedom is worth dying for would nevertheless state the
same thing about psychological and spiritual freedom—the right
to think and to command one's own attitude free from the 1984
type of spiritual surveillance. For reasons that are endless in their
variety and that are demonstrated from the beginning of history

3

down to the freedom marches and freedom rides of this century, the principle of freedom is considered more precious than life itself.

We have only to glance at the long line of illustrious persons to see that, in the past at least, freedom, in the words of Henrik Ibsen, was "our finest treasure." Jean Jacques Rousseau was profoundly impressed by the fact that people will "endure hunger, fire, the sword and death to preserve only their independence." About freedom he continues: Human beings "sacrifice pleasures, repose, wealth, power and life itself for the preservation of this sole good."* Kant joined in the defense of freedom against those who argued that the terror of the French Revolution showed that the masses of people were unfit for freedom. "To accept the principle," wrote Kant, "that freedom is worthless for those under one's control and that one has the right to refuse it to them forever, is an infringement of the rights of God himself, who has created man to be free."

Similarly Schelling made a passionate defense of freedom: "The whole of knowledge has no status if it is not supported by something which maintains itself by its own power," and "this is nothing but . . . freedom." Again, he writes, "Philosophy . . . [is] a pure product of a free human being, and itself an act of freedom. . . . The first postulate of all philosophy, to act freely

---

*A long line of people of wisdom have held that the capacity for and degree of freedom are the distinguishing qualities of the human being in contrast to other animals. Rousseau, I believe, oversimplified the problem of freedom in his creation of the "noble savage" and when he stated "man is born free, and everywhere he is in chains." Nevertheless, he had some profound insights. He scorned the presumption of those who attempt to explain human nature with the same mechanics they use for animal nature. The latter "cannot account for man's freedom and consciousness of his freedom."

The difference, Rousseau continues, is "that nature alone does everything in the operations of the beast, whereas man contributes to his operations by being a free agent. The former chooses or rejects by instinct and the latter by an act of freedom . . . it is not so much understanding which constitutes the distinction of man among the animals as it is his being a free agent. Nature commands every animal, and the beast obeys. Man feels the same impetus, but he realizes that he is free to acquiesce or resist; and it is above all in the consciousness of this freedom that the spirituality of his soul is shown." This is cited by Noam Chomsky, *For Reasons of State* (New York: Vintage, 1973), p. 392.

in its own terms, seems as necessary . . . as the first postulate of geometry, to draw a straight line. Just as little as the geometrician proves the line, should the philosopher prove freedom." In other words, the truth of freedom is self-evident; that is an inalienable right.

Though we shall later consider the empirical definitions of freedom, it is noteworthy that Schelling believed that freedom was axiomatic, that even to think and talk presupposed freedom, and hence no proof was necessary. The capacity to experience awe and wonder, to imagine and to write poetry, to conceive of scientific theories and great works of art presupposes freedom. All of these are essential to the human capacity to reflect. Indeed, in the same vein as Schelling, an intellectual of the modern day, Sir Isaiah Berlin, remarks: "Almost every moralist in human history has praised freedom."

Why these unending and extravagant panegyrics? Why should freedom be so venerated, especially in a world where practically nothing else is granted that devotion?

1. The Uniqueness of Freedom

To answer these questions we need to understand the uniqueness of freedom. Every other reality in human experience becomes what it is by its nature. The heart beats, the eyes see; it is their nature to do what they do. Or, if we take something inorganic like values, we know what the nature of truth is—e.g., to state things as close to the reality as possible. And we know the meaning, or the nature, of the value of beauty. Each of these functions in the human being according to its own nature.

What, then, is the nature of freedom? It is the essence of freedom precisely that its nature is *not* given. Its function is to change its nature, to become something different from what it is at any given moment. Freedom is the possibility of development, of enhancement of one's life; or the possibility of withdrawing, shutting oneself up, denying and stultifying one's growth. "It is the nature of freedom," Paul Tillich declares, "to determine itself."

This uniqueness makes freedom different from every other reality in human experience.

Freedom is also unique in that it is the mother of all values. If we consider such values as honesty, love, or courage, we find, strangely enough, that they cannot be placed parallel to the value of freedom. For the other values derive their value from being free; they are dependent on freedom.

Take the value of love. How can I prize a person's love if I know the love is not given with some degree of freedom? What is to keep this so-called love from being merely an act of dependency or conformity? "For love can take concrete shape only in freedom," writes Jacques Ellul. "It takes a free man to love, for love is both the unexpected discovery of the other and a readiness to do anything for him."

Take also the value of honesty. Ben Franklin proclaimed his alledgedly ethical principle, "Honesty is the best policy." But if it is the best policy, it is not honesty at all but simply good business. When a person is free to act *against* the monetary interest of his or her company, that is the authentic value of honesty. Unless it presupposes freedom, honesty loses its ethical character. Courage also loses its value if it is supposedly exhibited by someone who is coerced into it.

Freedom is thus more than a value itself: *it underlies the possibility of valuing; it is basic to our capacity to value.* Without freedom there is no value worthy of the name. In this time of the disintegration of concern for public weal and private honor, in this time of the demise of values, our recovery—if we are to achieve it— must be based on our coming to terms with this source of all values: freedom. This is why freedom is so important as a goal of psychotherapy, for whatever values the client develops will be based upon his experience of autonomy, sense of personal power and possibilities, all of which are based on the freedom he hopes to achieve in therapy.

Freedom endlessly re-creates itself, gives birth to itself. Freedom is the capacity, we have seen, to transcend its own nature— an occurrence in which that overused word *transcend* really fits.' We begin to appreciate the great fascination that freedom, phoenixlike in its capacity to rise from its own ashes, exercised on our ancestors. We begin also to experience the dangers in freedom. People will cling to freedom, treasure it, die for it if necessary, or continually yearn and fight others for it if they do not now enjoy it. And it is still true, according to the statistical studies of Milton Rokeach, that the majority of people place freedom highest on their list in the ranking of values.

This constitutes the radical difference between the slave and the free citizen in ancient Greece and Rome and in the South of the United States in the days of slavery. The slaves might have been well taken care of physically, well fed and well treated—in fact, often better than if they had supported themselves in freedom. But they did not have the "inalienable" human right to assert publicly their own beliefs or even to believe something different from what their masters believed. Taking the name of the master is a symbol of this built-in subordination to someone else in contrast to the free citizen; we recall the struggle of the chief characters in "Roots" to preserve their original name even on tombstones. This also is true in marriage and has been attacked by the women's liberation movement.

Everyone is aware that subordination to a master strikes at the core of human dignity of the slave, but we have not all realized that it does the same with the master. He who owns a slave is as much enslaved as the person he owns; slavery destroys the freedom of both. People will choose— the Grand Inquisitor notwithstanding—to lower their standard of living as free persons than to be well taken care of as slaves. Rousseau confesses that he is overwhelmed by the "marvels done by free peoples to guard themselves against oppression."

While this uniqueness of personal freedom has been tacitly recognized through history, it has remained for the existentialists to base their philosophy centrally on the concept. Schelling, an early existentialist who repeats again and again "Man was born to act and not to speculate," also proclaims, "The beginning and end of all philosophy is—Freedom." The contemporary existentialists see freedom as the quality most threatened by our modern age with its assembly-line objectification of human persons. In Jean-Paul Sartre's drama, *The Flies*, Zeus, frustrated in his attempt to exert his authority over Orestes, cries, "Impudent spawn! So I

am not your king? Who, then, made you?" Orestes retorts, "You.
But you blundered: you should not have made me free." Later,
Orestes summarizes it all: "I *am* my freedom!" he cries. Sartre is
stating point blank that freedom is not only basic to being human,
but also that *freedom and being human are identical.*

This identity of freedom and being is demonstrated by the
fact that each of us experiences himself as real in the moment of
choice. When one asserts "I can" or "I choose" or "I will," one
feels one's own significance, since it is not possible for the slave
to assert these things. "In the act of choice, in the original spontaneity of my freedom," writes Karl Jaspers, "I recognize myself
for the first time as my own true self." "Existence is real only as
freedom. . . . Freedom is . . . the being of existence." "Only in
those moments when I exercise my freedom am I fully myself."
"To be free means to be one's self."

The possibility of changing, which we have said is freedom,
includes also the capacity to remain as one is—but the person is
different from having considered and rejected changing. This
change, furthermore, is not to be confused with changing for its
own sake, as we shall see presently, or changing for escapist reasons. Hence, the gross confusion of license, so often pointed at in
American youth, with genuine freedom. I believe that Solzhenitsyn, who, by his own heroic struggle to be free, has earned the
right to speak of freedom, makes that error when he says:

Freedom! for adolescents of 14–18 years to immerse themselves in idle-
ness and amusements instead of invigorating tasks and spiritual growth.
Freedom! for healthy young adults to avoid work and live at the expense
of society."

Solzhenitsyn's objections confuse freedom with license and irresponsibility, and with acting out of boredom. He does not see
what his countryman, Dostoevsky, grasped so well, that freedom
is always a paradox.

License is freedom without destiny, without the limits that are as
essential for authentic freedom as night is to day. As we shall see,
freedom consists of how you confront your limits, how you
engage your destiny in day-to-day living. Proteus, the Greek god

who could continually assume a different form to escape being pinned down, may be a symbol in our day for noncommittal, but he is never cited as a symbol for freedom.

Even those who deny freedom presuppose it. In the act of denying freedom, their denial purports to be true—that is, dependent not on mere prejudice or their digestion for that day, but on objective norms which one is able to accept or reject. And what is this capacity to "accept or reject" but our freedom? As we shall discuss, determinism, as one point of view, is required and given by freedom. In this sense deterministic belief is part of, and is made necessary by, human freedom, just as darkness is required to make the light discernible.

There is solid reason, therefore, for concluding that freedom is essential to human dignity. Von Humboldt states this incisively: "I have felt myself animated throughout with a sense of the deepest respect for the inherent dignity of human nature; and for freedom, which alone befits that dignity." In the Renaissance Pico della Mirandola also identifies freedom with human dignity. He pictures the creator as saying:

Neither heavenly nor earthly, neither mortal nor immortal have we created thee, so that thou mightest be free according to thy own will and honor, to be thy own creator and builder. To thee alone we give growth and development depending on thy own free will. Thou bearest in thee the germs of a universal life.

Human dignity is based upon freedom and freedom upon human dignity. The one presupposes the other.

In the Renaissance, however, Pico could use terms that present difficulties in our own era, such as "free will." "Free will," in its traditional sense, seems to be a concept that has been the cause of years of fruitless arguments. It is the *whole human being* who is free, not a *part* of him or her such as will. Surely will is important, as we will later indicate when we emphasize freedom as the capacity to state "I will" and "I can." But this "I will" speaks not from a given faculty, as implied in "free will," but from the whole self, including such diverse aspects of the self as freedom to move one's muscles, freedom of imagination, freedom to dream, freedom to commit oneself—indeed, freedom of the total human being. Even the capacity not to believe in free will is itself an exercise of freedom.

"Freedom is the *possibility* of 'self-realization' based on personal choice, on free contract and spontaneous endeavor, or individual initiative," as the anthropologist Malinowski puts it.

Freedom is possibility. Kierkegaard stated this a century and a half ago, and it is still the best positive definition of freedom. Emily Dickinson has intuited it in a poem:

> I dwell in Possibility—
> A fairer house than Prose—
> More numerous of windows—
> Superior of Doors
>
> Of Chambers as of Cedars—
> Impregnable of Eye—
> And for an Everlasting Roof
> The Gambrels of the Sky

The word "possibility" comes from the Latin *posse*, "to be able," which is also the original root of our word *power*. Thus begins that long and tortuous relationship, interminably debated in the parliaments of the world and fought and bled over on countless battlefields, of the relationship between freedom and power. Powerlessness, we know, is tantamount to slavery. It is a truism that, if people are to have freedom, they must have the equivalent personal power in the form of autonomy and responsibility. The women's liberation movement has argued this point with cogency.

To be sure, one has to discriminate between possibilities: hectic acting, because it is more comfortable to act than not to, is a misuse of freedom. Nixon is guilty of this, as illustrated in his own writings about the "unbearable tensions that build up . . . tensions that can be relieved only by taking action, one way or the other. Not knowing how to act or not being able to act is what tears your insides out." This compulsion to act in any extreme form is what is meant by "acting out" in therapy and is often symptomatic of the psychopathic personality.

Personal freedom, on the contrary, entails being able *to harbor different possibilities in one's mind even though it is not clear at the moment which way one must act.* The possibilities must be there to begin with, otherwise one's life is banal. The psychologically healthy person is able to confront and manage the anxiety directly in such situations, in contrast to the neurotic, in whom anxiety sooner or later blocks off his consciousness of freedom and he feels as if he is in a strait jacket. Freedom always deals with "the possible"; this gives freedom its great flexibility, its fascination and its dangers.

2. The Hypocrisies of Freedom

Freedom is now in a crisis so serious that its meaning is obscured, and those who use the word are called, often justifiably, hypocritical. In our day freedom is beset by paradoxes, many of which we find surfacing on all sides. James Farmer, former director of CORE, writes about World War II:

Total war was being waged in the name of freedom and democracy. We were all mobilized to fight for the American Way of Life. Yet in the glare of the conflagration overseas we could see clearly how much unfreedom and inequality went into that way of life. Many victims of the Depression were still hungry and terrified; labor all over the country was bound to long hours and low wages. And always there was the Negro, a full-fledged soldier on the battlefields of France, but at home still the son of Ham, a servant of servants unto his brethren.

"Freedom's just another word for nothin' left to lose" demonstrates that multitudes of people whose convictions are expressed by such music believe that the word "freedom" is used as bait to entice them down heaven knows what primrose path. These people see the hypocrisies, the false dilemmas, the artificial decorations and gimmicks that now make this once noble word almost unusable. From its position as the "most treasured word" in our language, the most precious experience of mankind, "freedom" has now been reduced in many quarters to a synonym for mockery.

Like other erstwhile get words—"truth," "beauty," "God"

—the word "freedom" may soon be usable only in irony, as the poet W. H. Auden illustrates in "The Unknown Citizen." Auden describes a man against whom there can be "no official complaint," who

> held the proper opinions for the time of year;
> When there was peace, he was for peace: when there
> was war, he went.

And he concludes this picture of this completely conforming, "normal" man with:

> Was he free? Was he happy? The question is absurd:
> Had anything been wrong, we should certainly have heard.

The flagrant denial of personal freedom can be seen in precisely the shrillest and loudest protestations of *protecting* our freedom. One need only glance back at the McCarthys, the Dieses, and the Jenners to appreciate the song written by Kristofferson and Foster. We well remember how Joseph McCarthy, the most infamous of these self-styled "protectors," was able to crush many valuable citizens by scaring the country into believing there was a communist under every bed. The cruelty and destructiveness of McCarthy came from his capitalizing on the anxiety people had of losing their freedom. The great danger of freedom is its susceptibility to just such hypocrisy: for under the guise of saving our liberty, the greatest suppression of our freedom can be perpetrated. How many tyrants throughout history have rallied their supporters under the banner of freedom!

Such hypocrisy has become almost identified with the use of the word "freedom" in the minds and hearts of many people. When a high-school commencement speaker or a Fourth of July orator harangues us with phrases like "America, land of the free," we yawn and look up vaguely to see how he, in the pattern set by McCarthy, proposes to hoodwink us. The orators are generally persons who represent the "haves" in our society and have profited well under the present economic system. But most of the audience is aware that such orators would be horrified if they confronted a real rebellion like that of 1776.

In the speeches at the political conventions in the summer of

1980, it was notable that the more conservative and reactionary the speaker, the more he tended to use the term "freedom." One is reminded of Jacques Ellul's statement about man, that "he is most enslaved when he thinks he is comfortably settled in freedom."

One of the presidential candidates in the 1980 election, writes Eugene McCarthy, stated his religious belief that the "United States was strategically placed by God as an island of freedom between two continents in which freedom was either denied or un-recognized." This holier-than-thou claim seems to me to make a mockery of freedom.

Freedom is used and abused to rationalize our laissez-faire, "free"-enterprise economic system. A trustee of a large university who also was the president of one of the leading oil companies in this country argued in a private conversation, that his company was justified in cutting off the supply of gas to raise the price at the time of the shortage during the excessively cold winter of 1975–1976. His company had the "right" and "responsibility" to its stockholders, he stated, to make as much money for them as possible. Was he assuming that the preserving of the free-enterprise system is more important than the lives of the human beings, the American people who were suffering severely that winter, some of them literally freezing to death because of the unavailability of gas? "Right" and "responsibility" are moral words used here for the immoral purpose of defending an action that results in hardship to thousands of people struggling to survive the subzero cold.

The argument that such practices of the free-enterprise system must be defended at whatever price in human suffering is dubious indeed. Have we forgotten the wisdom of Richard Tawney, who pointed out four decades ago that modern "industrialism is the perversion of individualism"? For the "repudiation of any authority [such as social value and function] superior to individual reason . . . left men free to follow their own interests or ambitions or appetites, untrammeled by subordination to any common center of allegiance." Tawney pointed out that a self-contradiction is set up in industrialism itself: a "completely free" industrial system would destroy its own market and ultimately itself, as we see now happening in the automobile industry in this country. This seems to be also occurring in our curious phenomenon of simultaneous rising inflation and unemployment. The dilemma hinges on how we use the term "freedom." How important that we rediscover its authentic meaning!

Justice William O. Douglas, as well as numerous others, has remarked that there can be no freedom which does not begin with the freedom to eat and the right to work. "Freedom," writes Irwin Edman, "involves, as Marx and Robert Owen and Edward Bellamy were to discover, the economic conditions of action, and in the struggle for democracy economic security has only at late last been recognized as a political condition of personal freedom."

The same hypocrisy and moral confusion about freedom is described in a recent editorial in a news magazine. Referring to the abuse of privacy and the misuse of political freedom in the present and the past few years in this country, the editorial refers to a book about the Germans under Hitler entitled *They Thought They Were Free:*

Like the good Germans, we [in America] continue to think we are free, while the walls of dossiers, the machinery of repression, the weapons of political assassination pile up around us. Where is the movement to restore our freedom? Who are the leaders prepared to insist that it won't happen here?

We hear the haunting final chorus of the movie *Nashville:* "It don't worry me, it don't worry me. You may say that I ain't free, but it don't worry me." Is this to be the final epitaph of American liberty?

The possible demise of freedom in the modern world concerns Henry Steele Commager, a historian whose balanced eye and observant mind are beyond question. In "Is Freedom Dying?" he cites political and social evidence to demonstrate that we *are* losing our freedom. Already "freedom has lost its exalted place in philsophy and policy." Citing the old caution "The price of liberty is eternal vigilance," he notes sorrowfully that there is little vigilance in our country at present. Commager believes the main causes of this demise of freedom are the widespread growth of materialism and hedonism in America.

I believe that the materialism and hedonism, so often decried by Solzhenitsyn and now Commager, are themselves symptoms of an underlying, endemic anxiety. Men and women devote themselves to making money when they cannot get gratification from making anything else. It is above all a personal dilemma, whatever its economic repercussions. Couples develop sexual hedonism as an end in itself because sex allays anxiety and because they find authentic love so rarely available in our alienated and narcissistic culture. At present in our country there is a general experience of suppressed panic: anxiety not only about the hydrogen bomb and the prospect of atomic war, but about uncontrolled inflation, unemployment, anxiety that our old values have deteriorated as our religions have eroded, about our disintegrating family structure, concern about pollution of the air, the oil crisis, and infinitum. The mass of citizens react as a neurotic would react: we hasten to conceal the frightening facts with the handiest substitutes, which dull our anxiety and enable us temporarily to forget.

Commager emphasizes that the price of surrendering our freedom is much greater than most people are aware. For freedom is "a necessity for progress," he proclaims, "and a necessity for survival." If we lose our inner freedom, we lose with it our self-direction and autonomy, the qualities that distinguish human beings from robots and computers.

The attack on freedom, and the mockery of it, is the predictable mythoclasm which always occurs when a great truth goes bankrupt. In mythoclasm people attack and mock the thing they used to venerate. In the vehemence of the attack we hear the silent unexpressed cries "Our belief in freedom *should* have saved us—it let us down just when we needed it most!" The attack is based on resentment and rage that our freedom does not turn out to be the noble thing inscribed on the base of the Statue of Liberty or that Abraham Lincoln's "new birth of freedom" has never occurred.

In all such periods of mythoclasm, the great truths yield the greatest bootlegged power to their attackers. Thus, the attack on freedom—especially by those psychologists who use their freedom to stump the nation, arguing that freedom is an illusion—gets its power precisely from what it denies.

But the period of mythoclasm soon becomes empty and unrewarding, and we must then engage in "the long and lonely search for inner integrity," as Jerome Bruner puts it. The constructive way is to look within ourselves to discover again the reborn truth, the phoenix quality of freedom now so needed, and to integrate it anew into our being. This is the deepest meaning of Lincoln's "new birth of freedom."

For is not the central reason for the near bankruptcy of a once glorious concept that we have grossly oversimplified freedom? We have assumed it was an easy acquisition which we inherited simply by being born in the "land of the free." Did we not let the paradox of freedom become encrusted until freedom itself became identified with whites in the racial conflict, or with Protestants, or with capitalism, and ultimately with one's own personal idiosyncrasies? Thus the decline and fall of a great concept!

In our Declaration of Independence, there is a joyful enthusiasm for the "self evident" and "inalienable" right of individual freedom, which most of us lapped up with our mother's milk. But we find even there a pronounced lack of awareness of the social problems of responsibility and community—that is, a lack of realization of what I call destiny. True, there is the reference to the "Creator" and the phrase in this declaration "we . . . acquiesce in the necessity" after the long list of the oppressions of the British king. True, also, that in our Constitution the Supreme Court is charged with providing the necessary limits. But adjudication is not enough. The British historian Macaulay wrote to President Madison half a century after the Declaration was adopted that he was worried about the American Constitution because it was "all sail and no rudder." Thus, we have, marking the birth of our nation, the cheering for "full speed ahead" but with a lack of guiding limits. In the condition of "all sail and no rudder" freedom is in continual crisis; the boat may easily capsize. Freedom has lost its solid foundation because we have seen it without its necessary opposite, which gives it viability—namely, destiny.

That keen observer of America, Alexis de Tocqueville, wrote that people in America imagine that "their whole destiny is in their own hands. . . . The woof of time is every instant broken and the track of generations effaced. Those who went before are soon forgotten; of those who will come after, no one has any idea: the interest of man is confined to those in close propinquity to himself." As a result, Tocqueville states, "I know of no country in which there is so little independence of mind and real freedom of discussion as in America." In European nations like France, where the monarchy stood against the legislature, one could exercise freedom of mind since if one power sides against the individual, the other sides with him. "But in a nation where democratic institutions exist, organized like those in the United States, there is but one authority, one element of strength and success, with nothing beyond it." Tocqueville writes eloquently of the "tyranny of the majority" in America, which I call conformism of mind and spirit. We have recently seen this exhibited in the last election in the power of what is called the "moral majority." "There the body is left free, and the soul is enslaved." Tocqueville continues: "The master no longer says, 'You shall think as I do, or you shall die'; but he says, 'You are free to think differently from me, and to retain your life, your property, and all that you possess; but you are henceforth a *stranger among your people.* . . . You will retain your civil rights, but they will be useless to you." Other people "will affect to scorn you." The person who thinks freely is ostracized, and the mass of people cannot stand such alienation.

Have we not too easily and readily seized upon freedom as our birthright and forgotten that each of us must rediscover it for ourselves? Have we forgotten Goethe's words: "He only earns his freedom and existence/Who daily conquers them anew"? Yet destiny will return to haunt us as long as it is not acknowledged. Destiny is eternally present to remind us that we exist as part of a community. We cannot afford to ignore "those who went before," as Tocqueville puts it, and "those who will come after." If we are ever to understand what Milton meant when he cried "Ah, Sweet liberty," or what the Pilgrims sought in landing at Plymouth rock in search of religious freedom, or any one of the other million and one evidences of freedom, we must confront this paradox directly.

The paradox is that freedom owes its vitality to destiny, and destiny owes its significance to freedom. Our talents, our gifts, are on loan, to be called in at any moment by death, by illness, or by any one of the countless other happenings over which we have no direct control. Freedom is that essential to our lives, but it is also that precarious.

3. *Therapy: To Set People Free*

The same crisis of freedom is present in psychotherapy, this curious profession which burgeoned so fantastically in America during the past half century. The crisis can best be seen when we ask: What is the purpose of therapy? To be sure, to help people. And the specific purpose differs with the particular condition with which the person is suffering. But what is the overall purpose that underlies the development of this profession of psychological helpers?

Several decades ago, the purpose of the mental-health movement was clear: mental health is living free from anxiety. But this motto soon became suspect. Living free from anxiety in a world of hydrogen bombs and nuclear radiation? Without anxiety in a world in which death may strike at any moment you cross the street? Without anxiety in a world in which two-thirds of the people are malnurished or are starving?

Dr. Nicholas Cummings, in his inaugural address as president of the American Psychological Association, made a wise and insightful statement about the endeavor to avoid anxiety:

The mental health movement, in promising a freedom from anxiety that is not possible, may have had a significant role in the current belief that it is *a right* to feel good, thus contributing to the burgeoning consumption of alcohol and the almost universal prescription of the tranquilizer by physicians.

The mental health movement has emphasized "freedom from anxiety" as the definition of health. But finding that that is not possible in the general run of life, people have assumed that the quickest way to achieve this "freedom" is through alcohol and tranquilizing drugs.

Furthermore, if we did achieve freedom from all anxiety, we

would find ourselves robbed of the most constructive stimulant for life and for simple survival. After many a therapeutic hour which I would call successful, the client leaves with more anxiety than he had when he came in; only now the anxiety is conscious rather than unconscious, constructive rather than destructive. The definition of mental health needs to be changed to living without *paralyzing* anxiety, but living with normal anxiety as a stimulant to a vital existence, as a source of energy, and as life-enhancing.

Is adjustment the purpose of therapy—that is, should therapy help people adjust to their society? But this means adjusting to a society that fights the Vietnam war, a society in which the most powerful nation spends an enormous portion of its budget on armaments allegedly to defend itself from other members of that society. Adjustment as the purpose of therapy means that the therapist is the psychic policeman for the society, a role that I, for one, heartily detest. Ever since Lawrence Frank wrote in the middle 1930s on the theme "Society As the Patient," many of us have wondered who the psychotic was—the persons to whom the title is given or the society itself?

Is the purpose of the therapist to give people relief and comfort? If so, this can also be done more efficiently and economically by drugs.

Is the purpose of the therapist to help people to be happy? Happy in a world in which unemployment and inflation burgeon at the same time? Such happiness can be purchased only at the price of repressing and denying too many of the facts of life, a denial that works directly against what most of us believe is the optimum state of mental health.

I propose that *the purpose of the psychotherapy is to set people free.* Free, as far as possible, from symptoms, whether they be psychosomatic symptoms like ulcers or psychological symptoms like acute shyness. Free from compulsions, again as far as possible, to be workaholics, compulsions to repeat self-defeating habits they have learned in early childhood, or compulsions perpetually to choose partners of the opposite sex who cause continual unhappiness and continual punishment.

But most of all, I believe that the therapist's function should be to help people become free to be aware of and to experience their possibilities. A psychological problem, I have pointed out elsewhere, is like fever; it indicates that something is wrong within the structure of the person and that a struggle is going on for survival. This, in turn, is a proof to us that some other way of behaving is possible. Our old way of thinking—that problems are to be gotten rid of as soon as possible—overlooks the most important thing of all: that problems are a normal aspect of living and are basic to human creativity. This is true whether one is constructing things or reconstructing oneself. *Problems are the outward signs of unused inner possibilities.*

People rightly come to the therapist because they have become inwardly enslaved and they yearn to be set free. The crucial question is: how is that freedom to be attained? Surely not by a miraculous charming away of all conflicts.

When I was writing this chapter, a woman of twenty-eight came to me so that I could refer her to a therapist. Her problem was that she could never find the right job. She was intelligent and open, a person who, one would think, would be a success in the business world. She had had a good job as an executive secretary with interesting people in an organization she liked and believed in, and she did the work very well. But for some reason she could not understand, she hated this job, and her hatred took a great toll in nervous anguish. She quit the job, enrolled in a college, but was bored with studying and dropped out.

It turned out that her father was an executive, and at home he had been exceedingly authoritarian, blustering about the house and cursing at her mother, a weak person. The bind in which this would-be patient is caught and which radically curtails her freedom is that her father was the only image of strength she had, and in spite of her hatred for him, she also identified with him. The dilemma, then, is that she identifies with the person she feels she hates, and how could she then escape hating her executive job? But no other job would be interesting to her either, in as much as she identifies success, achievement, strength, and zest in life with her father. The upshot was that her freedom to do anything at all was blocked.

When a person loses his freedom, there develops in him an

apathy, as in the blacks in slavery, or neurosis or psychosis as in twentieth-century people. Thus, their effectiveness in relating to their fellow men and also to their own natures is proportionally reduced. Following Kierkegaard, we can define neurosis and psychosis as lack of communicativeness, "shut-up-ness," inability to participate in the feelings and thoughts of others or to share oneself with others. Thus, blind to his own destiny, the person's freedom is also truncated. These states of psychological disturbance demonstrate by their very existence the essential quality of freedom for the human being—if you take it away, you get radical disintegration on the part of the victim.

Neurotic symptoms, such as the psychosomatic paralysis of the leg which one of Freud's early patients developed when she could do nothing about being in love with her sister's husband, are ways of renouncing freedom. Symptoms are ways of shrinking the periphery of the world with which one has to deal to a size with which one can cope. These symptoms may be temporary, as when one gets a cold and takes several days off from the office, thus temporarily reducing the world that one has to confront. Or the symptoms may be so deeply set in early experiences that, if unattended, they block off a great portion of the person's possibilities throughout all of the person's life. The symptoms indicate a breakdown in the interplay of one's freedom and one's destiny.

This brings us to one of the gross abuses of freedom in our day: change for its own sake, or change as a flight from reality. This abuse of freedom is most egregious in what are called "growth centers." Let me hasten to say that impetus for the growth-center movement and the work of many individual centers I believe to be sound and admirable. This impetus is the courage to confront one's own self and one's problems in human relationships; it is the belief that one can take oneself in hand and establish some autonomy in one's life.

But anyone who reads the "Free Directory of Growth Centers" in Marin County can readily see the preponderance of "positive thinking" and self-delusion in its most blatant forms. From the brief individual ads for the 280 various centers given in this directory, one's impression is overwhelmingly of such purposes as "tapping your true potential and creativity," "finding more and more joy," "a perfect living guru is a 'must' on the path God-ward," and so on. Nowhere could I find words dealing with common experiences of anyone living in our day—namely, "anxiety," "tragedy," "grief," or "death." All is drowned out by endless joy and the fearless promises of triumph and transcendence, a mass movement toward egocentric "peace," self-enclosed "love," with its somnolescent denial of the realities of human life, the use of change for escapist purposes if there ever was one. And what a misunderstanding of the ancient religions of the East that in their name salvation is promised over the weekend!

The problem in these growth centers is the complete absence of any sense of destiny. Tocqueville is right: they seem to believe that all of destiny is controlled by themselves. The individuals will totally determine their fate. The leaders seem not to be aware that what they are espousing is not freedom at all, but sentimentality, a condition in which the *feeling alone is sought rather than reality.*

Such considerations as these lend urgency to our purpose to rediscover the meaning of personal freedom. The burgeoning of the growth-center movement does testify to the widespread hunger among modern people for some guidance so that life will not have passed them by. The mere existence of these centers—which could not survive were they not patronized—demonstrate that hordes of people feel there is something missing in their lives, some failure to find what they are seeking or perhaps even to *know* what they are seeking. One person, who apparently was well acquainted with the situation, wrote,

I've been ested, esaloned, Moonied, asserted, Krishna'd and Marin'd. And now I can't remember what a spontaneous feeling really is.

The root of the tree which has sprouted the infinite number of branches in different types of therapy—psychoanalysis, group psychotherapy, and even counseling in all its forms—is, of course, Sigmund Freud. I do not mean to imply there would have been no fantastic surge of methods of therapy, many of them claiming to be anti-Freudian, if Freud had not lived. It is not just that great men make history, as Tolstoy one-sidedly argued; but that history, in its various crises, also makes great men. Certain persons are called forth to spearhead a trend which is required by history. Hence, if there had been no Sigmund Freud at the beginning of the twentieth century to invent psychoanalysis, it would have been invented by somebody else with the same name.

Psychotherapy in all its branches is a response to the loss on a vast scale of people's inner mooring posts. It is symptomatic of the breakdown of freedom in our culture, the bankruptcy of our culturally inherited ways of dealing with our freedom and destiny. It is, thus, not by accident that Freud's work came at a time when personal inner freedom was becoming all but lost in the maelstrom of modernity. Confusion about human destiny and confusion about personal freedom go together, and they will be resolved, so far as resolution is possible, together.

Psychoanalysis—and any good therapy—is a method of increasing one's *awareness of destiny* in order to increase one's *experience of freedom*. In contrast to his technical determinism, Freud struck a significant blow on a deeper level for freedom. He set out to free people from the psychological entanglements they, like the executive secretary above, were embroiled in because of their failure to confront their own destinies.

What is most remarkable about Freud is his continuous wrestling with destiny. By showing the impossibility of shortcuts and the superficial by-passes to freedom, which break down at every turn, Freud required us to search for freedom on a deeper level. If freedom is to be achieved it will not be achieved overnight. In his theory of reaction formation, for example, he pointed out that altruism is the result of repressed stinginess (which surely a great deal of it is), and that religious beliefs are an opiate and a way for people to avoid facing death (which many of them are), and that the belief in God is an expression of yearning for the all-powerful father who will take care of us (which for multitudes of people it manifestly is).

If we are to achieve freedom, we must do so with a daring and a profundity that refuse to flinch at engaging our destiny.

II

One Man's Passage

*All I do to my disciples is to free them from their own bondage, by
any means their case may need.*

   *Whether you are bound by a gold chain or an iron one, you are in
captivity. Your virtuous activities are the gold chain, your evil ones
the iron one. He who shakes off both the chains of good and evil that
imprison him, . . . he has attained the Supreme Truth.*
     —FREDERICK FRANCK, *The Book of Angelus Silesius*

Let us begin our exploration of freedom with a detailed discussion of a man in his middle fifties, Philip, who came for therapy on the impetus of an intense and crippling jealousy. The
woman, Nicole, with whom he had been deeply in love for several years, as she apparently had been with him, was a writer in
her middle forties, intelligent, reportedly striking in appearance,
and the mother of two small children (not his). She had lately
insisted on the freedom to sleep with other men, arguing that it
had nothing to do with her love for him. But Philip could not
bring himself to accept this, and her going to bed with other men
threw him into agony. Nor could he break away from her. She
insisted that she would not be monogamous unless he married
her, a step he also could not bring himself to take since he
regarded his two previous marriages as partial failures and had
already raised a family of three children.

Philip presents the picture of a radically unfree man. He
resembled, as people who come for therapy regularly do, a Gul-
liver tied down by endless threads until he could not move one
way or another. Each fantasy about Nicole, he felt, seemed to
bind him tighter.

An architect, Philip showed me a vivid symbol of his psychological distress when, in one of our early sessions, he brought photographs of some churches he had designed. The buildings gave the impression of a great sweeping movement toward the sky, a yearning to pierce the heavens with their steeples. I could see why such architecture was often called "frozen music." But the foundations of these otherwise attractive and impressive edifices seemed overheavy—the stone and concrete seemed weighted down, bound to the earth. As I listened to him, this became a symbol for him in my mind—a man of powerful idealism, reaching upward toward the sky which promised freedom, but at the same time unintegrated with and hopelessly bound to the mud and stones at the bottom.

Half a year after he and Nicole had met, they had spent the summer together at his retreat, her children being with their father. Each morning Nicole had occupied herself with her writing, and Philip, in a separate studio on the land, worked on his architectural designs. Once at the beginning of the summer Nicole raised the question of their marrying. Philip had come out flatly against it, stating as reasons his previous bad luck in his marriages and the fact that, even though he was fond of her two sons, he could not conceive of himself as raising another family. Except for this interchange, they had had an idyllic summer together.

He apparently had gotten much tenderness and warmth from Nicole. Their sexual relations seemed to be the best he had ever experienced—sometimes ecstatic, sometimes giving them both the feeling of being totally merged with each other, but always rich and nourishing. Their intellectual discussions had also been especially gratifying to him, her ideas often giving him solutions to his design problems.

At the end of the summer Nicole had to fly back home half a week before him to put her children in school. The next day he had phoned her home, but he sensed something strange in her voice at the other end. The following day he phoned again, and it seemed to him that someone else was in the room. All afternoon he called back, only to find her line busy.

When he did get through to her, she answered his questions point-blank. Yes, someone had been there. An intimate friend from her college years had been staying with her for several days, and she had fallen in love with him. She had felt "dismissed" by Philip's supposed cavalier good-by when she left his farm and had been in a panic on the plane coming back about how she was going to take care of her children alone. The lover from bygone days, Craig, was "into" children, having two the same age as hers. The fine summer had convinced her how easy and gratifying it was to live with someone. She was planning to marry Craig at the end of the month and move across country, where Craig had promised to get her a job at his company.

Yes, she still loved Philip. She had thought Philip would be upset, but he would get over it.

Philip's world collapsed. He was overcome with feelings of betrayal. How could she do this after their idyllic summer? Coming back to the city, he lost fifteen pounds in the next three weeks. He resumed smoking, had no appetitie, and had to take Seconal to sleep at night.

When he saw her, he had thrown aside his usual politeness and told her in no uncertain terms that the whole plan was crazy. He continued to invite Nicole and her children to his house for weekends (when Craig was not visiting her) and to take her to the theater from time to time. During this period, while Craig was in the picture, Philip's potency was blocked off regardless of the fact that Nicole wanted to make love with him. "My body doesn't trust you," Philip had said.

Gradually Nicole got over her infatuation. After six weeks she was back in love with Philip and had written him, "You know I never could leave the place where you are." Philip was surprised at the message. He had consciously known no such thing, but it fitted into his own need for security, and he therefore didn't question it. He had given her a nominal research job in his corporation that she could perform at home and would yield her enough money to live on. He had also made her a gift of several thousand dollars, ostensibly because her family needed it to live on. But he told me in our sessions that he also did it as "insurance"—she would then be less apt to leave him. He tried to persuade Nicole to go into therapy at that time because of the great emotional confusion she had shown in her affair with Craig. But she would have none of it.

It might seem that his reactions are "normal" in such a situation for a man very much in love. But let me throw two other incidents into the hopper.

The incident that was the actual occasion for his coming for therapy occurred about a year after the "Craig affair." Philip had been under the impression that Nicole was going away to another state on an upcoming weekend to lead a workshop. It is interesting to note, as an example of the ESP that often appears in psychotherapy, that Philip, the Thursday morning before this weekend, had written in his diary about her trip to the workshop:

There is an ache in my heart. I am consumed by jealousy—a feeling of fear that I am losing Nicole. I have fantasies about her going to meet some man and spending the weekend with him. . . . I have the feeling she sticks with me only because I have a little money—which I know is utter nonsense. . . . But I am very lonely.

Philip had felt that he had to phone her on Sunday—so he stated to me—to decide on some plans on a trip they were to make. He got her phone number at her "workshop" from her babysitter. A man answered. Philip became aware that there had been no workshop at all, and that she had gone to spend the weekend—precisely as he had fantasied it—with this man at his home. Nicole on the phone refused to talk to him about where she was. She got angry when he asked whether she was staying with a man and hung up.

Exceedingly depressed and anxious, Philip had to leave the next morning for a five-day speaking trip. During these days he was filled with a maelstrom of emotions of anger, hurt, and betrayal. He resolved to break off the relationship as soon as he got back.

But during the last day, when he was flying back home, it occurred to him that perhaps he was being too harsh. Were there ways in which he, as a love partner, could accept this fact of extrarelationship sex? He had thought that one way would be to identify with the other man, imagine him as his friend. Then he would, in fantasy, be glad of the other man's pleasure with Nicole. He could also do what the younger generation did in the 1960s—decide that pure authenticity, pure feeling, is the important thing. Perhaps in a relationship like Nicole's and his this was the only criterion. Are we living in a new age, he asked himself, when promises and rules and roles are all thrown overboard?

These "principles" seemed to me to be rationalizations with a masochistic feature about the whole. But I did not want to cut off any associations by labeling experiences, especially so early in our therapy.

As soon as his plane landed, he went directly to Nicole's home. In their talk Nicole said, as Philip later wrote it down in his diary,

The weekend was not that important. What was good was that he gave me a lot of space by myself. What you, Philip, should understand about me is that I believe sex does not necessarily involve intimacy. The sex bored me. I was more attracted to women than to men. I've considered being celibate for a while. You don't understand me that way. And that's all I want to say about the weekend.

During their lovemaking later that day she had whispered in his ear that she loved him more than she'd ever loved anyone, and that she loved no one else. If he could get that through his head, she believed their problems would be solved.

A third incident occurred when Nicole, after spending an especially tender and ecstatic weekend with Philip at his home, asked him to drive her down to meet some friends from the college where she used to teach. The friends would then drive her the remaining fifty miles back to her home. She seemed nervous, and it turned out that she was to meet only one friend, Wilbur, who had been her passionate lover up until the time she moved from her previous town to her present home. She had often told Philip of the oceans of tears she had shed in the fruitless attempt to persuade Wilbur to leave his wife and marry her. As they arrived at the appointed house, Philip wished her luck—meeting an old lover is always an occasion—but he added that he hoped she would not go to bed with Wilbur.

After he had left them, Philip found himself deeply stirred up, smoked one cigarette after another, and spent a day and an evening filled with jealousy. At dinnertime he phoned Nicole's house and learned that she had been in to make her children's dinner and then had hurried out again. About midnight he reached her and poured out his jealousy over the phone. She reassured him that she no longer loved Wilbur; she found him very immature and wouldn't marry him on a bet. Philip then asked the inevitable question: Had she gone to bed with him? She replied that she did not like the question and refused to answer. Philip naturally assumed that she had, and then another quarrel ensued like the countless ones before.

Why didn't Philip break off this relationship? The fact that he felt himself deeply in love will not suffice for an answer. For a period of eight to ten months Nicole and Philip had both been committed to the relationship. But often—and before that— Nicole felt she needed her "space" and her "freedom." Were they both afraid of genuine intimacy? Was part of her attractiveness to him the fact that she *did* lead him on by jealousy? But if he could not stand her hopping in and out of bed with other men, why did he not find some other woman to love? If he was convinced that he could not marry her, why did he not act on that? In fact, why could he not act in any way at all? Except for these childlike outbursts toward Nicole and the painful gnawing he felt within himself, he was paralyzed.

He was, furthermore, entirely aware of the fact that his jealousy crippled him. It had been his Achilles heel all his life. Although he had initiated his two divorces, he felt that whatever the source of his jealousy, it was also a source of the breakup of those two marriages. And although a longish period of therapy he had undertaken some ten years ago had helped him a great deal, he had not been able to get to the roots of the jealousy. It seemed to have begun in the first years of his life, before he could talk and, therefore, before the development of his consciousness.

Philip and I had only six weeks in which to work (I had to leave for the summer months). But he was anxious that I see him as often as I could in a kind of "crash" program on the problem of his jealousy. This limitation of time accounts for the fact that I use some techniques here that I do not ordinarily employ.

1. The Fear of Abandonment

Philip's mother, now dead, seems to have been a borderline schizophrenic. She had been given to hysterical blowups and had been completely unpredictable in her emotions. Sometimes she treated Philip with tenderness and care, and the next hour she would turn into the personification of cruelty. An early memory of Philip's was from when he was three or four and the family was moving to a house several blocks away. Philip had felt that he had to go on his tricycle to show the movers where the new house was. His tricycle fell over on the brick sidewalk, and he skinned his knee. He went home to show his mother the injured knee. But she, apparently nervous because of the moving, threw a glass of water in his face.

For the first two years of Philip's life, the only other person in the household was his sister Maude, two years older, who was definitely schizophrenic and was later to spend some time in a mental hospital. The relations with this sister, to which we will refer below, seem to be secondary only to his relations with his mother. This sister had died just several weeks before Philip came to me and seems to play a curious and important role in his therapy. Philip's father was away most of these first years, and did not like infants in any case.

Thus, Philip endured his first years in the world learning to deal with two exceedingly unpredictable women. Indeed, he must have had inescapably imprinted on him that he needed not only to rescue women, but that one of his functions in life was to stick by them, especially when they acted their craziest. Life, then, for Philip would understandably not be free, but rather would require that he be continuously on guard or on duty. He recalled coming home from school and having to "case" the house on tiptoe to see what kind of mood his mother and sister were in, which would determine which tack was demanded of him. (As an aside, he remarked that often in driving down to Nicole's he had tried to list the pros and cons of various responses she might have so he would be prepared—i.e., he was mentally "casing the joint.") Freedom in such a situation would be like Michelangelo's half-finished statues of slaves: *freedom within the bonds of slavery.*

Nicole seemed, like Philip's mother, to be warm and tender at certain times and cruel at others. She not only did not make any attempt to keep her extrarelationship affairs private, but she apparently even went to the extent of making it impossible for Philip *not* to know about them—for example, by having him drive her down to meet and go off with Wilbur when she could have taken a cab. At her house she made a practice of leaving her calendar, on which were written her dates with other men, out on the desk where Philip could not help seeing it. "I have the right to do what I wish with my own body," she had said. The fact that these things were done "on principle"—i.e., on her belief that she was being "honest"—only made it all the harder for Philip to bear.

After the first two sessions, I found myself mulling over several aspects of Philip's problem. First, the unpredictability of Nicole—which was a repeat of an old pattern, established by his mother, that apparently cemented him to Nicole—seems to have been one of the central things which made her so attractive to Philip. Another reason he could not break free was his sense of responsibility for the woman; his survival as a child had depended on how he responded to his mother and sister. Both of his previous marriages had been with women who "needed" him. He had a strong sense of duty to take care of women; the more crazily they behaved, the stronger was his need to take responsibility for them. These things were in some way twisted into the cords that bound him to Nicole and enslaved him. Then there was the tenderness and nourishment that Nicole did actually give him, as did Philip's mother; Nicole did seem to be loving and warm during the many good times she and Philip were together. But these obvious points need to be brought together in a pattern in Philip that I had not yet grasped.

Nicole can be seen as his destiny, now visited severely upon him. In this sense Philip's problem is not a negative roadblock. It is, rather, an opportunity—indeed, a requirement—to work through the remaining problem with his mother and sister. This has to be done if he is to take another step, a giant step, in his achievement of personal freedom.

It is surprising how often neurotic problems seem "fateful" in that they appear at a given time in one's career as demands that the individual confront this or that particular complex within oneself. From this viewpoint, psychological problems are blessings in disguise. They come not by accident, but by an inner destiny that arises out of the needs of the person himself.

One of the things that gave us hope of getting to the origin of Philip's problems was the death of his disturbed sister several weeks before he came to see me. Simultaneously with her death, he had had an attack of very painful neuritis, which felt "like a sword thrust through my neck." One day in an early session, he had been talking about the pain and loneliness of his first two years of life, and he remarked that it was a relief to cry. At the utterance of the word "relief" the pain suddenly struck him in full force. In a few seconds he was writhing on the floor, grabbing at his neck as though to choke off the unbearable anguish. When the pain left and I helped him up, I asked whether he felt like continuing our session. He answered, "Yes. I have to get through this problem no matter how much it hurts." The pain, he felt, was his dead sister punishing him, as though she were crying out, "Where do you come off being so healthy and successful when I had to suffer so?"

But I took the pain to be something more than this physical torture. I felt it was a prediction of the pain he would have to endure psychologically if we continued our work. His determination to continue, come hell or high water, was an inspiration to me.

2. *The Acknowledging of Destiny*

In an early session in our work, I asked Philip to bring a photo of himself taken during those crucial first two years. The picture he brought showed him at about a year and a half being photographed with his sister, Maude. Her attention was elsewhere, but his hand tightly grasped hers, his wide eyes looking intently at the photographer. I could already see in that photo the dilated eyes that spoke of anxiety, the need in this child to keep a sharp sentinel's view of the world around him at all times. He must have imbibed with his mother's milk the fateful "truth" that one cannot basically trust the world.

The world, made up of his schizoid mother's hysterical state and his sister's disturbed mind, was the only world Philip had known for these two years. How was he to adapt to such a difficult and cruel destiny? There was no reason why it should have been Philip rather than one of a million other infants who was born into this house with a disturbed mother and psychotic sister. There he had found himself, and there he was left to grow up as best he could. It is sad to say but true: there is never any recompense for ills suffered as an infant.

One might think such an original environment would lead only to schizophrenia for Philip also. But already as a child of two he had escaped such severe disturbance by developing compensations—like his ability to detach himself when in danger, his capacity to keep his real thoughts secret, and his knack of getting along with everybody and placating other people by being charming. The hypersensitivity—indeed, the almost psychic quality—that people often develop in such unfavorable situations could be related to Philip's talents which led to his becoming a highly successful architect and a man with many friends and enough lovers. But one cannot make such compromises without penalty. The neurotic payment came from the fact that whenever a relationship got below a certain depth, Philip became panicky.

In such cases, the metaphor of "imprinting" comes into my mind. A newborn duck, when the myelinization of the duck's neurological pathways is right, will follow and stick to whatever object it first sees. I have watched a full-grown duck following a rabbit around because that was the creature to which it had been originally imprinted, even though the irritated rabbit regularly turned and nipped the duck to drive it away. The unfortunate duck, seemingly welded to a way of life that was continuously punishing, continued following the rabbit. Paradoxically, when the imprinting is made especially difficult for the creature being imprinted—say, by such punishment of the duck—the attachment becomes even stronger. I felt like crying out to the duck, "For God's sake, go away and find your own mother! Don't continue just being bitten and hurt."

Sometimes in my patients I see a similar blind, irrational attachment to a way of behaving to which the person has been conditioned by his fate at a very early age. The metaphoric relation of imprinting to human beings is that, in their early attachment to their mothers, human babies seem to follow their original attachment with a similar blind fidelity. And this behavior may be made even stronger by punishments or other difficulties put in its path.

Use of terms like "self-punishment" and "masochism" are to no avail. The original way the infant was taught to behave wins out. When the child becomes a little older, this emerges as the impossibility of basic trust, to use Erikson's words. Dr. John Bowlby, who has made the classic studies of attachment and separation of infants, writes:

The way in which attachment behavior develops in the human infant and becomes focused on a discriminated figure is sufficiently like the way in which it develops in other mammals, and in birds, for it to be included, legitimately, under the heading of imprinting.

Although there is doubt as to whether this original "imprinting" can be overcome, the person can build new experiences around and over it and thus compensate for an original unfortunate experience.

Even though he was in his fifties, Philip was still striving to find a "good" mother to make up for the "bad" mother of his experience, to bring him justice after the cruel first two years. He had gone through his life lonely, yearning for a love that would fill the large area of emptiness in his breast. He had lived on the edge of becoming the kind of person who goes on year after year looking in the face of every woman he meets with the silent question: Are you the one who will make up for my loss? One of my tasks in therapy with Philip was to get across to him that this struggle he was engaged in was bound to be self-defeating.

The first and fundamental challenge for such a person is to confront his fate as it is, to reconcile himself to the fact that he *did* receive a bad deal, to know that justice is irrelevant, that no one will ever make up for the emptiness and the pain of those first two years. The past cannot be changed—it can only be acknowledged and learned from. It is one's destiny. It can be absorbed and mitigated by new experiences, but it cannot be changed or erased. Philip only adds insult to injury by going on the rest of his life knocking his head against the same stone wall. Fortunately, psychotherapy can be a vehicle through which human beings may become more aware of and compensate for such implanted destiny.

I pointed out to Philip how hanging on to this way of life was also hanging on to his mother. It is an expression of the hope that someday Mother will reward him, someday he'll find the Holy Grail. Now he'll get the original care which was missing; now he'll get that restored! But there's no way to restore it, no matter how much of a loss it is. Bad fate, yes. But that's the way it is. The lost mother image, the lost chance, the great emptiness within him—they are all going to remain there. These things are the past; there is no way of changing them. You can change your attititude *toward* these tragic happenings, as did Bettleheim, describing his "ultimate freedom" as his command over his attitude toward the storm troopers in the concentration camp. But you can't change the experiences themselves.

If you hang on to an illusion of such change, always hoping for "pie in the sky by and by" you cut off your possibilities. You then become rigid. You don't let yourself take in the *new* possibilities. You trade your freedom for a mess of emotional pottage. And this way, as a corollary, you never use your anger constructively. You lose a tremendous amount of power, energy, and possibility. In short, you lose your freedom.

But is there no constructive value in coming to terms with one's early fate? Yes, there is—and a value potentially greater than what one gives up. The struggle to come to terms with such early relationships as Philip suffered as an infant has much to do with the emergence of creativity. Would Philip have developed these talents which led to his high status in the world of architecture if he had not experienced such a disturbed family life? Alfred Adler believed, indeed, that creativity was a compensation for such early trauma.

We know that creative people often come out of such unfortunate family backgrounds. Why and how they do is still one of the mysteries the answer to which the Sphinx of creativity has not revealed. We do know that unfortunate infants like Philip have never been permitted to take life lightly. They learn from the hour of birth not to accept Jocasta's advice: "Best take life easily, as a man may." They cannot coast along or rest on their laurels.

This exceptional achievement following a disturbed childhood has been documented in many cases. In his study of creativity Jerome Kagan writes:

Such freedom of the artist is not born. It is made in the pain of adolescent loneliness, the isolation of physical handicap, or, perhaps, the smug superiority of inherited title. The freedom that permits "generation of possibilities" . . . is the beginning of a creative product.

Similarly, Richard Farson finds his "calamity theory" fits such situations:

Many of our most valuable people have come from the most calamitous early childhood situations. Investigations of the childhoods of eminent people expose the fact that they did not receive anything like the kind of child rearing that a person in our culture is led to believe is healthy for children. . . . Whether in spite of or because of these conditions, it is clear that these children not only survived, but reached great heights of achievement, many after having experienced the most deplorable and traumatic childhoods.

The tension in these personalities between high aspiration and disappointment may well be the necessary matrix out of which creativity—and, later, civilization—is born. This type cannot slide into any "well-adjusted" syndrome. There is the outstanding exception of J. S. Bach, but his contentment—if it was that—seems to have been a combination of fortunate social conditions. The "well-adjusted" persons rarely make great painters, sculptors, writers, architects, musicians. Coming out of such a confused early childhood as Philip's, this creative capacity may be considered a later compensation. The question is: Can a person like Philip seize these possibilities—these new reaches of freedom not without cruel fate, but *despite* fate—and weld them into a significant building, a statue, a painting, or some other creative product?

There is another boon worth more than the loss in Philip's confrontation with his mother. If he can accept this deprivation of the care he had rightfully expected, if he can engage this loneliness face to face, he will have achieved a strength and a power that will be a foundation more solid than he ever could have achieved otherwise. If he can accept this aspect of his destiny, the fates will work *with* rather than *against* him. In this way one lives with the universe rather than against it.

These last things about the values in engaging one's destiny I did not express at this time directly to Philip, for I did not want him to accept his destiny *in order to* achieve creativity. That never works. I did strongly emphasize the need to engage and accept these cruel things in his background. I wanted him, to put it in our words rather than the words of the therapy, not to accept destiny *for* anything, but simply because it *is*.

3. The Confronting of Mother

At my suggestion, Philip had a conversation with his dead mother in my office. In the fantasy, his mother was sitting in the opposite chair.

> PHILIP: *Mother, you and I have come to the end of the road. I'm no longer going to cringe before you. In the past, if ever any of us children disagreed with you, you'd scream, get hysterical, and run to the window as though you were going to jump out. I used to lie awake at night when you were ranting and raving downstairs. You had us all scared to death. But you and I have reached the end of that road. Hereafter I'm going to speak out directly and straight. I am no longer afraid of you—as God knows I used to be. And I'm not going to lie or prevaricate to get out of saying what I think. Remember that time I received the award for that*

design of the church in New York City? You were there. The first thing you said to me, when you saw the model, was "Philip, I had all those ideas forty years ago." You took it all away from me. I felt depressed as hell. But I'm not going to let you do that any more.

He went on about how as a child he had never been able to feel any peace, and about his mother's part in the fact that being at home meant for him continuous anxiety and sharp pangs of psychological pain.

I asked him now to sit in his mother's chair and speak for her.

MOTHER: *Philip-boy, you may not believe it, but I was very proud of you. When you'd win those contests in school, I'd take the programs home and treasure them. I'd tell all the neighbors whenever you'd be on TV. I got a postcard photo of that very church for which you got the award, and I'd show it to everyone who came to the house. I said that about the model because I was so scared. With all those college professors around, who was I? Don't forget, I grew up as an orphan. I had no self-esteem at all. I was always tired from taking care of you children and trembling inside me with the fear that your father would leave me for good—like he later did. I know I had a bad temper . . . and I'm glad you stand up against it now. I used to lie awake nights regretting my blow-ups and making resolutions to stop them. But the next day my temper would be as bad as ever. You were my favorite child. I tried not to show it too much to the others, but you were. My oldest son. Whenever you'd design a building near us, I'd go to see it even while they were putting it up. Whenever you'd write something, I would look at it and hold it proudly, even though most of what you wrote I couldn't understand. You went with a crowd of intellectual big shots I never could feel at home with at all. But it was so hard to say these things when I was alive. I don't know why.*

PHILIP [moving to the other chair without my suggesting it]: *Mother, I want to set the record right. I've been deceiving myself without even knowing it. I think I did know all of my life that I was your favorite, but I never would admit it. To be rejected made a better excuse—to tell everyone how misunderstood I was, how I triumphed over great odds. The misunderstood genius, nobody to help me, and so on. I want to tell you now I do appreciate you. You had a lot of courage, which you passed on to me. You taught me what care is even though you couldn't let yourself use it very often. Remember that time when I was very small I broke a light bulb on a stone and the glass spattered into my eyes? You took me to the doctor, who took most of it out. He was quitting and you said, "Please go over his eyes once more." He did, and he found some more glass. Consequently, now I am not blind. Yes, you had courage, and you never quit while you lived. I want to thank you for these qualities.*

Back in his own chair, Philip sat silently, looking down at the rug. After a few minutes he turned to me and said, "I never in a thousand years would have imagined *that* would come out."

4. Little Philip

I got out the photo of Philip that I had asked him to bring me early on in our work. I said, "Philip, this little boy is in that period which you walled off, encapsulated. Please call him back to mind now. Have him sit in this other chair. Talk to him, and let him talk to you."

In this conversation between Philip and his fantasy counterpart of many years ago, the little boy first told how frightening it was to exist day by day in that atmosphere in the house with two hysterical zombies. It was constant inconstancy, unpredictability, insecurity, and especially loneliness. "Little Philip" (as Philip now called him) told how tremendously alone he felt, with the air so emotionally frigid that he'd go to bed at night with a feeling that no other person was in the house. The other two persons seemed a million miles away. Generally, the only connection he had with his mother and sister was in his having to be prepared for the times they'd get upset.

But the most remarkable thing in that session was the metamorphosis of Little Philip. As Philip mostly listened in this strange conversation, Little Philip seemed to get over his anxiety.

He now sat in the Lotus position, appearing like a little Buddha, wise beyond his years. Did this wisdom come from his having observed everything that had happened in those first two years, and then having kept all these thing bottled up in his heart?

Little Philip became a kind of guide and friend to Philip. Now he sat beside Philip. He was calm, cheerful, but not laughing, emanating peacefulness, as though he had, all these years unbeknownst to the grown Philip, triumphed over the problems that troubled the grown Philip so much—fear of abandonment, the unpredictability of women, the cruelty of being left alone.

"Yes, he *had* triumphed over these problems," I said, "since *you*—for he is you—did not succumb, but succeeded in life despite your problems."

Then Philip began to weep slowly, but he kept talking. "Little Philip says, 'I'll stay with you. . . . We'll be companions and friends. . . . When you want comfort, I'll be there, or when you just want to talk something over, I'll stick with you.'"

Philip's crying—I pointed out to him—seemed not to come from sadness but rather from gratitude at his finding this new part of himself. At last this reunion. Was not his crying simply an overflow of emotion, which everyone feels at the reliving of these early experiences? He nodded.

As a fantasy figure, but furnishing real comfort, Little Philip was later to go along with Philip on his plane trips across the country, on his way down to see Nicole, and everywhere Philip needed him. Indeed, every place Philip was, there also was Little Philip. He was always available, always ready to give the comments that were necessary, a constant companion, but mostly just a presence that greatly expanded Philip's self.

It all seemed a surprising discovery to the grown Philip. He said, as though he were the first person ever to experience this, "I'm not lonely any more. My loneliness seems to have been mostly my own abandonment of my early self." During the next weeks, whenever he would find some occasion to be jealous of Nicole, Philip had only to call to mind this friendly companion, and the little Buddha seemed to fill the emptiness that otherwise would have been a hollow in which anxiety and jealousy could fester. "I'm not abandoned any more!" Philip had said with amazed delight.

Philip was experiencing the birth in consciousness of a new—though old—part of his self. It was a dawning of awareness of new possibilities which had in effect been there all the time. This could be for Philip a giant step toward his personal freedom.

And it was actually the beginning of Philip's giving up his clinging to loneliness, the beginning of "accepting acceptance," the uniting of himself with that early self that he had had to lock up in a dungeon in order to survive when life was not happy but threatening. Although this does not alter the original lack of basic trust, it does *surmount* it in the literal meaning of that term.

5. Anger as a Path to Freedom

What we hear most about the psychology of anger is that it clouds our vision, causes us to misunderstand each other, and in general interferes with the calm necessary for a rational, clear view of life. People point out that anger curtails one's freedom. All this is true. But it is one-sided; it omits the constructive side to anger.

In our society, we confuse anger with resentment, a form of repressed anger that eats steadily away at our innards. In resentment we store up ammunition to "get even" with our fellows, but we never communicate directly in a way that might resolve the problem. This transformation of anger into resentment is, as Nietzsche so emphatically proclaimed, the sickness of the middle class. It corrodes our stature as human beings.

Or we confuse anger with temper, which is generally an explosion of repressed anger; with rage, which may be a pathological anger; with petulance, which is childish resentment; or with hostility, which is anger absorbed into our character structure until it infects every act of ours.

I am not referring to these kinds of hostility or resentment. I am speaking, rather, of the anger that pulls the diverse parts of the self together, that integrates the self, keeps the whole self alive and present, energizes us, sharpens our vision, and stimulates us to think more clearly. This kind of anger brings with it an experience of self-esteem and self-worth. It is the healthy anger that makes freedom possible, the anger that cuts one loose from the unnecessary baggage in living.

Philip told me about a trip that he and Nicole had made to Trinidad. One particular evening they had planned to go dancing. But upon returning to their room after several cocktail parties and wine at dinner before continuing on to the dance, Philip had unexpectedly passed out on the bed. Nicole, as usual desirous of dancing, was enraged. Philip awoke a few hours later to find himself, in the fog of half consciousness, making love to Nicole. She had gotten more and more upset at his having passed out and had pulled off his trousers and told him while he was still in a semiconscious state that she wanted to make love.

Still foggy and trying to orient himself to the gap in time, he asked her what she had been doing while he was blacked out.

She answered, "I went out on the lawn in front. There was a man from North Carolina. We got to talking, then fucking. He fucked me for a whole hour."

In his fogginess Philip didn't know whether her story was true or made-up. All night long he was prey to this ambivalence. In the morning he asked her what she had meant by the story, and she, blushing, had said it was meant to be funny.

R.M.: *What did you feel about the story?*
PHILIP: *Just that I was greatly upset by it.*
R.M.: *You didn't see its cruelty?*
PHILIP: *No, I didn't see it as cruel. I only know that every time I think of some stranger fucking her for an hour, it's like a red hot poker being shoved into my heart.*
R.M.: *Imagine Nicole sitting in this chair. She's just told you this story. What are your feelings? Speak them out to her. [A string of epithets toward Nicole comes from Philip, some about his anger at her, but mostly about how much she had hurt him.] Yes, you have felt her cruelty all the way along. Nicole's values are not your values. It's a conflict of two different value systems. If, as*

you say, her father left when she was four and she never had a firm father after that, she would naturally be confused about how to deal with men. She'd take revenge by punishing men as a whole. And you're also being punished for not marrying her. But none of these is our real problem here. You've left out your role in all this. Who was it who tried to buy Nicole off by giving her money? Who talked of insurance? Who puts himself through all of this pain, bears it all just to see Nicole again? Who humiliates himself time and time again just to be with her? Who follows these other fellows into her bed and, so long as he gets the nipple to suck, the lover to make love to, accepts the humiliation of it all? [Philip seems taken aback.] *Sure, it was a cruel story Nicole told you in Trinidad. But you notice you didn't feel its cruelty—only how much it hurt you. The reason you don't feel it is you can't admit your own cruelty—cruelty to yourself most of all. Today you are surprisingly like the little boy begging Maude and Mother, "Slap me, beat me, anything you wish, so long as you let me keep on living here!" Yes, I know that back in that home you had to be deceitful to survive, you had to cover up what you really felt and thought. You surrendered your freedom. You always tried to foresee what the other person's reaction would be before you spoke. You hid behind such laudable words as "responsibility," "dutiful," "noble son," and so on. But you must have hated those roles with Maude and your mother.*

PHILIP: *Christ, yes!*

R.M.: *Imagine Maude sitting in the chair now. She's been dead two months. Tell her what you really felt.*

PHILIP: *Okay. Maude, I always hated coming to see you. I never dared say it—you were in enough pain. I pretended to be the nice, responsible brother. You talked about your bowel movements, how much you hated all the doctors, how your niece was stealing your money, and all the people who had betrayed you. I kept secretly looking at my watch to see how much longer I had to endure this paranoid stuff. . . .*

Venting this anger gave Philip partial freedom. At least he began to know he could say what he feels. But it was still a freedom within a jail. There was lacking the surge of anger that leads to a changing of one's life, the willingness to cut loose all the barges one is pulling, to throw aside all one's luggage and one's overscrupulous cares.

Back in this country, a week after their trip to Trinidad where Nicole had told him the story about having intercourse with the man in the front yard, Philip had asked her point blank whether the story was true or made up. Surprised, she said that of course it was made up, and asked him rhetorically whether he knew anybody who would have actually done that? He had replied, "Yes, my sister."

This opened up a new dimension: the identification of Maude with Nicole and the probability of some projection on Nicole that actually came from his sister. Maude had been promiscuous—she had picked up men on the street. Philip was deathly afraid of being like Maude. Hence, his overcontrol, his fear of cutting loose. These were a protection against his sister's schizophrenic impulses.

> R.M.: *Philip, I notice that you show Nicole how much she hurts you. You react like Pavlov's dogs—you make sure she sees how you bleed. But you don't tell her how you really feel. You never simply say to her, "Look, I love you and I don't want you running around the country having sex with other men."*
>
> PHILIP: *I thought I had said that.*
>
> R.M.: *I haven't heard it. I've heard only how much her sleeping with so and so hurts you, how all your lacerations are bleeding from her going away for that weekend.*
>
> PHILIP: *I don't want to make demands on her.*
>
> R.M.: *You think you're not making demands on her by showing her all this blood? The only difference is, showing the blood is the more painful way for both of you. I hear you saying to the world "If I am hurt, they shouldn't do what they are doing" and "It's better to feel hurt than to make others cry." Whenever they do start to cry—your mother, Maude, or Nicole—you capitulate. . . . You always prefer to be hurt rather than to take care of yourself even if it hurts someone else.*

6. The Green-Blue Lad

At about this time in our therapy the green-blue lad appeared in Philip's fantasies. This figure—of indeterminate age but somewhere in his late teens—emerged as a personification of Philip's anger. Unknown to Philip until I told him, green and blue are the colors in Chinese tradition that signify anger and fear.* But the green-blue lad was not dour and glowering, as most people in our culture would expect since we are that way when angry, but, paradoxically, was completely open and honest and full of energy, never stooping to find the best possible face to put on regardless of what he was talking about. Most surprising of all, he was the stimulator of Philip's sense of humor. The green-blue lad laughed at defeat, somewhat like Zorba the Greek. He could pick himself up undaunted when knocked to the ground; he could "risk it all in one pitch and toss," to crib Kipling's line. He seemed to be free of all conformist luggage. He was spontaneous and seemed to move as though dancing and to be all the time on the point of breaking into laughter.

A couple of weeks after the green-blue lad made his appearance in Philip's fantasies, Philip wrote the following in his diary, which he read to me:

The green-and-blue lad comes to me when I'm feeling low, when I'm not able to do much except react. I may be low like Dickens' character Uriah Heep, cringing, ready to do anyone else's bidding. Suddenly, the green-blue lad appears and changes me by contagion. Just by my seeing his face and his energetic movements, I suddenly become a strong man, laughing at trouble and defeat. My self esteem is reborn. I feel strong, able to cope. There is then no such thing as defeat for me, for the issue is within me. Even a defeat on the outside in life is a victory for me within because *I have done it.* The green-blue lad and I know only the word *can;* we know only possibilities. There is no such word as *impossible* for the green-and-blue fellow and me when we stand together.

---

*I am told by Dr. Harold Bailen, doctor both of American medicine and acupuncture, that green is the color in Chinese tradition that signifies anger and its opposite, peace. Blue is the color that signifies fear and its opposite, courage. In Chinese tradition one must go through these to get to joy. Red, the color of fire, is also the color signifying joy.

Someplace in the session when the green-blue lad had first appeared, Philip had said, "If Nicole wants to continue her present bed-hopping, the hell with her. I'll make my life with someone else."

He left that session in a state of ecstasy. It was one of those moments of breakthrough in therapy when it seems that nothing can stop the client from asserting his freedom and from taking hold of his life and remaking it. I watched him from my window as he walked down the street. He seemed six inches taller.

Simultaneously with the appearance of anger, the gnawing jealousy in Philip vanished. I knew it would come back partially, but never as strongly or as overwhelmingly as it had been. The dread in Philip of being abandoned also vanished. He knew that if one person abandoned or rejected him, there were others who would not. Furthermore, he could choose with whom he wanted to be intimate from here on.

It may seem strange to some readers that the green-blue lad was for Philip the personification of anger and that he appeared at this particular time. To understand this we must realize that many people who come for therapy have lost their freedom because of their repression of anger, a repression generally caused by their learning early in life that any anger will be severely punished. They regularly adopt the pattern that Philip showed to start with: being deceitful, covering up what they really think, learning not to speak out directly but to foresee what the other person's reaction would be before they speak. The resentment into which their anger has been transformed in its repression is often a central cause of their lack of integration and their continuing to surrender their freedom and their possibilities of choice.

Whereas resentment is almost entirely subjective, this kind of constructive anger, symbolized for Philip by the green-blue lad, is generally objective. As long as Philip felt only resentment toward his mother, everything he would have said about her would have been negative. But when, in therapy, he got angry at his mother in his fantasy, this led him, to his great surprise, to reveal how he secretly was appreciative and proud of his mother's care for him and her gifts to him. We recall his objective statement that his mother had done the best she could bringing up the children with no help. It may seem that this is an "excuse." I do not think so. I think, rather, that it is an endeavor to ground the anger on the conditions which caused the anger in the first place. In other words, *one is angry against destiny.*

The concept of destiny makes the experience of anger necessary. The kind of person who "never gets angry" is, we may be sure, the person who also never encounters destiny. When one encounters destiny, one finds anger automatically rising in one, but as strength. Passivity will not do. This emotion is not necessarily negative; recall that the green-blue lad was permeated with humor and robustness. Encountering one's destiny requires strength, whether the encounter takes the form of embracing, accepting, or attacking. Experiencing the emotional state of anger and conceiving of destiny means that you are freed from regarding yourself as too "precious"; you are able to throw yourself into the game, whatever it may be, without worrying about picayune details.

Anger was, for Philip, a path to freedom. The times when he had become angry, we notice, were times when he had gained valuable insights, which he then expressed constructively—for example, the time when he told Nicole off about her plans to marry Craig and move across the country, which he had called "the craziest plan I ever heard."

Experiences like Philip's is analogous to a ship putting out to sea. It is cast loose from the dock, and, sailing in the open wind, it then gets its power from cooperation with wind and sea and stars, as we get our power by living in cooperation with destiny. Our freedom, like the ship's, thus comes from engaging destiny, knowing that the elements are there all the time and that they have to be encountered or embraced. Constructive anger is one way of encountering destiny.

But often sailors find that they have to fight the elements, as in the case of a storm at sea. We find our freedom at the juncture of forces we cannot control but can only encounter—which often, like the ship fighting the storm, takes all the strength we have. Now it is not only sailing *with*, it is sailing *against* the sea and the storm winds.

The constructive anger we have been speaking about is one

way of using our power to choose our way of encountering destiny. The possible responses to destiny range from cooperation *with* at one end of the spectrum to fighting *against* at the other. Our anger empowers us in the struggle against destiny. As Beethoven cried, "I will seize fate by the throat!" And out of that came the Fifth Symphony.

7. *Loneliness and Rebirth*

Several sessions later, Philip came to his last hour, at least for the time being, feeling sad, lost, and especially lonely. These moods—typical for patients in the last session—are mainly an expression of the confusion and loneliness at parting from the therapist, the helper. The sadness is despair on being cast loose, alone, into the world. It gives us a final chance to look into the client's despair.

Philip cried a little, which seemed to free him, and he then talked freely about this despair. "I feel that everybody has died. Mother is dead. Maude is dead. Nicole seems at the moment to be dying. And my relation with you will be dead. Everyone died at once."

I reminded him that I would be here in the fall and available to him if he wished to talk with me. Furthermore, I hoped we would remain friends. Then I asked him about his loneliness.

"I feel like one single spruce tree standing at the North Pole, with nobody or nothing around for a million miles. . . . . At the North Pole a great honesty strikes me—I mean loneliness." He smiled over that slip of speech, and after thinking a little he added, "Yes, I guess it is a great 'honesty'—the honesty that comes from being alone and feeling it alone. No mothering there."

His slip of speech says something important. Loneliness *is* honesty in one sense. In honesty you have to separate yourself from the impersonal mass—you are saved from conformism. To be honest is to be lonely in the sense that you individuate yourself, you seize the moment to be yourself and yourself alone.

There is an initial loneliness about being oneself, speaking out of one's own center.

I responded to him, "Isn't that the loneliness that we all experience at times, the kind that is inseparable from the human condition? If you dare to be honestly yourself, you will be lonely. At each moment in our self-consciousness we are alone. No one else can genuinely come into our sanctum sanctorum. We die alone. No one escapes. This is destiny in its deepest sense. When we recognize this, then we *can* overcome the loneliness to some extent. We recognize that it is a *human* loneliness. It means we are all in the same boat, and we can then choose to, or not to, let others into our life. Lo and behold, we then have used the aloneness to be less lonely."

For some reason not clear at the time but obvious later, Philip then told me about his three years at Robert College in Istanbul, where, on his graduation from college, he had gone to teach. The second year there he had felt painfully lonely, due chiefly to the isolation in a foreign land where the English-speaking group was small and boring. And teaching English to Turkish boys was not that absorbing. Philip had followed his usual defense: he threw himself into his work with ever greater zeal. But the harder he worked, the more isolated he felt. Finally he collapsed and had to go to bed for a couple of weeks. This he called his "nervous breakdown."

He had then changed his life style, he told me. He began to draw. He wandered around, drawing poppies in the fields and old mosques in Istambul. He gave up his habit of rigidly planning his life and began to take the flow of energy as it came. But all without aim or sense of direction, isolated, feeling often like a nonentity since all his old ways of proving his worth no longer worked.

> R.M.: *Please close your eyes and imagine yourself back at that time in your life. Listen to the things around you, the buzzing of bees, the songs of birds that spring. Be that young man who had that "breakdown." . . . What is he doing?*
> PHILIP: *He's just standing around in the college compound. He feels empty, lost. . . . There's a group of people nearby, mostly boys*

> *from the school. He walks a little bit toward them. . . . Is it time
> for supper? . . . There's nothing he wants to do . . . no direction
> at all. . . . He's like a deaf and dumb person . . . he doesn't say
> anything. . . .*
>
> R.M.: *What would you do with him?*
>
> PHILIP: *I'd walk over. . . . I'd put my arm around him. . . . I'd
> say, "We like you, Phil." . . . I'd go with him to supper. . . .*
>
> R.M.: *Others must have liked this young man, too. I see that you
> behave lovingly toward him. . . . What part of you is identified
> with this young man?*
>
> PHILIP: *My heart, my muscles. . . . I feel him all the way through
> me.*
>
> R.M.: *You see, you can give him love and tenderness.* [Now Philip
> starts to weep again.] *Is your crying because you have become
> aware that others could have liked and loved you and you
> wouldn't even have known it? . . . Aren't those tears of gratitude
> that you can now absorb these things?*

Philip then told me that that spring, when he'd been without
goals, undirected, and had given up his rigid mapping, had been
the prelude to the "best summer I ever had. I started out on my
summer vacation up toward the Caspian Sea with no plans, no
fixed guides to follow. By accident I met a group of fifteen or
sixteen artists traveling and doing art as a group, and I got a job
with them as a sort of fancy handy man. I traveled and made
sketches with them all through the villages along the Caspian Sea.
This was the birth of my becoming an architect. I fell deeply in
love that summer. I lost my virginity with the greatest of joy. It
was a fabulous summer!"

Should we call this "accident," as Philip describes his meeting
this group, really an expression of destiny? I think so. When he
gives up his rigid and compulsive demands on life, when he can
"let go and let be," unexpected possibilities may open up in
unpredictable ways which otherwise would never be known to
him. These are aspects of destiny become conscious.

Our therapeutic question is: Why did these associations about
the "fabulous summer" come up at that particular moment?
Because Philip subconsciously associated that summer with his

present moment. He is telling me symbolically that his present situation is similar to that spring and summer and will, he hopes and believes, lead from despair to joy, will lead to "the best summer I ever had."

In that hour with Philip, I wanted to support his confidence without taking away the force of his despair, since despair may well lead to the deepest insight and the most valuable change. For Philip it certainly did that in the incident of the "nervous breakdown" and the subsequent summer in which, as he put it, he experienced more sheer joy than ever before. It is true that most people shrink when in despair or depression—they tend to retreat into their hopelessness. I hoped that Philip would experience his despair constructively, as an opportunity. The despair can then act upon the person like the flood in Genesis: it can clear away the vast debris—the false answers, false buoys, superficial principles—and leave the way open for new possibilities. That is, for new freedom.

We know in psychotherapy that times of despair are essential to the client's discovery of hidden capacities and basic assets. Those therapists are misguided who feel it incumbent upon themselves to reassure the patient at every point of despair. For if the client never feels despair, it is doubtful whether he ever will feel anything below the surface. There is surely value in the client's experience that he has nothing more to lose anyway, so he may as well take whatever leap is necessary. That seems to me to be the meaning of the sentence from folklore "Despair and confidence both banish fear."

III

The Dynamics of Freedom

I have no need to see and to test in order to be set free. I am free even in the confusion of servitude. I enjoy the freedom of the future, generations in advance. And when I die, I shall die a free man, for I have fought for freedom my whole life long.

—NIKOS KAZANTZAKIS, *Freedom or Death*

Man is free, in so far as he has the power of contradicting himself and his essential nature. Man is free even from his freedom; that is, he can surrender his humanity.

—PAUL TILLICH

Freedom, by its very nature, is elusive. The word is difficult to define because of its quicksilver quality: freedom is always moving. You can state what it is *not* or what you desire to get free *from*—which is why the phrase "freedom from" should never be disparaged. But it is difficult to designate what freedom *is*. Thus we always hear of the struggle *for*, the fight *for* freedom. But when someone tells us "how I found freedom," we have a feeling that something is being faked. Kazantzakis rightly states, "The greatest virtue is not to be free, but to struggle ceaselessly for freedom."

Freedom is like a flock of white butterflies bestirred in front of you as you walk through the woods: rising in cluster they flit off in an infinite number of directions. "Using the word 'freedom,' " Loren Eisley writes, "immediately eliminates the entity it is meant to describe." In other words, once you become self-konsciously sure of your freedom, you have lost it.

Hence we find ourselves almost always describing what freedom is *not* rather than what it *is:* "I am free tomorrow" means I do not have to work; "I have a free period" means I do not have any class then. Malinowski points this out: "freedom is frequently and persistently conceived of as a negative quality. Freedom is very much like health or virtue or innocence. We feel it most intensely after we have lost it." The dictionary does nothing to relieve our frustration. In the eighteen different meanings in Webster's, fourteen of them are negative, such as "not held in slavery" or "not subject to external authority." Of the remaining four, one is "liberty"—which deals with political freedom—and the others are simply tautological, such as "spontaneous, voluntary, independent."

Freedom is continually creating itself. As Kierkegaard puts it, freedom is expansiveness. Freedom has an infinite quality. This ever-new set of possibilities is part of the reason psychology has by and large evaded the subject, for freedom cannot be pinned down as psychologists are wont to do.

In psychotherapy the closest we can get to discerning freedom in action is when a person experiences "I can" or "I will." When a client in therapy says either of these, I always make sure he knows that I have heard him; for "can" and "will" are statements of personal freedom, even if only in fantasy. These verbs point to some event in the future, either immediate or long-term. They also imply that the person who uses them senses some power, some possibility, and is aware of ability to use this power.

1. Freedom of Doing, or Existential Freedom*

Knowing that the ultimate meaning of *freedom* will elude us, let us still endeavor to define the term as best we can. The first

---

*I use the term *existential freedom* to mean the freedom that occurs in our day-to-day existence. I do not wish it confused with existential philosophy. I have learned much from the tenets of existential philosophy, but the particular view of freedom offered here is my own and should not be identified with the philosophy of that name.

definition is on the psychological level, the domain of everyday actions:

> Freedom is the capacity to pause in the face of stimuli from many directions at once and, in this pause, to throw one's weight toward this response rather than that one.

This is the freedom we experience in a store when we pause over the purchase of a necktie or a blouse. We summon up in our imaginations the image of how we will look in this or that tie, what so-and-so will say about it, or how the color will fit such and such a suit. And then we buy the tie or we move on to something else. This is *freedom of doing*, or existential freedom.

This freedom is shown most interestingly in the supermarket, when we push our carts through the aisles between the tumultuous variety of packages and cans of food on the shelves, each one silently shouting through its bright-colored label "Buy me!" We see the shoppers with expressions of hesitancy, vacuity, wonder, pausing for some inspiration as to which of all these foods will be good for dinner tonight. The shoppers seem hypnotized, charmed, preoccupied. Like patients on a ward in a mental hospital, they do not see me as I walk directly across their line of vision. The expressions of wonder and hesitancy are a readiness, an invitation, an openness to some stimulus on the shelves to persuade them to throw the balance this way or that in making their choice.

This first freedom is experienced by each of us hundreds of times every day. It is decked up in respectable terms like *decision/choice* when we discuss freedom in psychology classes—if we ever discuss freedom in psychology classes at all.

The most profound illustration of this kind of freedom is our ability to ask questions. Take, for example, my asking a question after listening to a lecture. The very fact that the question comes up in my mind at all implies that there is more than one answer. Otherwise there would be no point in asking the question in the first place. This is freedom; it implies that there is some possibility, some freedom of selection in what I ask. The speaker then pauses for a few seconds after I've asked it, turning over in his mind the possible answers.

We sense that there is, in asking and answering questions, a good deal more going on, and it is of a richer nature, than the mere responding to various stimuli and selecting a response. Questioning implies some value judgment, some investment of the person's life, some invitation to share, to make contact, some challenge to consider a new idea.

So we must move on to the second level of our definition. Solzhenitsyn sees the trend toward superficiality in any definition that includes only the freedom of doing. In his speech at Stanford, in accepting the American Friendship Award from the Hoover Institution, he stated:

Regrettably, in recent decades our very idea of freedom has been diminished and grown shallow in comparison with previous ages; it has been relegated almost exclusively to freedom from outside pressure, to freedom from state coercion—to freedom understood on the juridical level, and no higher.

2. Freedom of Being, or Essential Freedom

Whereas the "freedom of doing" refers to the act, the "freedom of being" refers to the *context* out of which the urge to act emerges. It refers to the deeper level of one's attitudes and is the fount out of which "freedom of doing" is born. Hence, I call this second kind of freedom *essential freedom*. This is illustrated in Bruno Bettelheim's testimony concerning his two years in a concentration camp during the Second World War. He had no freedom of doing at all; he was powerless to change the actions of the SS. But he did have what he calls "ultimate freedom," the freedom to choose his attitude toward his captors. This freedom of being, or essential freedom, involves the ability to reflect, to ponder, out of which the freedom to ask questions, whether spoken or not, emerges.

A prisoner in San Quentin, interviewed by Philip Zimbardo, gives us our springboard here. This prisoner was a Chicano and a poet. He could not take the pushing around in the prison, and hence for five years he had been held in solitary confinement, which, with a strange irony, is called in San Quentin "Maximum Adjustment Center." I quote from his words in the interview:

They have separated me from my family, deprived me of touching my young boy. They have hidden the sun, moon and stars from my view, exchanged their concrete and steel for earth and flowers and everything warm and soft.

The wind through my hair is replaced by their rules in my ears.

All tears are forbidden on the tier. The strength in my muscles is bound by chains and shackles.

They have tried to negate my existence—and almost succeeded.

They have left me with nothing, nothing except an inner core, a secret, private place they have not yet found how to get to.

The speaker of these words is obviously not trying to select among "stimuli." This is clearly a different kind of freedom, expressed in such phrases as "inner core" and "a secret, private place where they have not yet found how to get to." He goes on:

It is where I think of who I am, where I try to understand the what and why of my enemies, and where I keep alive my will to live in a hell where I am made to feel like a nothing, at best an animal, a wild animal in captivity.

We notice that he does not say, "What shall I *do*," but rather "I try to understand." He is engaged in a succession of leaps in his own thoughts, leaps which imply breakthroughs to a new dimension in his relation to himself. This is clearly not a freedom of *doing*; it is a freedom of *being*.

He tells us also—and this is of great importance—that this is where he keeps alive his will to live. This is a freedom that invigorates, that inspirits, and he rightly interprets it as that to which he owes his survival in the agonizing loneliness of solitary confinement. He concludes:

Although I sometimes get depressed and feel like giving up, the discovery of my thoughts gives me joy. For until they find a way to take my thoughts away, I am free.

Knowledge is freedom, and is the source of hope in this most hopeless of all places.

A man can live without liberty but not without freedom.

In that mind-blowing last sentence, he is using the terms as I have chosen to define them in this book, "liberty" referring to the political state. We could survive if we had to live under fascism or in prison, hate it as we may. But freedom is essentially an inner state. This "core," this "secret place," is absolutely necessary for our survival as humans. It is what gives the person a sense of being; it gives one the experience of autonomy, identity, the capacity to use the pronoun "I" with its full range of meaning.

I do not wish to have this inner freedom confused with the sentimentally subjective statements of it. In the Civil War play *Shenandoah*, there is a song and dance performed by a black boy with the words "Freedom's just a state of mind." Was freedom just a state of mind for Martin Luther King? Was it just a state of mind for the freedom marchers? Was it just a state of mind for Washington and the Continental Army at Valley Forge? Is it just a state of mind for those in the women's liberation movement?

There is no authentic inner freedom that does not, sooner or later, also affect and change human history. This includes Bruno Bettelheim's "ultimate" freedom, the affecting of history coming in his insightful books after the concentration camp. It includes the freedom described by the prisoner in San Quentin, its effect on history consisting, for one thing, in our quoting him here. The subjective and objective sides of freedom can never be separated from each other.

I propose that the prisoner we quoted is freer than his guards at San Quentin. In a poem he wrote in prison we find the words, "though we're wrapped in chains/The jailor is not free!" No one can deny that Epictetus, as a slave, was freer than this owner and master. Our prisoner also is experiencing freedom as an inner condition of life, the source of his human dignity and the source of his strength to write poems, "Scratched out from the pit of prison with a worn pencil from my cell."

The prisoner's statement "the discovery of my thoughts gives me joy" is a profound comment with far-reaching implications for our lives as well. His freedom is not a freedom of security, but a freedom of discovery. The joy of the discovery of one's own thoughts is a truth that we rarely hear from anyone who has not hammered it out on the anvil of years of solitude.

The prisoner in San Quentin also tells us that his "knowledge is freedom" and his "source of hope." In the freedom of being, new possibilities continually surge up, possibilities of new discoveries about oneself, new flights of imagination, new visions of what the world and living in it might be. Talamantez does not say "hope *for*" something; he proclaims that to have the freedom to know is *itself* hope, regardless of whether anything concrete eventuates or not.

What I am here calling the *freedom of being*, or essential freedom, is parallel, I assume, to what Augustine called "freedom major," as his "freedom minor" is parallel to what I call *freedom of doing*. Essential freedom is the essence out of which other forms of freedom flow.

Schelling similarly writes: "In the concept of freedom we have what Archimedes sought but did not find, a fulcrum on which reason can rest its ladder, without therefore placing it in the present or in a future world but only in the *inner sense of freedom*, because it unites both worlds in itself and must also be the principle of explanation for both."

As the prisoner in San Quentin demonstrates in his interview, this essential freedom is the source of his joy and his spirit. The former is shown in his own words "[it] gives me joy." The spirit is shown in his courage, his hope, the very fact that he survived and preserved his sanity and his sense of possibility in a situation in which many people would long before have given up in despair and probably taken refuge in psychosis. He says in a poem written while he was in prison that insanity was his constant companion, but he managed to avoid it by his absorption in his writing.

Survivors of the concentration camps give similar testimony to this essential freedom and to the fact that the inmates who could choose their own attitudes toward the SS were not spiritually enslaved. This is pragmatic proof, if it were necessary, of the reality of their essential freedom.

Picasso provides us with an illustration of freedom of being in contrast to freedom of doing. In 1904 Cézanne had advised other painters to "interpret nature in terms of the cylinder, the sphere, the cone." Picasso, a young artist prodigy at the time, had absorbed the rules and discipline of his craft. He could draw beautifully, and he knew the laws of perspective and proportion. All these are "givens," which I will refer to as destiny. Picasso had come to terms with this discipline: in his early blue period, especially in those paintings of Spanish peasants, every expression is superbly drawn. This, however, is still *freedom of doing*, or existential freedom.

But Picasso, an artist of courage and zest, struggled against the boundaries. Was there a way of transcending the old rules, a way of pushing on to new dimensions?

In 1907 came the breakthrough with his painting *Les Demoiselles d'Avignon*. This marked the birth of cubism. No longer was it a question of drawing arms and legs accurately in an academic sense; no longer was it a matter of rendering the fingers exactly as they are in reality. The challenge now was to see the human body as embodying the forms of nature, which Picasso did in this painting with a completeness never before achieved. The question now was how the lines of the arms and legs of the women in this painting relate to the space, how they fit on the canvas and with each other. The "cylinder, the sphere, the cone" were now visible before us. The cones that we see when we look at mountains, the curved lines that mark the sand where waves sweep in, the perpendicular lines of the plains cut by the vertical lines of trees rising up from horizontal lines of the fields—all these are part of our bodies and ourselves as shown in the amazing balance with which we walk, the rhythm with which we breathe and with which our hearts beat.*

This breakthrough of cubism, foreshadowed by Van Gogh and Gaugin, and certainly by Cézanne and Matisse, demonstrates the freedom of being in contrast with the freedom of doing. The "leap" was to a new context in which paintings were to be seen. It changed the attitudes with which we look at painting, and it changed the questions artists ask about their work. It cast a new light on our relation to nature.

Cubism opens up a host of new possibilities and gives a new unity to ourselves and our universe. The new way these artists

---

*We are not saying that cubism is the highest form of art or that everyone must like it, but only that it represents an important—and, for our day, crucial—development.

related to space in the first decade of this century, for example, predicted the "space age," which was to be taken up and re-expressed by intellectuals and scientists in the 1960s. It illustrates how one artist speaks for the whole community of his colleagues as well as for himself and for his culture.

3. Is There a Conflict between Freedom of Doing and Freedom of Being?

An interesting question confronts us here. Are freedom of doing and freedom of being contradictory? Why is it that some people achieve essential freedom only when everything in the existential world becomes unfree? This seems to have been the experience of the survivors of the concentration camps. Solzhenitsyn testifies that this was true in his years in the Russian work camps—when all freedom of doing was taken away, he felt himself pushed back to the level of essential freedom. It was, moreover, the experience of freedom marchers who were thrown into prison, as shown by the several books that subsequently came out by the marchers with titles like *I Found My Freedom in Jail*. Saint Paul states that in bondage the Christian is freed, a sentence that seems hopelessly paradoxical at first but takes on meaning the more one thinks about it.

Do we get to essential freedom only when our everyday existence is interrupted? For as long as most human beings can settle for bread and comfort, they will do so, the Grand Inquisitor argues. But when bread and comfort are no longer available, are people then—and only then—pushed to their essential depths of experience? If we answer "yes" to these questions, we deny the popular idea that human beings move up through a hierarchy of needs from the biological to the psychological to the spiritual. It would mean, rather, that people evolve by conflict and struggle, and there is no simple and placid evolution from lower needs to higher ones. When lower needs are not met, they are forced into higher needs. Fasting as a way of reaching religious truth is one example of this. "Calamity theory," as Richard Farson elucidates it, is another example. It says in effect that in calamity, in hardship, many people are forced to look inward and to take the necessary leaps to higher levels, as we have noted above.

Is confinement, including the simple fact of having time to think, one aspect of what is necessary for the experience of essential freedom? Talamantez was, of course, in jail. John Lilly also thinks confinement is essential in his experiments in isolation tanks: the person floats in complete darkness in a tank in which he is weightless and without any stimuli from the outside world. Then apparently radical and often highly positive things happen to some people in their sense of freedom of being. When human beings can no longer escape—when they can no longer run about, go to this movie or that, surrender to their TV addiction, or fill their time with diversions—when these escape avenues are no longer open to them, they must listen to themselves.

But here we arrive at a fascinating question: *Is not our destiny itself our concentration camp?* Is not the destiny that impinges upon us that which forces us to see our bondage? Does not the engaging of our destiny—which is the design of our life—hedge us about with the confinement, the sobriety, indeed, often the cruelty, which forces us to look beyond the limits of day-to-day action? Is not the inescapable fact of death, whether we are young or old, the concentration camp of us all? Is not the fact that life is a joy and a bondage at the same time enough to drive us to consider the deeper aspect of being? This is the greatness of life and our "quiet desperation," which Thoreau talks about, in the same instant.

James Farmer tells of the struggles of CORE to help black people turn the simple proclamation of freedom put on paper by Abraham Lincoln into real and actual freedom. Out of the battles he and his followers went through and the violence they had to endure, Farmer writes:

In the very act of working for the impersonal cause of racial freedom, a man experiences, almost like grace, a large measure of private freedom. Or call it a new comprehension of his own identity, an intuition of the expanding boundaries of his self.

He identifies this as the "radical source" of freedom; I call it the freedom of being. He describes one incident in which he and his followers endured the brutality of police, and "the men and women who stood between me and the lynch mob gradually, during the course of those two violent days, made the decision to act instead of being acted upon."

4. Growing in Freedom

Our capacity as human beings to imagine, to think, to wonder, to be conscious are all degrees of freedom. "In the realm of the mind," wrote Bertrand Russell, "there are no limits." In our imaginations we can instantaneously transport ourselves back three thousand years and listen to blind old Homer reciting his tales around a campfire in Macedonia. Or we can take our place, again instantaneously, on a stone seat in the theater of Dionysus in classical Athens and be enthralled by the dramas of Sophocles and Aeschylus. Or we can project ourselves into the future any number of years we wish. The fact that all of these acts can be done instantaneously—that we can *conquer space and time simultaneously*—is itself indicative of the nature of freedom.

Personal freedom can be seen as the *range of movement* possible for the organism. Saint Thomas Aquinas stated that there are four kinds of existence. First are inert things, like rocks, which simply *exist*. Second are the things that *exist* and *grow*, like plants and trees. Third are things that *exist* and *grow* and *move about*, like animals. Fourth are creatures that *exist, grow, move*, and *think*, like human beings. (For us the term *consciousness* would be more accurate.) Each of these stages represents a radically increased freedom, seen in the range of movement, over the preceeding one.

As Swiss biologist Adolf Portmann phrased it, we are born with freedom in the sense of the potentiality for movement of the infant. "The free play of the limbs, which gives to the human nursling so much richer possibilities than the new-born monkey or ape reminds us that our own state at birth is not simply helpless but is characterized by a significant freedom." This freedom of movement, which, contemporary experiments demonstrate, begins even in the uterus, is given a great boost when the umbilical cord is cut, and continues as the newborn grows. One leap ahead in the infant's range of movement is when the child can crawl, another leap when it learns to walk, another when he or she goes off to school. All of these are quantum increases in the range of movement of the human child—in nautical terms, the "cruising range." The movement is increasingly psychological as well as physical, the psychological having its roots in the great leap in the child's learning to talk.

All of these "leaps" from birth on, these events in which one differentiates oneself from parents, can be seen as psychological rebirth experiences. Hence, they are anxiety-creating as well as challenging. At adolescence there are other quantum leaps that increase the young person's range of movement, most notably in the sexual realm. One experiences the "alarming possibility of being able," as Kierkegaard puts it. Going off to college, marrying, earning a living, moving to a new city—all can be seen as increases in the person's range of freedom.

Freedom is a moving *out* while retaining the human bond to the persons, particularly the mother, *at home*. There is a delicate balance between these two poles. If there is too little wandering out and too much dependence on the home, freedom is being surrendered in favor of security, which turns out then to be an escape from freedom. If there is too much wandering out and too little security at home, the person may get pathologically anxious and may retrench in other ways that cut off his or her freedom. Each of these new levels of movement consists of the enlarging of one's cruising range by cutting the biological ties with home and mother and father and establishing psychological and spiritual ties in their place. We saw, in the case of Philip, as he came to terms with past and present in his talk with his mother, that he no longer talked about what she should have done for him, but rather what she *did* do for him. He admired and valued her. Obviously his mother had not changed: the change in memory really came from a change in Philip's attitude. At his stage in life, the dynamic question is very rarely "What happened?" but rather *"What is your attitude* toward what happened?" The achievement of freedom now makes it possible for Philip *to change the context* for viewing his mother. It is freedom of being.

The last and ultimate leap in this growth of movement, in this pilgrim's progress, occurs on one's death bed, when, as Otto Rank puts it, we go through the last stage of differentiation.

In therapy—the central purpose being, as I have said, to help the patient discover, establish, and use his or her freedom—I find it important, when the patient pleads total powerlessness, to remind him that he put one foot in front of the other to get to my office. And he *can* leave. On that range of freedom, minute as it is, we can begin building.

Each step in the growth in differentiation carries a new sense of responsibility equivalent to the new freedom. The sense of response-ability, as the word may be understood, involves an awareness of others' needs as we live in the community of the family or the village together with a capacity to respond to the needs also of one's own self. We choose our way of responding to the other people who make up the context in which our freedom develops. The paradox that one can be free only as one is responsible is central at every point in freedom. But the converse is just as true: one can be responsible only as one is free. This is the reason why the argument that we are totally determined breeds irresponsibility. You have to have some sense that your decisions genuinely *matter* to take responsibility for them.

The sense of responsibility begins in the relation of infant to mother: as he grows older, the infant learns that mother has her own needs. She does not come every time he cries, and he cannot bite his mother's nipple without eliciting a look of pain on her face. Thus growth always has two simultaneous sides: freedom *and* responsibility, one equivalent to the other, one necessary for the other. We do not let our three-year-old child cross Broadway in New York by himself; he has not yet developed sufficient responsibility to be permitted this freedom.

Albert Camus expresses this well:

The aim of art, the aim of a life can only be to increase the sum of freedom and responsibility to be found in every person and in the world."

Since it limits freedom, responsibility is one aspect of the destiny pole. So long as we are born of woman (in contrast to cloning) we shall have to come to terms with mother not only as a source of food, but increasingly as a person carrying her own destiny. Freedom for oneself increases as one's awareness of the destiny of others increases.

It is significant that the new capacity for freedom related to movement is actualized as a form of art. Human beings dance—ballet and folk and jazz and ballroom and T'ai Chi—as an expression of aesthetic possibilities. Each art form is developed as a ritual to express one's exhilaration and freedom. "To us," writes Alan Oken in the *Age of Aquarius,* "rock music represents freedom . . . the freedom to feel, to be one with a higher collective force, to move together in one cosmic rhythm." One "dances for joy," or to express sexuality or religious feelings, as in the whirling of Muslim dervishes, or to "drum" up emotion for battle, like the war dances of the Native Americans.

Movement and the expansion of freedom are symbolic expressions of the individual's career from birth to death.

IV

The Paradoxes of Freedom

See how everything instantly creates its opposite! War continues in the midst of peace. Want is born from abundance. In one and the same laboratory, the same men search for what will kill and what will cure, cultivating both good and evil. . . .

—PAUL VALÉRY

Freedom, we have stated, is fraught with paradoxes because of its unique character. Before there could be any freedom to walk on the streets or to raise cattle in frontier towns, for example, law and order were necessary. Security is the opposite of freedom, yet a certain degree of security is essential if freedom is to exist at all. Spinoza held that the purpose of government is to preserve sufficient security so that each man may live without fear of his neighbor. "*Have to,*" the anthropologist Dorothy Lee speaks paradoxically, "is strangely *freeing.*"

I use the word *paradox* to describe the relationship between two opposing things which, even though they are posited against each other and seem to destroy each other, cannot exist without each other. God and the devil, good and evil, life and death, beauty and ugliness—all these opposites appear to be at odds with each other. But the paradox is that the very confrontation with the one breathes vitality into the other. Life is more alive, more zestful, when we are aware of death; and death has significance only because there is life. God needs the devil. Freedom comes alive only when we see it in opposition to destiny, and destiny is significant only when it is in opposition to freedom. The opposites fructify each other: each gives dynamism, power, to the other.

66

The emotions elicited in us by a paradox are surprise and amazement. The assertion that God cannot exist without the devil catches short those who believe life is a one-way ticket to paradise. That male and female need the differences between each other gives pause to those who dabble in simplistic hopes for a future brave new androgyny.

Heraclitus proclaimed that people "do not understand how that which differs with itself is in agreement: harmony consists of opposing tension, like that of bow and the lyre." This he illustrated by the bow and cord; one can shoot with the bow because of the tension set up by the string pulling against it. Or the frame of the lyre and its strings. Each of these opposites is useful to us by virtue of the tension set up between the two forces.

The paradox we confront in this chapter is that between freedom and destiny. It can be stated in many ways. One is that freedom gets its vitality, its authenticity, from its juxtaposition with destiny. And destiny, such as in death, is important to us because it perpetually threatens our freedom; the Grim Reaper stands at the far end of any path we take. But no matter how scant at any given moment our freedom is, new possibilities beckon us in our dreams, in our aspirations, in our hopes and actions, and the possibility pushes us to acknowledge, encounter, confront, engage, or rebel against our destiny.

The paradox is fundamental in psychotherapy, a point not realized by most therapists. Philip, for example, attained his personal freedom only when he came to terms with the paradoxes of his life. The chief one was his love-hate relation with his mother. But there were other derivative paradoxes such as his dependency-love relation with Nicole. The major experiences such as birth, death, love, anxiety, guilt are not problems to be solved, but paradoxes to be confronted and acknowledged. Thus in therapy we should talk of solving problems only as a way of making the paradoxes of life stand out more clearly.* Just as the

---

*One of the most sensitive and skillful of the British analysts, D. W. Winnicott, writes perceptively that he wishes to draw "attention to the *paradox*. . . . My contribution is to ask for a paradox to be accepted and tolerated and respected, and *for it not to be resolved*. By flight to a split-off intellectual functioning it is possible to resolve the paradox, but the price of this is the loss of the value of the

acceptance of normal anxiety is necessary if we are to be able to free ourselves of neurotic anxiety, so the acceptance of the normal paradoxes of life—love-hate, life-death—is necessary if we are to achieve freedom from the compulsive and neurotic aspects of our problems.

The confusion with regard to freedom in our day is that we have conceived of freedom as a bow with no string to hold it in tension or a lyre with no frame to give it tautness and hence produce music. We were created free, the American Declaration of Independence tells us, and hence we assume there are no limits. Freedom thus has lost its viability; it has vanished like the flame going out in our fireplace just when we need it most.

1. The Grand Inquisitor

The most penetrating and profound picture of the paradox of human freedom versus security is presented by Dostoevsky in his legend of the Grand Inquisitor in *The Brothers Karamazov*. The legend begins in Seville in the sixteenth century with the burning of a hundred heretics in the town square. This "magnificent *auto da fé*," as Dostoevsky calls it, was presided over by the cardinal of the church, the Grand Inquisitor, in the presence of the king, the knights, and the ladies of the court. All of the townspeople were there, and they heaped faggots on the fires under the dying heretics.

The next morning, before the burning recommenced, Jesus returned to Seville. "He came softly, unobserved, and yet, strange to say, everyone recognized Him. . . . The people are irresistibly drawn to Him, they surround Him, they flock about Him, follow Him. He moves silently in their midst with a gentle smile of infinite compassion. . . . The crowd weeps and kisses the earth under His feet. Children throw flowers before Him, sing, and cry 'Hosannah.' 'It is He—it is He!' "

---

paradox itself" (*Playing and Reality* [Harmondsworth: Pelican, 1974]; italics are Winnicott's). And again: "I should like to put in a reminder here that the essential features in the concept of transitional objects and phenomena . . . is the paradox, and the acceptance of the paradox" (*Ibid.*, p. 104).

Coming out of the cathedral, the Grand Inquisitor, a tall and erect man of ninety with sharp eyes "in which there burns a sinister fire," observes everything. After watching for a few moments, he motions his palace guards to arrest Jesus and throw him into prison. That night under the cover of darkness, the Inquisitor comes to the prison and speaks to his silent prisoner: "Is it You? you? . . . Why have you come to hinder us? . . . Tomorrow I shall condemn you and burn you as the worst of heretics. And the very people who have today kissed your feet . . . at the faintest sign from me will rush up and heap embers on your fire."

The kernel of his accusation is that Jesus taught people freedom, promised them freedom, expected them to be free. "Did you not often say then, 'I will make you free'? . . . Yes, we've paid dearly for it," the old man goes on. "For fifteen centuries we have been wrestling with your freedom, but now it is ended and over for good. . . . Let me tell you that now, today, people are more persuaded than ever that they have perfect freedom, yet they have brought their freedom to us and laid it humbly at our feet. . . . You gave them a promise of freedom which in their simplicity and their natural unruliness they cannot even understand, which they fear and dread—for nothing has ever been more insupportable for a man and a human society than freedom."

Jesus' great mistake, the old Inquisitor argues, was His refusal to accept Satan's magical power. "Turn [these stones] into bread, and mankind will run after you like a flock, grateful and obedient, though forever trembling, lest you withdraw your hand and deny them your bread. . . . Oh, never, never can they feed themselves without us! No science will give them bread so long as they remain free. In the end they will . . . cry, 'Make us your slaves, but feed us.' . . . I tell Thee that man is tormented by no greater anxiety than to find someone quickly to whom he can hand over that gift of freedom with which the ill-fated creature is born."

Although the Grand Inquisitor argues that human beings will choose bread and the security that bread symbolizes rather than freedom, he is no simple materialist. He is aware that the Church, to take away man's freedom, must take charge of the human conscience, appease it, and relieve men and women from

the burden of the knowledge of good and evil. For moral choice—
or the freedom of conscience—is the most seductive thing of all.
Human beings must have some stable conception of the purpose
of life or else they will commit suicide. Indeed, human beings
need three things, he states, all of which the Church furnishes:
"mystery, miracle, and authority." These relieve people not only
from physical hunger but from the struggles of conscience—and,
I would add, relieve them of wonder, awe, independence, and a
sense of autonomy. In the world the Grand Inquisitor presents,
the yearning for security on all levels of life has triumphed.

The people will be told what to believe: the Church will
inform them when they can sleep with mistresses or wives and
when they can't. The Grand Inquisitor presents an enticing picture: there will be no crime anymore and, therefore, no sin. Yes,
the Church will have to lie to do these things, he admits—particularly when it tells people they still follow Christ; and this
"deception will be our suffering," the Inquisitor puts it. The
Church has been following Satan, he admits, the "wise and dread
spirit, the spirit of self-destruction and non-existence." The
Church made this bargain eight centuries before, in 756, when
Pepin the Short, King of the Franks, granted Ravenna to Pope
Stephen III, thus establishing the pope's temporal power.

But all this will enable the Church to "plan the universal happiness of mankind." The Church will devote itself to "uniting all
in one unanimous and harmonious anthill." Humans are like "pitiful children," but "childlike happiness is the sweetest of all."

Every sin will be expiated if it is done with the Church's permission. If the people are obedient—obedience has now been
elevated to the highest virtue—they will be allowed to have children of their own. Everyone, the millions of them, will be happy.
Everyone, that is, except those who direct this great program.
Only we, "the hundred thousand who rule over them," will be
unhappy, says the Inquisitor, only those "who guard the mystery," only those who have taken upon themselves "the curse of
the knowledge of good and evil."

He finally looks directly into Jesus' face and challenges Him,
"Judge us if you can and dare. . . . I too prized the freedom with
which you have blessed men. . . . But I awakened . . . and joined

the ranks of those *who have corrected your work*. . . . I shall burn you for coming to hinder us. For if anyone has ever deserved our fires, it is you. Tomorrow I shall burn you. *Dixi."*

What strikes us most sharply is the contemptuous image the Inquisitor holds of humankind. Human beings are weak, base, vicious, vile, ill-fated, pitiful, helpless, sinful, and tend toward rebellion if they are not kept rigidly in restraint. The highest moral principle for such creatures—and what the Church teaches—is absolute obedience. Then human beings will express their childish mirth, contentment, and other emotions, all within the jurisdiction of the Church: "I swear," cries the Inquisitor to Jesus, "human beings are slaves by nature." They cannot, on their own power, confront the "curse of the knowledge of good and evil." Thus, the Inquisitor pushes mankind back again into the preconscious state of innocence in the Garden of Eden. No stronger demonstration that freedom is a sign of the nobility of human beings could be imagined than this, that without it they are so base.

The legend of the Grand Inquisitor asks sharp questions of each of us. Do we choose comfort rather than risk, stagnant certainty rather than creative doubt? Do we choose to remain in a dull and uninteresting job because the pay is certain, or choose to remain in a destructive marriage because of fear of loneliness if we left, or choose to cling to the security of the doll's house, as Ibsen would put it? Do we choose to walk out on marriage quarrels rather than confront the inevitable misunderstandings and blows to one's narcissism in working the problems out?

The Grand Inquisitor confesses, symbolically, that he knows the paradox of freedom is all too real. *They*—the officials of the Church—must face the paradox, even though they may succeed in protecting humankind from it. The paradox, he admits by implication, is present in all persons who seek to realize themselves. But the Church will protect humankind as a whole from self-realization, from going through the crises of freedom that should occur in everyone's growth. They will keep humankind as children who never taste failure, struggle, aspiration, rebellion, and the joy of life that comes from a sense of human dignity. They never will understand the irony in that enticing character

in Aldous Huxley's *Brave New World*, the Indian who quotes
Shakespeare continually and wanders about longing to suffer.
Those "children" of the Grand Inquisitor will never be gripped
by the drama of *King Lear* or know the delight of *A Midsummer
Night's Dream* or be shaken by Beethoven's Ninth Symphony.

2. Freedom and Rebellion

The thing that stirs the Grand Inquisitor, that threatens his
smug complacency, is the human spirit of rebellion. He is ob-
sessed with it; he comes back to it again and again. "Man was
created a rebel," he states regretfully, "and how can rebels be
happy?" and "What though he [man] is everywhere rebelling
against our power, and proud of his rebellion? It is the pride of a
child, and a schoolboy." "Humankind are slaves of course," he reassures himself, "though rebellious by nature." He vows that such
oppositional efforts will be useless, "though man might be a hundred times a rebel."

There is good reason for his concern. Rebellion is the one way
human beings can demonstrate that they are not what the Grand
Inquisitor called them: "slaves, base, vile, weak and cowardly."

This stubborn, oppositional tendency in humankind raises
the question, Is the possibility for rebellion necessary and inevitable for human freedom? I answer yes. Freedom, we have seen,
is known only when something opposes it, takes it away. Hence
the word *freedom* exists always in the company of such verbs as
resist, oppose, rebel. I do not mean rebellion in the sense of fixation
on childish patterns of defiance nor in the sense of sheer destructiveness, or rebellion for its own sake or for the sake of diversion-
ary excitement in one sector of one's life to avoid commitment in
another.

I mean the capacity for rebellion as the preservation of human
dignity and spirit. I mean the act of coming to terms with one's
own autonomy, learning to respect one's own "no." Thus, the
capacity to rebel is the underpinning of independence and the
guardian of the human spirit. Rebellion preserves the life core,
the self as conscious of its existence as a self. The capacity to rebel

gives one's cooperation efficacy. Otherwise one is simply inert human weight rather than a cooperating human being. And if one senses these characteristics as important in himself, he must, if only to preserve his own psychological integrity, grant this sense of dignity and the respect that it rightly demands to other persons in the world as well. "Without rebellion," wrote Bertrand Russell, "mankind would stagnate, and injustice would be irremedial. The man who refuses to obey authority has, therefore, in certain circumstances, a legitimate function, provided his disobedience has motives which are social rather than personal."

Our Declaration of Independence puts it politically: "That whenever any Form of Government becomes destructive of these ends [Life, Liberty and the pursuit of Happiness], it is the Right of the People to alter or to abolish it." Our nation was born in 1776 by virtue of the spirit of insurgency of our forefathers.

This rebellious quality was the turning point in Philip's therapy. His cry "If Nicole wants to continue her present bed-hopping, the hell with her—I'll make my life with someone else" was the crucial step in his asserting his freedom from his neurotic tie to her.

Even in creativity the "rebellion" is present in a different sense. Every act of creation is preceded by an act of destruction, as Picasso was fond of saying. The scientific aspect of creativity is not different here from the artistic; the essential characteristic of a creative contribution is that it transcends prior experience and contains a revolt against it. Concerning inner values, it is significant that this capacity to preserve one's freedom by insurgency is present in artists. Henry Miller expresses this beautifully:

When I reflect that the task which the artist implicitly sets himself is to overthrow existing values, to make of the chaos about him an order which is his own, to sow strife and ferement so that by the emotional release those who are dead may be restored to life, then it is that I run with joy to the great and imperfect ones, their confusion nourishes me, their stuttering is like divine music to my ears.

The function of the artist in overthrowing existing values is to construct a new order, and he sows ferment so that emotionally dead people will be restored to life—a laudable purpose, indeed!

No wonder Joyce proclaims that the artist creates the uncreated conscience of the race.

Rebellion may be discerned in the rebirth experience we endure at every point of psychological growth. The "normal" rebellion is, of course, most clearly seen in adolescence, in the fight against what one's parents stand for in favor of creating a new, free world of one's own. In psychotherapy it is often the function of the therapist to support this rebellion of the adolescent against his parents when the young person himself has not yet developed enough courage to declare his independence and to begin to take responsibility for his own life.

Frantz Fanon argued in two persuasive books that rebellion for the blacks of Africa is the only way they will earn their freedom. Rebellion is the anvil on which these blacks can hammer out their new ability to assert "I can" and "I will." Freedom to govern oneself is not conferred simply by the erstwhile master signing a decree of independence and moving out. ("Freedom is not a cake that drops into one's mouth and is there for the swallowing, but a citadel to be stormed with the saber. Whoever receives freedom from foreign hands remains a slave," Kazantzakis proclaims.)

An African trained in France as a psychiatrist, Fanon's belief was that Africans must go through this stage in which they commit their all to some ideal, that is more important to them than life itself. By "earn" Fanon meant the developing of the dignity, the sense of interdependence, and the collective mythology that one experiences in the trenches—all of these psychological experiences forming the structure on which a free nation composed of free individuals can be established. This rebellion is most significantly an inner process that *changes the character of the people who have become free, a process that involves the building of human dignity into each one of the now free persons.*

The sense of solidarity binding each member to the group, the collective consciousness now oriented toward freedom in the whole community—these are a necessary part of the welding together of people who have been slaves into a nation conscious of itself. Some feminists hold that the strident quality in the movement is inevitable, and that the liberation movement cannot escape being oppositional since it has to fight so much opposition. The struggle may be women's way of earning their own freedom and equality. When, in Ibsen's drama *The Doll's House*, Nora finally walks out of her house and marriage, one breathes a deep sigh of relief. For at last she has been able to rebel against a destructive and stultifying entanglement.

If I have the possibility of rebellion, it is implied at the same time that I do not need to rebel. I am free to choose to cooperate instead. Then my cooperation has a reality and an authenticity. It would not be thus if I were coerced into cooperating—i.e., if I had no possibility of rebellion; the cooperation of a slave is not cooperation at all, but slave labor.

Or I can rebel nonviolently. Whatever one thinks about Gandhi's nonviolence, it was essentially a form of rebellion. Martin Luther King wrote in 1958:

We will take direct action against injustice without waiting for other agencies to act. We will not obey unjust laws or submit to unjust practices. We will do this peacefully, openly, cheerfully because our aim is to persuade. We adopt the means of non-violence because our end is a community at peace with itself.

King knew what a high price this might entail. But it would achieve the sense of dignity, the rebirth, the self-esteem among the blacks—it would *earn* freedom for his people. He stated later:

The way of non-violence means a willingness to suffer and sacrifice. It may mean going to jail. If such is the case the resister must be willing to fill the jail houses of the South. It may even mean physical death. *But if physical death is the price a man must pay to free his children and his white brethren from a permanent death of the spirit, then nothing could be more redemptive."*

What is the inner dignity, the experience of rebirth, that occurs as one takes one's stand? Let us note two cases.

Something happens inside a person, Pat Cusick says, when he is arrested for the first time. He crosses a barrier. It's an emotional experience which jars and confuses him; later, after the emotional impact has worn thin, he *is left with a new sense of himself as a citizen.* Pat sensed this, at least, and suspected that it was true of others. They had all broken a law. They had contended that they were obeying a higher law. Be that as it may, they had broken a law of society, of the town. In doing so, they had crossed a barrier. Now that they had a police record they were freer than ever to follow the dictates of their consciences.

James Farmer wrote that the blacks who

refused to be victimized any longer by the troopers, had been transformed into a community of men, capable, despite the severest limitations, of free and even heroic acts. Their subsequent activity at the polls and in initiating a school boycott suggests that this kind of freedom, though essentially personal, will inevitably lead to social action, and that freedom once won is not readily surrendered.

Again, Farmer speaks from his experience:

If we do not encourage impoverished communities to engage in direct action-picket lines, boycotts, rent strikes—all the money and loving care in the world will not succeed in providing them with a dignified life. . . . Our people must feel that *they are shaping their own lives;* that they have forced changes in the politics of the powerful. You cannot engineer freedom. *A freed man is not yet free.*

Thus people do *earn* their right to be free. They experience the birth of themselves inwardly, shape themselves, experience the dignity of an independent human being. Farmer goes on to picture this inner change as a religious rite.

We might think of the demonstration as a rite of initiation through which the black man is mustered into the sacred order of freedom. It is also a rite the entire nation must undergo to exorcise the demons of racial hate. If in a spasm of emancipated exuberance these rites should cause inconvenience or violate the canons of cultivated good taste or trouble the dreams of some good-livers—I think it is forgivable. . . . exuberance and . . . inconvenience are small prices to pay when a nation is undoing historic wrong.

Freedom is an art demanding practice, and too many of us are unpracticed.

Freedom is not an end; it is a beginning and a process. We feel further from the end now than we did before a decade's progress was wrought. . . . This is part of the fact that freedom is never static, never gained once and for all; and this is because essential freedom is an inner state that must be re-affirmed in each act.

We need here to emphasize, as we have throughout this book, that destiny, which is always present as the limiting factor, may make the struggle to attain freedom more difficult than at first envisioned. This certainly was true of the feminist movement; the members did not put their roots down deep enough to sustain the later shocks.

Farmer is right in stating that essential freedom is an inner state that is reaffirmed in each act. He writes that the struggle is surely more complex than they had foreseen, but the "complexity is splendid; perhaps that is freedom too." Freedom of being is gained only when the persons can feel in their own muscles, in their own hearts, that they have risked themselves, that they have "leaped," that they have gained the sense of dignity necessary for the real experience of freedom. Thus, they will develop *their* collective mythology as we developed ours in 1776. In the words of the ex-slave Frederick Douglass:

Those who profess to favor freedom and yet deprecate agitation are men who want crops without plowing up the ground. They want rain without thunder and lightning. They want the ocean without the awful roar of its many waters. The struggle may be a moral one; or it may be a physical one; or it may be both moral and physical. But it must be a struggle. *Power concedes nothing without demand. It never did and it never will.*

3. Freedom as Participation

Freedom is a species phenomenon—that is, all human beings experience it to some degree. But it is also a cultural creation, and hence there are many variations in the meaning and significance of freedom throughout the world. In these years the most crucial distinction is between freedom in the West and in the East.

In the Western world we experience freedom as individual self-expression. In the East, on the other hand, freedom is experienced as participation. In the latter, one lives more in the context of the community, and one's freedom comes from participating in the group.*

When Shirley MacLaine's trip with a small group of Americans to China was shown on television, there was one amazing interchange about art. MacLaine asked the Chinese Maoist guide—who was obviously friendly and wanted to answer the questions as completely as possible—what would happen if some citizen had an inner, personal vision that he wanted to express in a poem or painting? The guide immediately answered that they would put him in a group and recondition him to be more in line with Maoism. MacLaine hastened to respond that she had not meant that there was anything wrong with this hypothetical person, just that he had a vision of his own. The nonplused guide finally answered something along the same line as before. What I found fascinating was that the guide was obviously perplexed and couldn't really take in the meaning of the question.

In the Eastern societies freedom is mediated by tradition, a group phenomenon in which the person participates. In contrast to Henry Ford's notorious proclamation "History is bunk," Eastern societies venerate tradition and ancestors; their freedom exists by virtue of their tradition rather than in spite of it. This means there is an upset greater than in the West when college students and women cast off tradition in favor of modernism. In seeking to be free, they may in fact lose their freedom since it consists of their participation in their group and its tradition.

Freedom today is a pressing and urgent issue all over the world—for the East and especially for the West, for men and especially for women. The objection that our view of freedom of the individual would not make sense in India is beside the point.

---

*Freedom as participation was illustrated to me by Professor Richard Falk, who speaks out of his personal experience of several years of contact with and especially extensive visits to the Near East. In discussion groups so characteristic of religious life in the mosques in the Near East, for example, where the group sits in a circle, there is automatic participation. Everyone may speak up; each participant helps as he sees fit to add clarity or depth to the religious leader's viewpoint. No one expects personal credit for the point he makes; one merely tries to help the group along. There is no hierarchy in the Western sense.

The fact that Easterners have a different kind of freedom does not mean that for them freedom is nonexistent or meaningless. Anthropologist Dorothy Lee points out that, while only in Western culture are the terms *freedom* and *free will* used extensively, other cultures she has studied achieve the same thing by other means. They may express their freedom by valuing the autonomous activities of the individual, or by insisting on the worth of the person, or by guarding the originality of each human being, or by furthering other routines or patterns in their culture which results in the same thing as our Western emphasis on freedom.

Eastern society tends to generate more warmth, more communal feeling. In the efforts to answer the question of why the Japanese factories could produce automobiles so efficiently, it was brought out that the factory worker in Japan enjoys some genuine aspects of community. Once the worker has begun to work at a given factory, he is assured of a job for life. If the product is discontinued, he must be given another post. When the managers and workers arrive for work in the morning, they engage in communal setting-up exercises. They then belt out in unison a song describing their loyalty to their factory and the excellence of the products it produces. "It seems silly to Westerners," says one executive of Matsushita, "but every morning at 8:00 A.M., all across Japan, there are 87,000 people reciting the code of values and singing together. It's like we all are a community."

The Japanese worker gets a sense of freedom from being valued; workers are consulted often, and the books of the company are open to the union at all times. Later in this book we shall point out the close relation between human spirit and human freedom, and it is relevant in this regard that the authors Pascale and Athos, of the excellent book *The Art of Japanese Management*, speaking of the Matsushita Corporation as representative of the Japanese attitude, write: "Spiritual is an unlikely term in a narrative of corporate life. Yet nothing else suffices to capture the strong belief system that underlies Matsushita's philosophy." Matsushita states, "Profits should not be a reflection of corporate greed but a vote of confidence from society that what is offered by the firm is valued." In view of our reference above to Tawney's criticism of laissez-faire practices, it is relevant that Matsushita insists that the "management of his corporation serve as developers of character, not just as exploiters of human resources."

But when tradition—and, therefore, the order of the societies—breaks down, Eastern countries are apt to resort to force in an effort to hold the structure of society together. Eastern societies are thus more open to Marxism with its collective emphasizes and its outright attack on individualistic concepts of life. Lenin spoke of that "quaker prattle about individual rights." Maoism is the obvious example of how naturally Marxism fits into the Eastern concept of freedom by participation.

The Russian poet Yevtushenko illustrates the communal feeling in a way which has nothing to do with communism as such but shows an unusually strong concern for interdependence in the community. His poem is entitled "On the Question of Freedom":

> You talk to me of freedom? Empty question
> under umbrellas of bombs in the sky
> It's a disgrace to be free of your own age
> A hundred times more shameful than to be its slave
>
> Yes I'm enslaved to Tashkent women
> and to Dallas bullets and Peking slogans
> and Vietnam widows and Russian women
> with picks beside the tracks and kerchiefs over their eyes
>
> Yes I'm not free of Pushkin and Blok
> Not free of the State of Maryland and Zima Station
> Not free of the Devil and God
> Not free of earth's beauty and its shit
>
> Yes I'm enslaved to a thirst for taking a wet-mop
> to the heads of all the bickerers and butchers of the world
> Yes I'm enslaved to the honor of busting the mugs
> of all the bastards on earth
>
> And maybe I'll be loved by the people for this
> For sending my life
>   (not without precedent in this iron age)
> *glorifying unfreedom from*
> *the true struggle for freedom*

But the tension between the Eastern and Western approaches to freedom is shown in the fact that this Russian poet Blok, whom Yevtushenko mentions, attacked the Soviet authorities in the early days of communism in 1921 for taking away *"creative tranquility . . .* not the freedom to play the liberal, but *the creative will*—the secret freedom. And the poet is dying, because there is no longer anything to breathe." This "creative will—the secret freedom" sounds like the Western concept of freedom.

There will always be tension between freedom as individual self-expression and freedom as participation. In America we cling to such diverse forms of institutionalized self-expression as laissez-faire doctrines in economics and industry, the Horatio Alger myth in which anyone who has enough "spunk" can outstrip his competitors and marry the boss's daughter, our mottos of the self-made man and "every man for himself and the devil take the hindmost," and our ego psychology. It is even present between the lines in the Declaration of Independence: "We hold . . . that all men are created equal, that they are endowed by their Creator with certain unalienable Rights."

Especially in America, the land of individualism *par excellence*—with our pioneer spirit and our Horatio Algers and our Gatsbys—we have underestimated the significance of community. The East can provide us with a corrective, and this is what is happening with the advent of Buddhism and Zen and Taoism into the West. But this is very different from renouncing our own tradition—as though it were possible to leap out of our own skins and into another's.

We need to develop our forms of community in the West in ways that spring out of our own natures. In an article entitled "Freedom As Participation," Peter Stillman holds that both Hegel and Arendt believed that "in order to be free, individuals must participate actively, continually and directly" in the public domain. He continues:

For Hegel and Arendt, only revolutions that aim at freedom as participation and that concurrently see the value of structured participatory institutions can be successful at gaining power, attaining ideals worth attaining, and transforming the polity.

Our tradition of self-realization in the West is one of our great ideas. It has brought forth some magnificent creations—of which Western science is not the least, if the most dramatic—no matter how open to criticism these creations may be. The landscape paintings of the East generally show human beings as small and insignificant. But no one can glance more than once at Greek statues or Renaissance paintings without realizing that the individual person is of great significance. The Hebrew-Greek sources out of which our Western ideal of freedom was born furnished a new vision of the dignity and value of the individual person. These seminal concepts must not be overlooked—for example, the Hebrew concept that man cooperates with God as God works through human history, and the Greek love of individual wisdom and veneration of a courage that transcends life itself. The yearning of educated persons in Eastern cultures for these contributions of the spirit of the West is partially a demonstration of this.

V

On Human Destiny

The free man is he who wills without arbitrary self-will. . . . He believes in destiny, and believes that it stands in need of him. . . . He must sacrifice his puny, unfree will, that is controlled by things and instincts, to his grand will, which quits defined for destined being.

—MARTIN BUBER

As freedom and destiny, so arbitrary self-will and fate belong together. But freedom and destiny are solemnly promised to one another and linked together in meaning.

—MARTIN BUBER

Metaphorically, freedom in its essence is the acceptance of the chains which suit you and for which you are suited, and of the harness in which you pull towards an end chosen and valued by yourself, and not imposed. It is not, and never can be, the absence of restrictions, obligations or law and of duty.

—BRONISLAW MALINOWSKI

What is the relationship between freedom and determinism? Both of them operate in our day-to-day lives. If we refused to accept either freedom or determinism, we would diminish our possibilities for living. Without determinism and the predictability of plane schedules that goes with it, for one example, our lives would be lost in anarchy. But without freedom and the exuberance that goes with it, without poetry and flights of imagination that freedom entails, we would be swallowed up in apathy.

I read everything on the topic I could find, and I pondered

the question at length; but, as Omar Khayyám put it, "Evermore I came out by the same door I went in."

One morning, having gotten up early to go to my study, I walked out to get the morning newspaper, which is thrown on the curb in front of our house. When I was about fifteen steps from the house, in this relaxed, preworking mood, there suddenly came into my mind—so clearly that it seemed like someone speaking out loud—these sentences: *Freedom and determinism give birth to each other. Every advance in freedom gives birth to a new determinism, and every advance in determinism gives birth to a new freedom.* Freedom is a circle within a larger circle of determinism, which is, in turn, surrounded by a larger circle of freedom. And so on *ad infinitum.*

Immediately there crowded also into my mind the demonstrations for this hypothesis. Take Freud and his description of the unconscious. In his deterministic theory of the mind, he demonstrated that our needs are determined by unconscious childhood experiences and that our so-called "rational" values are really not rational, but are compensations for their opposites in our unconscious, irrational urges. Freud seemed to be taking our freedom away.

But soon we began to see that the real effect of Freud's determinism was to increase the breadth and depth of the human mind. He was, in our present terms, simply clarifying one aspect of destiny. For hereafter the mind would include not only the conscious, rational mind, but also the subconscious, the preconscious, the unconscious, and, with an assist from Jung, the collective unconscious. Lo and behold, the determinism in Freud's theory actually gave us far-reaching possibilities for freedom in self-development, freedom in directing our minds, and freedom in enjoying the ecstatic possibilities of intellectual exploration.

Another illustration was Darwin and the determinism of his theory of evolution. A great hue and cry of protest greeted *Origin of Species.* Was Darwin, trying with his determinism to make us all into a bunch of monkeys? But after the anger had cooled, we began to see that Darwin's new theory, deterministic as it was, actually gave us a new intellectual freedom for understanding our past and new freedom in possibilities, especially in the twentieth century, for controlling and directing our evolution.

All this ran through my mind in a few seconds. Immediately after that flood of ideas, I picked up the newspaper and started back toward the house. But in the few seconds it took to retrace my steps, I became acutely aware of a fragment of poetry running through my mind:

> . . . "Other friends have flown before—
> On the morrow *he* will leave me. . . ."

I had no idea where this intrusive and surprising couplet came from, and at that moment I had not the slightest hint as to what it meant.

But I became aware that I was instantaneously filled with anxiety. My frightened mind was now totally occupied by thoughts completely contrary to my exhilaration of minutes before. I began to recognize an old shadow-companion, an enemy-friend who always put in his leering appearance at just such moments. The context surrounding this verse in my mind indicated that it expressed the anxiety projected by this uninvited and obtrusive guest who spoke so stridently I could not help but listen. It was as though my enemy-friend was saying, "Come off it. Forget these new ideas you've gotten, which you fondly imagine were original. People have known these things for centuries. Forget it all and go in and enjoy your breakfast."

Now very anxious but exhilarated, I hurried into the house not to eat my breakfast, but to scribble down these ideas before they should be lost in the confusion that anxiety creates.

Later on in the morning, I recalled where the couplet came from. It was the last two lines of a stanza in Poe's "The Raven." As every schoolboy knows (although later we may have forgotten) the scene of the poem is Poe's room late at night. Oppressed with feelings of loneliness and alienation, and possibly under the influence of drugs, Poe carries on a conversation with this raven who flew into his room and perched on his window sill. Poe gradually begins to feel an affection for this strange bird, and he fears, in the couplet mentioned, that the bird will desert him—"On the morrow he will leave me." But the raven answers this one word, as he does at the conclusion of half of the stanzas in the poem: "Nevermore."

Being a psychoanalyst, I could not resist pondering the significance of this word "nevermore." Could it mean "nevermore" will we escape from the human paradox? That is, when we gain enough freedom to get new insights, new visions, will we be attacked by the anxiety that accompanies freedom like a shadow? We may block off our new thoughts by apathy or by dogmatism, hanging on to the tried and true ideas that never upset anyone. Yet whatever form of denial we choose, this "nevermore" says that we never will be completely free from this human paradox: that with the freedom presupposed in every new idea, there comes the equivalent anxiety to plague us. This is the curse and the blessing of being human—that we are free but destined at the same moment. But at the same time this "destiny," of which this black bird was a part, is saying something helpful: that its presence, as Poe experienced it, will "nevermore" desert us.

1. From Determinism to Destiny

True and useful as the hypothesis may be that freedom and determinism give birth to each other, I became aware that it also had a serious difficulty. This difficulty hovered around the nature of the word *determinism*. Does not that term severly limit the reality with which we deal, which is shown in this very example? Does not the word *determinism* omit the richness, the hopes and fears, the very human anxiety mediated by the "enemy-friend"?

Determinism is borrowed from physics and is particularly adequate to describe physical movements on the model of billiard balls: when one ball hits another, it imparts to it a completely predictable direction and movement. To the extent that one is unaware of his physiological and neurological reactions, the term *determinism* may also fit those realms as well. Hence, *determinism* is at least partially adequate in describing the conditioning of Pavlov's dogs and Skinner's pigeons. But when consciousness enters the picture, as it does with human beings, we find ourselves forced to search for a more inclusive word, a word that will do justice to the infinite number of nuances in human experience.

Also, being limited itself, the word *determinism* forces us into a limited view of freedom. One of the reasons our concept of freedom has become so confused is that we have tried to cut it down on a Procrustean bed until it is parallel to determinism. The only kind of freedom that turns up then is that of picking and choosing, the freedom of doing. It is called in psychology classes "decision-choice," and it can be reduced to discrete items. But there is then no place for ultimate freedom, as Bettelheim calls his freedom in the concentration camp or what I call in this book essential freedom, the freedom of being.

And the inadequacy of the term *determinism* is shown in the fact that it leaves no place for mystery. It takes no special acumen to see that mystery is a part of all human experience. It is a mystery that any of us was born at all and, especially for me, a mystery that I was born at eleven o'clock at night in a little village in Ohio; a mystery that sometimes we meet a particular person with whom we fall in love; and a mystery that we ultimately die at an unpredictable place and by unpredictable means. "The sense of the mysterious stands at the cradle of true art and true science," said Albert Einstein.

It is important to see that the mystery does not deny that there are causes. But the argument that we will sooner or later discover the determining elements in the situations that now seem mysterious does not apply, since the mystery has to do with the *pattern* by which these elements are related to each other, not the elements themselves. *How* a person responds to a situation already involves his freedom, and that freedom may combine a number of different causes. This is what Freud called "overdetermined," determined by many causes at once. Falling in love may be determined by one's libido, one's culture, one's early family background, one's personal plans, or a combination of several of these things. A "pattern" means that different events or causes are put together in a particular form, as a snowflake is put together in a certain pattern of crystals. This form cannot be broken into parts, for the form *is precisely the relationship* between the parts, as Pythagoras said. We need a new word to do justice to such human phenomena, a term that can take in the richness, the complexity, the mystery, the artistic elements in form.

Hence I reserve *determinism* for inanimate things like billiard balls. For human beings I will use the term *destiny*. Paul Tillich writes that human freedom is "a finite freedom with all of its potentialities being limited by the . . . opposite pole, destiny."

Determinism is one part of destiny. That we have to die, that we are conditioned, that we can so easily be taught to behave like robots—is not all of this part of our destiny? We reflect on our lives, we anxiously anticipate our death, we are conscious of the fact that we never know when we are to leave this earth or how—does not all this refer to destiny?

The radical shift from determinism to destiny occurs when the subject is self-conscious about what is happening to him or her. The presence of consciousness creates the *context* in which the human being's responses to his or her destiny occur. Albert Camus describes the relation between consciousness and destiny in his essay "The Myth of Sisyphus":

That hour like a breathing space which returns as surely as his suffering . . . is the hour of consciousness. . . . [Man] is superior to his fate. He is stronger than his rock. . . . If there is a personal fate, there is no higher destiny. . . . Sisyphus teaches the higher fidelity that negates the gods and raises rocks. . . . Each atom of that stone, each mineral flake of that night-filled mountain, in itself forms a world. The struggle itself toward the heights is enough to fill a man's heart. One must imagine Sisyphus happy.

2. What Is Destiny?

We saw in the case of Philip the confrontation of one man with his destiny. We observed that he had been searching for someone who would make up for his having been born into an unwelcoming world consisting of a disturbed mother and a schizophrenic sister, a destiny that he did not in the slightest choose. Up to this point in his life he had tried to cover up this early background, to compensate for it, consciously to deny it—anything to avoid facing directly this aspect of his infancy. But this only contributed to resentment, a longing and yearning that he could not understand, a Quixote-like tilting at windmills.

So long as he continued this, he would remain bound to his mother, his very resentment furnishing the motive for this binding. He would also be doubly sensitive to Nicole's affairs with other men; he would always be trapped by the question, Why does this woman, who should give me security and recompense for the past, continually cut my heart in two? But as he began to confront his destiny as a given, unchangeable series of events which, no matter how painful, needs to be acknowledged and accepted, he became able to experience the relief of one who was a slave and is now free.

The freedom of each of us is in proportion to the degree with which we confront and live in relation to our destiny.

Unfortunately, the term *destiny* has been so used and misused by Hollywood films that the word has almost solely the connotation of inescapable catastrophe, secret doom, irrevocable ruin— all of which gives a curiously erotic flavor to the films, as though the secret urge to be carried off for sexual purposes by Zeus camouflaged as a bull were present in the subconscious of all of us, male as well as female.

True, the definitions of destiny do include "irrevocable fate," but they also include much more. The verb form of the word, *destine*, is defined as "to ordain, to devote, to consecrate." Destiny is a cognate of the term *destination*, which implies moving toward a goal. We discern two trends in these different meanings: one the element of direction, and the other the sense of plan or design. These are all aspects of the human condition; our billiard balls have been left far behind.

I define *destiny* as the pattern of limits and talents that constitutes the "givens" in life. These may be on a grand scale, like death, or on a minor scale like the gasoline shortage. As we shall see below, it is in the confronting of these limits that our creativity emerges. Our destiny cannot be canceled out; we cannot erase it or substitute anything else for it. But we can choose how we shall respond, how we shall live out our talents which confront us. *Destiny* is a term that describes our condition *prior* to sociological and moral judgments. One's destiny is archetypal and ontological; the term refers to one's original experience at each moment. *It is the design of the universe speaking through the design of each one of us.*

Destiny confronts us on different levels. There is our destiny on the *cosmic* level, like birth and death. We may postpone death slightly by giving up smoking, for example, or we may invite it by suicide; but all the while death stands there irrevocably waiting. Dylan Thomas's poem on the death of his father is an impassioned and arresting creative work. But it did not cancel out the fact that his father had to die.

Also on this cosmic level are earthquakes and volcanoes, curiously called "acts of God" in insurance policies. We can choose to flee from the vicinity of earthquakes or volcanoes, or we can take our chances, remaining in the path of the eruptions. But we cannot escape the fact that volcanoes and other such eruptions of the universe do occur without the slightest concern for us. When we admit these so-called destructive aspects of destiny, we also see that the positive side of the pattern includes the "pleasure in the pathless woods" and "the rapture by the lonely shore."

There is a second group of "givens," *genetic*. Our destiny is expressed in our physical characteristics, like the color of our eyes and skin, the race we happened to be born into, whether we are male or female, and so on. "Anatomy is destiny" is the famous statement by Freud. One's talents—such as special gifts for music, art, or mathematics—are part of this bundle. One feels possessed by them. There is no denying talents without penalty, and one name for the attempt at denial is neurosis.

Third, there is the *cultural* aspect of destiny. At birth we are "thrown," to borrow Heidegger's term, into a family we did not pick, into a culture about which we knew nothing, and into a particular historical period about which we had no say. We may, and sometimes need to, fight our family, but there is no successful way of disowning this fount from which we sprang. "Freedom's great emotional potency," writes Bronislaw Malinowski, "is due to the fact that human life and indeed the pursuit of happiness depend upon the nature and the efficiency of those means which culture gives man in his struggle with the environment, with other human beings, and with Destiny herself."

A fourth group of givens is *circumstantial*. The stock market rises and falls; a war is declared; Pearl Harbor is attacked. Once these happen, they cannot be reversed nor avoided nor ignored nor done over again.

One can think of the different forms of destiny on a spectrum with various gradations. On the left-hand extreme position I would put what the philosophers call necessity and the poets call fate, like earthquakes or volcanoes. These are scarcely at all susceptible to human change. Determinism I would place near this end also. In the middle I would place the unconscious function of the human mind, since this is partly determined and partly influenced by human activity. The cultural aspects of destiny I would place nearer the right end of the spectrum, since, though we have no voice in choosing our society or historical period, we have a good deal of freedom in how we use them. On the extreme right hand I would put talent, for though it is given in one sense, we have considerable freedom with respect to how we use it.

There are also varying ways of relating to one's destiny. *One is to cooperate with it.* The aspects of destiny that Marcus Aurelius, the Roman Stoic, had in mind best fit this cooperation: "The destiny assigned to every man is suited to him, and suits him to himself." Another way is *be aware of and to acknowledge* one's destiny. Most of us do this, at least superficially, with physical size, anatomy, and death. A third way is more active—namely, *engaging* one's destiny. A fourth way is the outright *confronting and challenging* of one's destiny. Philip's conversations with his dead mother are examples of this. A fifth and the most active response is *encountering* and *rebelling* against destiny. Dylan Thomas's "Rage, rage against the dying of the light" is an example of this. These ways are not mutually exclusive, to be sure, and we all use all of them at different times.

The role of talent as a form of destiny is shown in a letter Beethoven wrote when he was twenty-eight and becoming so deaf that others "heard the shepherd singing and I heard nothing":

Oh, if I were rid of this affliction I could embrace the world! I feel that my youth is just beginning and have I not always been ill? . . . Grant me but half freedom from my affliction and then—as a complete, ripe man I shall return to you and renew the old feelings of friendship. You must see me as happy as it is possible to be here below—not unhappy. No! I

cannot endure it. I will take Fate by the throat; it shall not wholly overcome me. Oh, it is so beautiful to live—to live a thousand times! I feel
that I am not made for a quiet life.

We can, of course, spend our lives trying to falsify or flee from
our destiny. F. Scott Fitzgerald's *The Great Gatsby* is the story of
a young man who tried to falsify his past. Gatsby changed his
name, disowned his parents, cultivated a British accent, and
spent the crucial years after the world war trying to win back
Daisy, the rich girl with whom he had fallen in love when he was
in military training. In Fitzgerald's words,

The truth was that Jay Gatsby of West Egg, Long Island, sprang from
his platonic conception of himself. . . . So he invented just the sort of
Jay Gatsby that a seventeen-year-old boy would be likely to invent, and
to this conception he was faithful to the end.

At the tragic ending, the fabulous dance orchestras were silenced,
the last person had left the once-crowded parties, Gatsby's big
house was empty, Daisy had gone back to her rich husband. And
Gatsby's body floats dead in his own swimming pool. Fitzgerald
sums up the tragedy and relates it to us all:

Gatsby had come a long way to this blue lawn, and his dream must have
seemed so close that he could hardly fail to grasp it. He did not know
that it was already behind him, somewhere back in that vast obscurity
beyond the city, where the dark fields of the republic rolled on under the
night.

   Gatsby believed in the green light, the orgiastic future that year by
year recedes before us. It eluded us then, but that's no matter—tomorrow we will run faster, stretch out our arms farther. . . . And one fine
morning—

   So we beat on, boats against the current, borne back ceaselessly into
the past.

With beautiful insight, Fitzgerald sees the human compulsion
to repeat behavior: "tomorrow we will run faster." Is this not our
universal hubris? "No man of woman born / Coward or brave,
can shun his destiny," Homer proclaimed centuries ago. We
human beings beat on like "boats against the current," while we
are all the time "borne back ceaselessly into the past." Fitzgerald
rightly observed that each of us to some extent falsifies, denies, or

dodges his destiny—to commit the errors is all too human. He himself was especially of this type, as imaginative writers often are, and his special difficulty with his own destiny, which obviously included his early fame, led to his alcoholism and early death. So he knows whereof he speaks.

Looking at destiny from within the person, Ortega y Gasset calls the destiny of each of us our "vital design." This puts the accent on destiny as destination, or the significant direction or conflict of directions each one of us senses within himself. "Our will is free to realize or not to realize this vital design which we ultimately are, but we cannot . . . change it, abbreviate it, or substitute anything for it." The environment we live in, the outside world we face, and our own character as it had developed up until that moment simply make this task easier or harder. "Life," continues Ortega, "means the inexorable necessity of realizing the *design* for an existence which each one of us is. . . . The sense of life . . . is nothing other than each one's acceptance of his inexorable circumstance and, on accepting it, converting it into his own creation."

Destiny in this sense is that design of our lives that we spend our years trying to find, seeking and groping, trying this job and that one, loving this woman or man and that one, stumbling into this therapist's office or that one, sometimes with success and sometimes with failure. The tendency, present especially in America, to believe that we can change everything at any time we wish, that nothing in character or existence is fixed or given (in Los Angeles not even death) and that now with psychotherapy or the cults we can remake our lives and personalities over the weekend is not only a misperception of life, but is also a desecration of it.

Psychoanalysis and its offspring provide varied ways of trying to discover this vital design of each of us. Gurus—or other persons who claim to have some transterrestial connections—are so prized in our day because they presume to tell us what our vital design is.

To the extent that we are able to live out our destiny, we experience a sense of gratification and achievement, a conviction that we are becoming what we were meant to become. It is an experience of authenticity, a feeling of being in accord with the universe, a conviction of genuine freedom. William James would have understood what we are talking about:

The huge world that girdles us about puts all sorts of questions to us, and tests us in all sorts of ways. Some of the tests we meet by actions that are easy, and some of the questions we answer in articulately formulated words. But the deepest question that is ever asked admits of no reply but the dumb turning of the will and tightening of our heartstrings as we say, "Yes, I will even have it so!"

When the vital design is covered up and silenced, however, the sensitive person has the experience of acting like a prig—he feels unreal, ungenuine, inauthentic. "This design," Ortega states, "is not an idea or plan thought up by the person involved, and freely chosen. The design is anterior to all the ideas one's intellect forms, and to all the decisions of one's will. Life is essentially a drama, because it is a desperate struggle—with things and even with our own character—*to succeed in being in fact that which we are in design.*"

Often our pressure to deny our destiny comes from such things as our insecurity, our dread of ostracism, our fear and anxiety, and our lack of courage to risk ourselves. These, in turn, come largely from the pressure to conform: it is safer to be like everybody else. The vital design, the authentic pattern to which we are called can then be left far behind.

But the tendency to deny our destiny may also come from a conflict between possibilities—between, say, being a scientist or a poet, as in Goethe's life. There is the conflict in classical tragedy, for example, between Orestes' love and pity for his mother and his need to avenge his father, the love-hate dilemma that arises from a fundamental human conflict between desire and destiny.

There is a tendency among us to separate that which has an evil connotation in destiny, which we generally call fate, from that which is constructive, which we call destiny. Martin Buber, who has said important things about destiny, also seems to make that mistake when he writes in *I and Thou* of the need to avoid the "fate-will" and to choose instead the "destiny-will." He distinguishes "between fated self-will and destined free-will." But this emasculates destiny and makes it insipid. It is crucial to remember that the concept of destiny is *prior* to the moral criteria of good and evil, as we stated earlier. "So let there be no confounding the *ought to be* of morality, which inhabits man's intellectual region, with the vital imperative, the *has to be* of personal vocation, situated in the most profound and primary region of our being."

We need to accept the negative *fate* element together with the positive destiny elements if we are to experience the power of destiny. Hitler developed his great power over the German people by his use of destiny, demonic as this power was. When he spoke of the destiny of the German people, he was using the term correctly no matter how destructive his campaigns turned out to be. "The devil can quote scripture" has a meaning far beyond what we normally assume.

Destiny and freedom form a paradox, a dialectical relationship. By this I mean that they are opposites that need each other—like day and night, summer and winter, God and the devil. Out of the encountering of the forces of destiny come our possibilities, our opportunities. In the engaging of destiny our freedom is born, just as with the coming of the light the day overcomes the night. Destiny, as we have said, is not to be thought of as a ball and chain that afflict human beings. It is true that

> There's a divinity that shapes our ends,
> Rough-hew them how we will.

But it is likewise true, as Shakespeare also points out,

> The fault, dear Brutus, is not in our stars
> But in ourselves, that we are underlings.

These statements sound like a clear contradiction. But they are paradoxes instead. Freedom is by no means the absence of destiny. If there were no destiny to confront—no death, no illness, no fatigue, no limitations of any sort and no talents to pose against these limitations—we would never develop any freedom.

The meaning of the dialectical relation between freedom and

destiny is that, even though they are opposites, they are still bound together. They imply each other. If destiny changes, freedom must change, and vice versa. As Hegel put it, first comes a *thesis;* this then gives rise to its *antithesis;* and this, in turn, leads to a *synthesis.* Destiny is the thesis; this gives rise to freedom, which is its antithesis; and this, in turn, leads to a synthesis. Each not only makes the other possible; each stimulates activity in the other pole, gives power and energy to the other. Thus we can truly speak of destiny being born out of freedom and freedom being born out of destiny.

For freedom is honed in the struggle with destiny. The freedom that develops in our confronting our destiny produces the richness, the endless variety, the capacity to endure, the ecstasy, the imagination, and other capacities that characterize the world and ourselves as conscious creatures, free but destined, moving in it. In this sense destiny is personal: "Each of us suffers his own destiny," as Virgil puts it. It is out of the dialectical relation of destiny and freedom that creativity and civilization are born. Karl Jaspers agrees: "Thus freedom and necessity [destiny] meet and fuse not only in my present and future choices but in the very individuality of my existence. Each and every decision establishes a new foundation for the formation of my real historical self: I am bound by the decisive character of my choices; in virtue of these choices I have become what I wanted myself to be."

Hence, there are all the paradoxical statements about freedom. "We are 'doomed' to be free by the very fact of being born," states Hannah Arendt. She is here in agreement with Saint Augustine, who said the same thing. Or, as Sartre puts it, "We are condemned to freedom." Or Ortega: "Man is the being condemned to translate necessity into freedom."

3. Destiny and Responsibility

Are we responsible for our destiny? If we dare to answer that by saying "Partly so," we then face another question just as difficult. That is: If destiny is a given, a vital design that gives us talents and limits and that we cannot revoke, how can responsibility have any meaning?

The ancient Greeks faced this problem, together with the moral implications of destiny, when the ethical consciousness of the Greek civilization was being formed. During this period, around 1000 B.C., Homer relates the following fascinating incident from the Trojan War.

The combined Greek forces were encamped around the walls of Troy. Agamemnon, the general in chief of the Greek armies, had stolen Achilles' mistress from the Achilles' tent. When Achilles returned and discovered this, his rage knew no bounds. He was not only a man of fiery temper, but also the best fighter in the Greek army. There hung in the balance the portentous question: Would the whole Greek expedition be destroyed by the enmity between these two men?

As these two heroes confront each other, Agamemnon says:

Not I . . . was the cause of this act, but Zeus and the furies who walk in darkness: they it was who . . . put wild até [madness] in my understanding, on that day when I arbitrarily took Achilles' prize from him. So what could I do? Deity will always have its way.

In other words destiny—Zeus and his "wild até"—will brook no denial. Is Agamemnon saying "I was brainwashed; not I but my unconscious did it"? It may seem so, but he is not. He is preparing the way to assume his own responsibility. He then goes on:

But since I was blinded by até, and Zeus took away my understanding, I am willing to make my peace and give abundant compensation.

Ah! Since destiny did these things to me, *I* will give compensation.

Cooling down, Achilles answers:

Let the son of Atreus [Agamemnon] go his way. . . . For Zeus the counselor took away his understanding.

The Greeks are saying here that a person is responsible even though the gods work inwardly, even though they take away one's understanding. That is, one is destined, but one is responsible for what this destiny makes one do. Although Agamemnon is driven by destiny, which works through powers in his unconscious mind, he is nevertheless responsible. And responsibility is inseparable from freedom. Freedom and responsibility on one side, and até and destiny on the other—these operate simultaneously in this dialectical and intimately human paradox.

Julian Jaynes reminds us of another incident from Homer and the Trojan War. Hector finds himself confronting Achilles in the heat of battle. Hector does not want to fight Achilles at that moment, so he backs away. His withdrawing is not determined by cowardice; i.e., he is not forced by Achilles' sword to back up. Instead, the goddess put her shield around Hector in the form of a cloud under which he could back out of the battle without any loss of self-esteem.

The furies who walk in darkness and the goddess surrounding Hector with a cloud are superb synonyms for destiny. Indeed, the gods and goddesses were personifications of destiny; they set the ultimate limits on human actions and opened up possibilities for human beings. Anyone who opposed them outright was brought to ruin by such means as a bolt of lightning—what we moderns call an "act of God," carryover of this ancient belief—from the hand of Zeus.

This sense of responsibility is partly the impingement of culture upon us. We have to have responsibility if we are to live with any harmony in community. Culture can help us mitigate or meliorate destiny: through culture we learn to build houses to keep out the snow and the winter cold. Through culture we barter our services for food so that we do not starve. But culture cannot overturn destiny, cannot erase it. We can collectively cover our eyes to the results of our actions, blind ourselves to the full import of our cruelty and our responsibility for that cruelty, as we did in the Vietnam war. But this requires a numbing of our sensitivity and will sooner or later take its toll in neurotic symptoms.

For Homer the acknowledging of destiny was by no means a wallowing in guilt, but an acceptance of personal responsibility. Homer has the gods proclaim in the *Odyssey:*

O alas, how now do men accuse the gods! For they say evils come from us [the gods]. But they themselves, by reason of their sins, have sufferings beyond those destined for them.

In these Homeric tales the early Greeks were learning—an arduous task in civilization requiring hundreds and hundreds of years—that freedom and destiny require each other, that they are in dialectical relation with each other. Agamemnon knows that he must assume his responsibility by compensating Achilles for what he believes the gods—i.e., destiny—made him do.

The Greeks found, furthermore, that their belief in destiny, expressed in the gods and goddesses, *energized and strengthened them individually.* The typical Greek citizens, as anyone who reads Herodotus or Thucydides knows, were amazingly self-reliant and autonomous. We look at their activities and realize that it is not true that belief in destiny tends to make one passive and inert. The opposite is true—namely, that belief in unlimited freedom, as the flower children demonstrated, tends to paralyze one. For unlimited freedom is like a river with no banks; the water is not controlled in its flow and hence spills out in every direction and is lost in the sands.

Hence the seeming paradox that the deterministic movements, like Calvinism with its predestination, and Marxism with its economic determinism of history, have such great power. One would think that since people are the result of their predestination or their economic status, not much change is possible. But the Marxists and Calvinists work energetically to change people and often with great success. In other words, their belief in their particular form of destiny gives them power.

Once in a while a person, after going through innumerable smaller decisions, arrives at a point where his freedom and destiny seem united. This was true of Martin Luther, who, when he nailed his ninety-nine theses on the door of the cathedral at Wittenberg, said, "Here I stand, I can do no other." Such acts are the fruition of years of minor decisions culminating in this crucial decision in which one's freedom and destiny merge.

By encountering destiny directly, the Greeks had their own

ways also of mitigating it. The clever man, like Ulysses, could know which gods to set against other gods in his sacrifices. The Greeks could guarantee an auspicious wind with which to sail from Aulis to Troy by sacrificing Iphigenia, daughter of Agamemnon. This cruel act, incidentally, clinched Agamemnon's destiny—he would later be murdered by his wife for his part in the bloody heritage of Mycenae.

In Aeschyus' drama, when Agamemnon came back from Troy, he marched in as the proud conqueror, one who could scarcely restrain his boasting that *he* had accomplished the laying low of Troy. The chorus hastens to warn him not to commit *hubris*, the sin of overweening pride, which makes the gods jealous and incites their revenge. It is parallel to our modern, weaker form of the same wisdom "Pride goeth before a fall." But Agamemnon, with his bluster, does commit hubris, and this leads directly to his death.

Hubris is the refusal to accept one's destiny. It is the person's belief that he performed great acts all by himself. It is the tendency to usurp the power of the gods. It is also the denial of how much one is always dependent upon one's fellow man and woman and one's society. Destiny itself is the source of our talents and aids the victors in these great projects like the Trojan War, and when we lose sight of this—as we do when we commit hubris—evil consequences ensue.

Does not the *possibility* or the power to do something about the situation at hand confer on one some *responsibility* to do it? I choose to answer yes. Responsibility is no longer simply tied to past causes—i.e., what one *did*. It must be geared also to present freedom—i.e., what I can do. The freedom to act confers on me the responsibility to act. In this sense freedom and responsibility are united. Responsibility is more than a moral teaching, more than another rule of the ethical life. It is part of the underlying ontological structure of life. This means, obviously, that there is a host of things that we are responsible for that we will never be able to discharge. But it is better to carry unfulfilled responsibility than to act on some pretense of "pure" conscience.

Such is the interdependence of people in the collective nature of the human community that we need to assume responsibility for a multitude of things. Obviously, I am not saying that we develop neurotic consciences—there may be many reasons for not doing the given thing. For example, my friend brings up his child wrongly, and I had better not act on my hunch that I know how and he doesn't. But the freedom inherent in a friendship does confer on me the responsibility to be open to talk with him about it and to share whatever insights I have. Thus, I am not suggesting we be busybodies. I am suggesting we be sensitive, compassionate, and aware of the complex interdependence of our human community.

VI

Destiny and Death

Forget your personal tragedy. We are all bitched from the start and you especially have to hurt like hell before you can write seriously. But when you get the damned hurt use it—don't cheat with it. Be as faithful to it as a scientist.
>   —ERNEST HEMINGWAY, writing to F. Scott Fitzgerald

It is only in the face of death that man's self is born.
>   —SAINT AUGUSTINE

Our awareness of death is the most vivid and compelling example of destiny. I say awareness of death rather than simply death, for everything in nature dies in its own time. But human beings *know* that they die. They have a word for death, they anticipate it, they experience their death in imagination. This experience of imagining one's own death is seen in such diverse events as seeing a dead bird in the road, or crossing a trafficked street, or buckling a seat belt, or having an orgasm.

A genius in physics as well as in moral insight, Blaise Pascal tells us this most beautifully:

Man is only a reed, the feeblest reed in nature, but he is a thinking reed. There is no need for the entire universe to arm itself in order to annihilate him: a vapour, a drop of water, suffices to kill him. But were the universe to crush him, man would yet be more noble than that which slays him; because he *knows* that he dies, and the advantage that the universe has over him; of this the universe knows nothing. Thus all our dignity lies in thought. By thought we must raise ourselves, not by space and time, which we cannot fill. Let us strive, then, to think well—therein lies the principle of morality.

This awareness of death is the source of zest for life and of our impulse to create not only works of art, but civilizations as well. Not only is human anxiety universally associated with ultimate death, but awareness of death also brings benefits. One of these is the freedom to speak the truth: the more aware we are of death, the more vividly we experience the fact that it is not only beneath our dignity to tell a lie but useless as well. Rome will not burn a second time, so why fiddle during this burning? We can then say with Omar, "The bird of Time has but a little way to flutter—and the Bird is on the Wing."

The men of wisdom throughout history have understood the value for life in our awareness of death. "To philosophize," said Cicero, "is to prepare for death." And Seneca stated, "No man enjoys the true taste of life but he who is willing and ready to quit it."

A young man who was studying to be a psychotherapist and who was at this time my patient told me how intensely anxious he had been for several days prior to reporting on a case before a group of older practicing therapists, where he anticipated being attacked. Driving to the meeting, the thought suddenly occurred to him, "We'll all be dead some day—why not forget this neurotic anxiety and do the best I can?" Strange to say, this gave him a sudden, temporary relief from his anxiety. Another client told me about his having gone to a therapist several years earlier also with the problem of being so anxious he felt he could not stand it when his work required him to travel around the country. The other therapist had remarked, "You can always put a revolver in your suitcase and shoot yourself." This also gave the man a considerable relief from his anxiety.

Both of these persons experienced, with this reference to death, a relief from the feeling of being trapped. The anxiety lost its power when they realized that, if they had to, they could get out of the victim's role. We see what Nietzsche meant when he said, "The possibility of suicide has saved many lives."

1. The Poignance of the Transient

To admit genuinely one's mortality is to be released, to achieve a sense of freedom. The immortal gods on Mount Olympus were not free in any real sense. They were bored, empty, and uninteresting creatures—except when they got involved with mortals. Zeus and his cohorts could liven things up only by vagrant trips to earth to have a love affair with a human being. Those figures in Greek mythology whose careers are genuinely interesting are the demigods who do things for mortals, like Prometheus, or the gods or goddesses when they concern themselves in human affairs like the Trojan War or like Athena when she presided at the trial of Orestes. In other words, *mortality must be brought in to liven up immortality.* The drama *Amphitryon 38*, written by a contemporary Frenchman, illustrates this point. Zeus goes down to seduce the beautiful wife of a soldier away at war, and he later tells Mercury about making love to a mortal:

She will use little expressions and that widens the abyss between us. She will say, "When I was a child"—or "When I am old"—or "Never in all my life"—This stabs me, Mercury. . . . We miss something, Mercury—*the poignance of the transient*—the intimation of mortality—that sweet sadness of grasping at something you cannot hold.

Homer, in the same vein, tells us how Odysseus refused immortality when he was tempted by the beautiful goddess Kalypso, who says to him:

"Son of Laertes and seed of Zeus, resourceful Odysseus, are you still all so eager to go on back to your own house and the land of your fathers? I wish you well, however you do it, but if you only knew in your own heart how many hardships you were fated to undergo before getting back to your country, you would stay here with me and be the lord of this household and be an immortal, for all your longing once more to look on that wife for whom you are pining all your days here. And yet I think that I can claim that I am not her inferior either in build or stature, since it is not likely that mortal women can challenge the goddesses for build and beauty."

Then resourceful Odysseus spoke in turn and answered her: "Goddess and queen, do not be angry with me. I myself know that all you say is true and that circumspect Penelope can never match the impression you make for beauty and stature. She is mortal after all, and you are immortal and ageless. But even so, what I want and all my days I pine for is to go back to my house and see my day of homecoming. And if some god batters me far out on the wine-blue water, I will endure it, keeping a stubborn spirit inside me, for already I have suffered much and done much hard work on the waves and in the fighting. So let this adventure follow."

So he spoke, and the sun went down and the darkness came over. These two, withdrawn in the inner recess of the hollowed cavern, enjoyed themselves in love and stayed all night by each other.

At dawn Odysseus arises, cuts down trees to build his ship, and sails away three days later. As Kalypso had foretold and Odysseus had feared, his journey home was long and filled with hardships. He nevertheless had chosen Penelope, home, and mortality rather than the pleasant life of immortality with Kalypso.

This is what Abraham Maslow meant when he wrote, while recuperating from his heart attack: "Death and its ever present possibility makes love, passionate love, more possible. I wonder if we could love passionately, if ecstasy would be possible at all, if we knew we'd never die." This is not simply an expression of "I almost lost this . . . I almost died," but is a sensing of the rich depth that comes from awareness of destiny and the new possibilities, the new freedom of aesthetic sensibility, that then opens up.

No one knows what lies beyond this pale. But if there is anything other than extinction, we can be sure that the best preparation for it, in this brief interval when the bird of time is still on the wing, is to live out our lives and our creativity and as fully as we can, experiencing and contributing what we can.

If, however, we defend ourselves against the dread of dying by the belief that death is simple and easy, life becomes insipid and empty and the concept of freedom has no meaning.

Like most of the people who have read and heard Kübler-Ross, I have been impressed by her stories of her self-sacrifice in dealing with dying patients. I don't wish to detract from that or from her right to believe what she thinks is correct. But this should not prevent us from looking clearly at the implications of the conclusions she draws. Kübler-Ross states that death is like the opening of the chrysalis of the caterpillar and the emergence of the butterfly. This, I propose, is a form of denial; it takes away the person's impetus to make the most of this life. Kübler-Ross also quotes some of her patients as saying, "I cannot wait to die and see my friends." If death is so nice, then we would hurry toward it, with no poetry, no attention to building civilization for our children, no painting to pass on to posterity, no Ninth Symphony of Beethoven. And freedom would not even be a relevant concept.

This leads to the real hopelessness, for it robs human beings of the poignancy of living. In vain, then, we listen for the song of the Ulysses:

> . . . I will drink
> Life to the lees . . .
> . . . Life piled on life
> Were all too little . . .

Tennyson then describes the confronting of destiny and the living out of one's possibilities . . .

> . . . Come, my friends.
> 'T is not too late to seek a newer world.
> We are . . .
> One equal temper of heroic hearts,
> Made weak by time and fate, but strong in will
> To strive, to seek, to find, and not to yield.

But immediately we run up against the omnipresent denial of death in our culture, the fact that our society is sick in its pretenses in song and ritual that we never really die. When Hubert Humphrey, wizened and thin from cancer, made his last appearance before Congress, the senators, in their speeches, spoke optimistically: "Get well soon, Hubert. We need you back here." Who were they kidding? Not Humphrey, who courageously knew his death was only several months away. Not the millions watching on television, who could see clearly he was dying. Themselves? How much in contrast is Senator Richard Neuberger's statement, which he wrote shortly before his own death from cancer, that there had come

a new appreciation of things I once took for granted—eating lunch with a friend, scratching Muffet's ears and listening for his purrs, the company of my wife, reading a book or magazine in the quiet cone of my bed lamp at night. . . . For the first time I am savoring life. I realize, finally, that I am not immortal.

But what a tragedy that one waits until one is dying before savoring life!

The denial of death is the more amazing because it is clearly exhibited by many of the famous psychoanalysts themselves. Erich Fromm, in his book *The Heart of Man*, states, "The good man never thinks of death." In this book he sets "biophiliacs," the lovers of life, against "necrophiliacs," the lovers of death. In the latter, which Fromm obviously hates, were gathered the destructive persons of history—Hitler, Napoleon, and so forth. "Good is all that serves life; evil is all that serves death." The problem is that one then represses all thoughts of death, and this leads directly to the denial of death and of evil. In those thoughts there is no understanding of Goethe's statement in *Faust*:

> LORD: *Man's active nature, flagging, seeks too soon the level;*
> *Unqualified repose he learns to crave;*
> *Whence, willingly, the comrade him I gave,*
> *Who works, excites, and must create, as Devil.*

And when Mephistopheles reveals himself to Faust:

> FAUST: *Who art thou, then?*
> MEPHISTOPHELES: *Part of that Power, not understood,*
> *Which always wills the Bad, and always works*
> *the Good.*

In his denial of death, Fromm was but following the lead of most Freudians and of Freud himself. The originator of psychoanalysis set the fashion in arguing that anxiety about death is generally castration anxiety, because no one has ever actually experienced literal death, and, therefore, death cannot be in the unconscious. But as Yalom pointedly asks, Who has ever experienced literal castration? Freud deals with death only in his theory of Thanatos and in some essays inspired by World War I. But the theory of Thanatos—whatever its mythic values, which I think are great—never became part of the main body of psychoanalytic thought and is widely rejected by orthodox Freudians. With the exception of Otto Rank and Melanie Klein, both of whom broke off from the master and founded their own schools, this blindness about death seems more or less universal in orthodox psychoanalytic circles.

It is indeed a puzzle as to why Freud and his orthodox followers have so blocked off death and left the area for the existential therapists to bring back into its own. I suggest that the reason is the illusion of the *invincibility* of psychoanalysis. For to confront and acknowledge death—our own death and the death of others—is the central statement of human vincibility. The awareness of death is the emergence of destiny, now in the sense of necessity, in its extreme and ultimate form. To admit this aspect of destiny, this confession of finitude, would be to admit that psychoanalysis—and Freud and Fromm and all the rest of us mortals as well—would have to give up the craving for invincibility. This is to accept our finiteness and our mortality. It is to join the club of the human, the club of the finite, the vincible, the vulnerable; the club of the poignant mortals.

The awareness of death is required by the yes-no characteristic of human consciousness. Consciousness is never static: it knows one thing because that is opposite to something else. It experiences things dialectically, like an electric current with positive and negative poles. Or, as Gregory Bateson often said, we become aware of something by virtue of its contrast with its background. If the fly were perfectly still, the frog would never see it. But the fly moves once, and the frog takes aim; the fly moves again and the frog gobbles it up. Again, we hear the echo of the ancient wisdom of Heraclitus: "People do not realize that what is opposed to something is also identical with it."

Life is the opposite of death, and thoughts of death are necessary if we are to think significantly of life. Who has not thought at some moment of great joy "I hope I never die!" Or on seeing some breathtakingly beautiful view of the Alps "This makes me feel like eternity—I'm beyond life and death." Or on toiling at some challenging task "May heaven help me to live long enough to finish my work." Or at some moment of discouragement "Death would be better than this!" Or at a time of great fatigue, "He giveth his beloved rest." We need not talk about thoughts of suicide at all. For all the above illustrations are of the poignancy of life, and they all contain references to death. The most intense experiences of life bring with them the most intense experiences of death.

2. *Witchcraft and the Projection of Destiny*

When persons cannot or will not acknowledge and confront aspects of their destiny—such as a sudden illness, an inexplicable death, the birth of a malformed baby—the destiny becomes repressed. It is then often projected on figures outside themselves, such as gods, sorcerers, demons, and witches. I do not use the word *project* pejoratively. Projection is a common and normal function of the human mind, and we all do it continuously in less portentous ways then those cited here. Many talented people experience their visions in art or music as coming at least partially from outside themselves. As an artist paints a landscape, it is impossible to tell how much comes from the landscape that he presumably sees and how much is projected from his own sense of form. Indeed, his genuine art depends on what he projects rather than on what exists objectively "out there." The line between inner and outer reality is impossible to draw sharply, as the physics as the brain studies of Karl Pribram make clear. But here we will be talking mainly about the destructive aspects of the projection of destiny as it shows itself in witchcraft.

Witchcraft has been a sad and serious problem in Europe and the West since the twelfth century, particularly in the Catholic and Protestant churches. In the thirteenth century the Inquisition petitioned Pope Alexander IV (1254–61) for permission to add witchcraft to the ecclesiastical functions to be judged by the Inquisition. The pope refused, but he left the door open by stating his belief that all witches were the servants of Satan. By the end of the fifteenth century, witchcraft was assimilated with heresy, and those found guilty by the Inquisition of practicing witchcraft were burned at the stake.

If a person did not believe in witchcraft, his very disbelief put him in danger of being accused of heresy. If you believed that "no compact does or can exist between the Devil and a human being" or "that there is no sexual intercourse between the Devil and human beings" or that neither "devils nor witches can raise tempests, rain-storms, hail-storms and the like," you were already suspect of being in league with Satan. Even the leaders of the Protestant Reformation believed in witches. Luther wrote, "Paul reckoneth witchcraft among the works of the flesh, which . . . is not lust or lechery, but a kind of idolatry. For witchcraft covenanteth with the devil." John Calvin also was a believer in such sorcery and frequently quoted a passage from the New Testament: "Put on the whole armour of God, that ye may be able to stand against the wiles of the Devil. For we wrestle not against flesh and blood, but against principalities, against powers, against the rulers of the darkness of the world."

Witchcraft not only denied the ethical standards of the day, but also the aesthetic ones. The customary repulsive aspects of the witch's sabbath are present in extant documents: "The corpses of newly-born children were eaten by them; they had been stolen from their nurses during the night; all manner of revolting liquids were drunk and there was no savour in any of the food."

It is easy to understand that the aspects of destiny that we have called "cosmic," like the eruption of volcanoes or earthquakes, associated as these phenomena are with emotions of awe and terror, should be seen as the workings of some supernatural power. But the commonplace things of life were also susceptible, in any imaginative or hysterical person, to being called the work of witches. Thus, "continued sterility of many years was caused by witches through the malice of the Devil."

Male impotence, to cite an example among the many things projected, was widely cited as being caused by witchcraft. A couple, let us say, had been preparing for weeks to be married, and in the evening, after the strain and stress of the marriage ceremony, the groom finds himself impotent. Out of his bewilderment, anger, and feelings of inferiority, he could well have fantasies that some enchantment caused this embarrassing phenomenon. Pierre Bayle wrote in the early eighteenth century: "Several men are unable to consummate their marriage, and believe that this impotence is the effect of a spell. From then on, the newlyweds regard each other with an evil eye, and their discord at times descends into the most horrible enmity; the sight of one makes the other shiver." It is said, he adds, that witches say certain words during the nuptial benediction, which is called "knotting the braid." "That is why there are some good mothers who consent to anticipating the wedding night in order to foil the witch."

Thomas Aquinas takes up this question under the rubric "Whether the effects of sorcery are an impediment to matrimony." While he concludes that witches cannot impede the consummation of a marriage, the stronger spirits of evil, like demons and the devil, can do so. "The catholic faith . . . insists that demons do indeed exist and that they may impede sexual intercourse by their works."

The data in the witch trials are often sexual, and, indeed, sound like the precursor to today's pornography.

Anne Marie de Georgel declares that one morning when she was washing clothes near Pech-David above the town, she saw a man of huge stature coming towards her across the water. He was dark-skinned and his eyes burned like living coals; he was dressed in the hides of beasts. This monster asked her if she would give herself to him and she said yes. Then he blew into her mouth and from the Saturday following she was borne to the [witch's] Sabbath, simply because it was his will. There she found a huge he-goat and after greeting him she submitted to his pleasure. The he-goat in return taught her all kinds of secret spells; he explained poisonous plants to her and she learned from him words for incantations and how to cast spells during the night of the vigil of St. John's day, Christmas Eve, and the first Friday in every month. He advised her to make sacrilegious communion if she could, offending God and honouring the Devil. And she carried out these impious suggestions.

Anne Marie de Georgel then admitted that she had not ceased to do evil, practising all manner of filthiness during the years which passed from the time of her initiation to that of her imprisonment.

Sometimes these victims make theological statements of considerable sagacity. This Anne Marie went on to say that "the struggle between God and the Devil had gone on since eternity and would have no end. Sometimes one is victorious, sometimes the other, and at this time the situation was such that Satan was sure to triumph." How ironical that her being burned at the stake was itself a demonstration of the "triumph of Satan"!

Why are witches predominantly female? Whereas some of the pronouncements from the Inquisition use the phrase "witches of both sexes," there is no doubt that witches are chiefly women. (The term for a male witch, *warlock*, is unfamiliar and rarely used.) The *Malleus Maleficarum* (1486) written by two leaders of the Inquisition in Germany, H. Institoris and Jacob Sprenger, often called an "encyclopedia" of witchcraft, has one section entitled "Why is it that Women are chiefly addicted to Evil Superstitions?" The authors write (with seemingly perverse delight) "concerning the witches who copulate with devils," and they seek

the methods by which such abominations are consummated. On the part of the devil: first, of what element the body is made that he assumes; secondly, whether the act is always accompanied by the injection of semen received from another . . . whether he commits this act more frequently at one time and place . . . [and] whether the act is invisible to any who may be standing by.

These authors speak often of the "fragility" of females and state, concerning women, that "when they are governed by a good spirit, they are most excellent in virtue; but when they are governed by an evil spirit, they indulge [in] the worst possible vices." Indeed, "the word woman is used to mean the 'lust of the flesh.' " But women also have brought beatitude to men, and have "saved nations, lands and cities," as did Esther, Judith, and Deborah. Referring to the fact that original sin is blamed on Eve, Institoris and Sprenger remark that "we find a change of name, as from Eva to Ave [as in 'Ave Maria'] . . . and the whole sin of Eve is taken away by the benediction of Mary."

This condescending diatribe against women makes one wince, but it also casts light on the dynamics of the repression and projection of destiny. It seems obvious that this "lust of the flesh" is largely a projection of the men's own unacknowledged sexuality. The *femme fatale* phenomenon throws light on the helplessness a man may feel under the attraction of a beautiful woman, especially if she is unavailable to him. Many men resent such attraction, as though these waves of passion take the control of their own lives away from them. Throughout history, paintings of the courtesan, the prostitute, the beautiful but possibly insensitive woman bear witness to the power of the *femme fatale*.

Sex is a vivid part of our destiny in that we had no say about whether we were born male or female. Sex seems to take over our bodies willy-nilly. Our biological development brings with it new and, to the pubescent, strange and powerful desires and fantasies. Growing boys and men often experience sex as an intrusion and the powerful yearnings as something beyond their control. The conflicts males have about their sexuality can be accentuated by monastic life, as illustrated by Saint Anthony's sexual temptations in the desert and by Origen's self-castration.

All of this generates hostility toward the women on the man's part. But "good" men repress this hostility—perhaps under a Victorianlike code of putting women on a pedestal—even though this hostility is shown in semirecognizable form in men's groups, men's humor, and so on. Male anger arises from the situation in which the woman seems to hold power over his own glands, some secret influence over his internal organs that may be shown in his involuntary erections. This at first surprises him, then bewitches (the word is apt) him, and finally enrages him. It is easy to imagine these uncontrollable and tantalizing surgings of emotion as evidence that one has been bewitched. So strong can the repression be that one never pauses to consider that the source may be one's own destiny in one's reference to sexuality.

What better way to handle this bewildering attraction, this succumbing to the charms of the *femme fatale*, than by ascribing the secret influence to a witch? Sometimes the witches are young girls whose only crime is their beauty, and sometimes the witches are old and wizened and senile. But the man can easily remind himself that the old witches had this magic power in their youth, and they still remember the secret of it even though they don't tell. The "bewitched" man, attracted in ways he can do nothing about, passes on to another his suspicion that so and so has witchly powers. Others become suspicious, and soon so and so "becomes" a witch. Her denial only adds to the conviction. The erstwhile attracted man can tell himself he acted righteously and helped rid the world of the harmful one. Thus, his hostility and his erotic passion are relieved a thousandfold as the woman is burned at the stake.

All along there were protests against the cruel and inhuman treatment in the attack on so-called witchcraft, but the protesters objected at the risk of being accused themselves. One Jesuit and poet, Frederick Spee, assigned to the task of confessor to witches condemned to death in Würzburg, was appalled by the method of the trials and in 1631 published an anonymous attack on the persecutions.

In 1584 Reginald Scot subtitled his book on witchcraft *proving that the Compacts and Contracts of Witches with Devils and all Infernal Spirits . . . are but Erroneous Novelties and Imaginary Conceptions,* and laying bare *The Unchristian Practices and Inhumane Dealings of . . . Witch-tryers upon Aged, Melancholly and Superstitious people in extorting Confessions by Terrors and Tortures.*

Toward the end of the period a number of people argued that the fears of witchcraft were themselves the result of superstition and the human imagination gone wild. Pierre Bayle, in 1703, in a public letter, asserts that one hears among the common people that "an illness has been given to such and such persons by a witch." But he argues that these "are an effect of the dominion that the imagination exercises over the other faculties of the body and the soul." The diseases mentioned are "maintained by the anxieties of the mind and by the panic-stricken terrors of the soul." He tells of a nun who sincerely felt herself possessed and adds, "see what the imagination is capable of, once unhinged by too contemplative a life." Bayle reminds the person to whom he is writing that "you did not put too much stock in what I wrote to you about the bitterness that accompanies the devout life. You have persisted in telling me that mystics seem to you to be the happiest men in the world. It was thus necessary to convince you by means of a great example that they do not always enjoy those ineffable sweetnesses that you have read in their writings." We note here Bayle's insight that the evil projected on witches was the result of mental difficulties on the part of the mystics and others who repressed their own evil tendencies and pretended to experience perpetual sweetness and peace.

Bayle points out that witchcraft is the effect of an intense but twisted imagination. "Remove this cause," he states like a modern psychotherapist, albeit in overly simplistic terms, "give a full confidence to the ill person, and he will have a tranquil mind, and that will be his cure."

In the sixteenth century Montaigne tells of talking at length to "a prisoner . . . a real witch in ugliness and deformity, long very famous in that profession," and gives his conclusion: "It seemed to me a matter rather of madness than of crime."

In the seventeenth century Hobbes also became convinced that the belief in witchcraft was a delusion based on self-persuasion. Even the Grand Inquisitor of Spain came to see the self-delusion in the persecution of witches, and the fact that the presentation of witches itself led, by its suggestive self-fulfilling effects, to the appearance of the symptoms of witchcraft. There was, finally, the touching recantation of the twelve jurors of Salem (where a score of convicted witches had been put to death), who solemnly stated: "We justly fear we were sadly deluded and mistaken, . . . [and] do therefore humbly beg forgiveness."

Witchcraft and the persecution of witches were ultimately overcome by Cartesian rationalism, the philosophical belief that the body and the mind were separate and did not influence each other. In our day this rationalism takes the form of the factual, "scientific" explanation of the adversities that befall us.

I propose, however, that this solution is not enough. What are we to do with the destructive projections (which have been and can be shifted to Jews and blacks as well as witches) that are not cured by the "clear and simple" ideas of the rationalist? Parents may want to know the facts concerning the crippling of their child in an auto accident, but this does not assuage their grief. Sadness and grief, joy and exultation are emotional responses, while scientific explanations are rational phenomena. Thus the acknowledging and confronting of death, serious illness, the fact that one was born into a certain race and culture at a certain historical period (to cite some random aspects of destiny) are essentially feeling, emotional phenomena. Logical data are on a different plane. A healthy society must make room in poetry, art, and music for the expression of those emotional and mythic activities.

This is why our forbears, like Bayle and Hobbes, spoke so often of the role of *imagination* in the projections on witches. It also may throw light on why women were regarded as being "more disposed to superstition," since women in Western culture by and large react more emotionally than do men.* In witchcraft women were being punished for being more poetic, more emotionally sensitive, more intuitive than men (all things that could be regarded as "fragile").

This is also why our argument here does not fall under Calvin's stricture when he attacks the "trifling philosophy about the holy angels which teaches that they are nothing but good inspirations or impulses which God arouses in men's minds, [and] those men . . . who babble of devils as nothing else than evil emotions or perturbations which come upon us from our flesh." But the acknowledgment of fate and other aspects of one's destiny is by no means a "trifling" matter. On it depends our freedom as human beings and our very existence.

We note that it is the conventionally "good" people—the faithful Catholics and Protestants, the ethical bourgeois citizens, the monks and nuns—who seem to have been most ready to ascribe witchcraft to other persons living on the fringes of their communities. These "good" people are most apt to repress the evil tendencies within themselves and to pretend that fate does not exist, and, therefore, they are most likely to project their

---

*Light is thrown on this by contemporary research into the differing functions of the right and left hemispheres of the brain, begun by Dr. R. W. Sperry at the California Institute of Technology and now generally accepted in scientific quarters. These studies demonstrate that the left hemisphere, broadly speaking, channels logical, rational aspects of our experience, and the right hemisphere channels mainly the emotional, poetic, artistic ones. In our culture, women are reputed to develop the right-brain functions, and men depend more on the left brain. Thus, it can be asked whether women, in our culture, are more addicted to what Institoris and Sprenger called "evil superstitions." We here state that this was simply a question of women being emotional, poetic, and imaginative.

This can be said only in a general sense, and should not be made into a rule. There are many exceptions, one of which we shall see presently in the personalities of Macbeth and Lady Macbeth.

unacceptable urges on to other persons. Thus, goodness without the humility that John Bunyan expressed on seeing a condemned man being taken to the gallows, "There but for the grace of God go I," can itself lead to evil. Whenever I hear the customary platitudes "I love everyone" or "I have no enemies" or "Illness does not exist since God is spirit," I sigh and find myself wondering: Which aspect of destiny is the person repressing? Where will the projected energy rear its destructive head?

A classic portrayal of the projection of destiny is found in Shakespeare's *Macbeth*. In the fashion typical of the times, Shakespeare uses the three witches, called by him "the Weird Sisters," as the screen on which Macbeth's drive for power and ambition are projected. In this tragedy it is crucial that Shakespeare present Macbeth in the beginning as a good man, universally admired and respected by his peers. This sets the stage for Macbeth's profound and tragic conflict between this, the "public," side of his personality and his repressed power drives. A character sketch of Macbeth is given to us by Lady Macbeth near the beginning of the play:

> . . . thy nature;
> It is too full o' th' milk of human kindness
> To catch the nearest way. Thou wouldst be great,
> Art not without ambition, but without
> The illness should attend it. What thou wouldst highly,
> That wouldst thou holily; wouldst not play false,
> And yet wouldst wrongly win. . . .

Macbeth is presented in the hour of his greatest success as leader of the army on the day of victory. This is the moment when we are all open to the greatest temptations of power and ambition and the time when Macbeth is most open to his own sense of destiny. As one Shakespearean scholar states: "Experience has taught that to good men the day of greatest achievement proves too often the day of fate; that few natures can withstand the evil promptings to greater glory which come in the day of success."

Macbeth also possesses a poetic nature and an active and portentous imagination, which reminds us of the role of imagination in the witchcraft of the times. He is always communicating asides to the audience, telling us his inner thoughts: he sees ghosts and apparitions and hallucinates the dagger hanging in the air before him. Lady Macbeth rightly states, "Your face, my thane, is as a book where men/May read strange matters." During the drama he vacillates between his power drive and his human compassion, as illustrated in his cry after murdering Duncan the king, "Wake Duncan with thy knocking! I wouldst thou couldst!"

The play opens on a stormy day with the witches dancing around their fire as they chant on the heath: "Fair is foul, and foul is fair." Thus, as was the practice of witches, they deny the standard of ethics in their first line. They likewise destroy the standard of aesthetics: the brew around which they dance is made up of such things as "Finger of birth-strangled babe" and "grease that's sweatn'd/From the murderer's gibbet."

Macbeth's first words as he comes on the stage with Banquo echos what the witches have just said, "So foul and fair a day I have not seen." He is wholly unconscious of any relation with these supernatural agents of evil. The audience knows that this signifies some link between Macbeth and the witches, some unconscious relationship with the Weird Sisters.

The witches then predict that Macbeth will be Thane of Cawdor and king and that Banquo's children will be kings to come. Banquo brushes off the witches' message, saying it is nothing: "The earth hath bubbles, as the water has,/And these are of them." He asks Macbeth whether they have "eaten on the insane root/That takes the reason prisoner." But Macbeth, with his poetic nature and already drawn into a relationship with occult powers, cannot brush the witches' prediction aside, especially since they are the screen on which he projects his unconscious urgings. The witches, indeed, are constituted by Macbeth's own unconscious.

One might ask: Why does Banquo see the witches at all if they are projections of Macbeth's suppressed evil hopes and fears? Shakespeare was writing a drama, not a psychoanalytic paper, and took whatever poetic license he needed. But it is a fact that when we project our own evil, we can make it sound rational enough to get our friends to "see" it even though they do not take it as seriously as we do. Macbeth cannot rid his imagination of these prophecies from the witches. When other lords arrive to inform him that he has indeed been rewarded for the victory by being appointed Thane of Cawdor, Banquo cries, "What, can the devil speak true?" But Macbeth ponders the dilemma in an aside,

> This supernatural soliciting
> Cannot be ill, cannot be good. If ill,
> Why hath it given me earnest of success,
> Commencing in a truth? I am Thane of Cawdor.
> If good, why do I yield to that suggestion
> Whose horrid image doth unfix my hair
> And make my seated heart knock at my ribs,
> Against the use of nature? . . .

He is so caught up and overwhelmed by these thoughts that he can only add another paradox: "nothing is/But what is not." Thus, he again agrees with the witches' denial of the base of ethical standards. But his vacillation goes on: "If chance will have me King, why, chance may crown me/Without my stir."

We see in this the drama of the damnation of a great soul, the struggle of a once good man with his destiny. Lady Macbeth plays the part of a human representative of fate, a situation similar to Macbeth's own projection on the witches. Her portrait is drawn by Shakespeare as the opposite of Macbeth's: she is not poetic but practical, cold, calculating, even ruthless. She cries in speaking of nursing her baby, "I would, while it was smiling in my face,/I have pluck'd my nipple from his boneless gums/And dash'd his brains out, had I so sworn as you/Have done." As the representative of fate, she uses every kind of persuasion from scorn to cajoling to force Macbeth "to screw his courage to the sticking point," until finally her husband, in a salute to her steel-like will, adjures her to "bring forth men-children only!"

Murder follows murder as this fate is lived out—the assassination of Banquo and the killing of Macduff's wife and children. Macbeth is vacillating and remorseful all the while, until at the end he becomes desperate. The "milk of human kindness" is now lost in his deeper and deeper inner conflict, depression, and ultimate destruction.

Like the rest of us, Macbeth cannot take responsibility for his own fate. He goes back three times to the witches for reassurance. Hecate, queen of the witches, states to her minions, "Thither he/Will come to know his destiny." And she instructs her witches on how they will delude Macbeth further:

> . . . raise such artificial sprites
> As by the strength of their illusion
> Shall draw him on to his confusion.
> He shall spurn fate, scorn death, and bear
> His hopes 'bove wisdom, grace, and fear.
> And you all know, security
> Is mortals' chiefest enemy.

Macbeth's life has become empty, as in the "tomorrow, and tomorrow" speech, but more than that: "There's nothing serious in mortality;/All is but toys."

True to Hecate's prediction, Macbeth does come back again "to know his destiny" and is bolstered by the witches' statement that he will not die "till Birnam wood do come to Dunsinane," and no one "born of woman" will be able to kill him. Both of these turn out to be illusions. And in the last scene Macduff marches on stage with Macbeth's head.

It is not by accident that this drama, which is so psychoanalytic, is also the one where Shakespeare makes his most specific references to mental healing. After Lady Macbeth, herself at last the prey of overwhelming guilt, walks in her sleep, trying to wipe out the blood on her hand, and Macbeth and the doctor he has called watch her, Macbeth pleads with the physician,

> Canst thou not minister to a mind diseas'd,
> Pluck from the memory a rooted sorrow,
> Raze out the written troubles of the brain . . .

When the doctor answers, "Therein the patient/Must minister to himself," Macbeth expostulates, "Throw physic to the dogs; I'll none of it." Relevant also is the doctor's earlier remark: "More needs she the divine than the physician."

The destiny of Macbeth, we assume, is a combination of the design of his own nature in conflict with the external situation in which he finds himself. This conflict confronts us all, and to the extent that we can embrace it, we avoid the need to repress it and then to project it upon somebody or something outside ourselves.

Dramatic tragedies have such a powerful impact on us because we observe on the stage a good person who, like Macbeth, may be universally admired and respected by his peers but who succumbs to the conflicts that were always present in himself and who then slowly disintegrates before our eyes. Good people, as we have said, have a capacity for evil that balances their goodness. The saints throughout history have declared—and there is no reason to doubt their judgment—that they were also great sinners. This does not necessarily mean that they did specific evil things—which may or may not be the case. It does mean that, ethically speaking, goodness and evil are to be understood as one's sensitivity to the effect of one's actions and thoughts on oneself and on one's community. Holy men are saints precisely because of their highly developed sensitivity to goodness and evil.

I borrow from Carl Jung the concept that, in the unconscious mind, a person's goodness is in direct proportion to his potentialities for evil. The unconscious thus compensates for and balances consciousness. As one becomes sensitive to one's greater good, one also has the potentiality for greater evil. It is the latter that the witches represent. The higher we are able to go, the lower we can sink.

The necessary thing is to be able to acknowledge and confront one's evil fate. A tragedy is a situation, like Macbeth's, in which the person cannot admit and confront the aspects of his destiny nor even rebel against his destiny, for it is already blocked off from awareness. When Macbeth cries "Stars, hide your fires;/Let not light see my black and deep desires," he is describing the fissure that leads to projections of the repressed elements on witches or other unfortunate, albeit supernatural, agents.

Societies also go through the process of repression and projection that produces witches and witchcraft. Sometimes it takes the form of scapegoating, as when it was used against the Jews and the blacks in our own time. Every nation in wartime shouts out to its people the atrocities committed by the enemy and projects its own repressed aggression on the enemy. Thus freed of their own guilt at killing and given tangible "devils" to fight, the people can unite on the side of "God," "democracy," and "freedom." Like the "good people" of the Middle Ages, we are the righteous ones, struggling against the representatives of Satan.

We can see this in our own country, when we are told that we cannot talk with the Russians because they do not believe in God and an afterlife. Whether the statement is sincere or is made by officials simply as a way of enlisting the support of the religious masses, the dynamics are the same. It is the dynamics of witchcraft all over again. Witchcraft led to torture and burning at the stake in past centuries, and such behavior can lead us and our world into unimaginable tragedy—atomic warfare. Coming to terms with our own destiny is essential if we are to have compassion and empathy for others who are different from us, but with whom we must co-exist in a world with possibilities of unprecedented cruelty.

3. Destiny and the Poets

Engaging destiny is seen most brilliantly in poets, partly because of their genius with words, but mainly because they live in and write with the awareness of deeper dimensions of consciousness than the rest of us. Whether or not we call these depths subconscious, unconscious, or collective unconscious, they still are arrived at only by an intensity of feeling and vision, an ecstasy or a rage that cuts through superficial existence and reveals the profound forms of life. We should expect poets to have a great deal to communicate about destiny and about their own struggles to confront it. And we are not disappointed.

The poet's way is the opposite to the opaque, placid life. In authentic poetry we find a confrontation which does not involve repression nor covering up nor sacrifice of passion in order to avoid despair, nor any of the other ways most of us use to avoid direct acknowledgment of our destiny. The art of the poet teases out our awareness of our fate; the energy that goes into the making of the poem adds to our passion; and by means of the music poets combine with words, the poem takes on a power to express the dignity of our state as human beings.

Matthew Arnold begins his sonnet entitled "Shakespeare" with the line "Others abide our question. Thou art free." The reasons Shakespeare is free are revealed in the remainder of the sonnet:

> All pains the immortal spirit must endure,
> All weakness which impairs, all griefs which bow,
> Find their sole speech in that victorious brow.

Shakespeare thus expresses for all of us the passions and griefs experienced in engaging our own destinies. The joy and ecstasy of Shakespeare are noted by Matthew Arnold in his reference to "that victorious brow." From this level freedom takes off. All possibilities then open up—"Thou art free," as Arnold puts it.

John Milton contended, in his approaching blindness, against a bitter fate without becoming bitter. We find in his poetry not self-pity, but a courageous statement of his life's circumstance:

> When I consider how my light is spent
> Ere half my days in this dark world and wide,
> And that one talent which is death to hide
> Lodged with me useless. . . .

Blindness is a cruel fate for anyone, and especially for a poet in which it covers over this "talent which is death to hide."

In another sonnet to a friend, Milton is more explicit about "this three years' day these eyes":

> Bereft of light, their seeing have forgot;
> Nor to their idol orbs doth sight appear
> Of sun or moon or star through-out the year,
> Or man or woman.

For many people this loss of the precious capacity of seeing would eat their souls. But Milton had available what we do not generally have in our culture—namely, a religious faith that could help him to accept such a harsh destiny. He speaks of the "mild yoke" that he is assigned to bear:

> Against heavens hand or will, Yet I argue not
> Nor bate a lot of heart or hope, but still bear up
> And steer right onward. . . .

> This thought might lead me through the worlds vain mask
> Content, though blind, had I no better guide.

The above lines may sound like resignation, but they are not a giving-up. Resignation usually drains away one's power and productivity. But this is the Milton who was passionate in his defense of freedom, who wrote the "Areopagitica," who cried "Give me the liberty to know, to utter, and to argue freely according to conscience, above all other liberties." This is the Milton who in Italy went to see and to support Galileo, at that time a victim of the Inquisition, the Milton who devoted his energy to producing passionate pamphlets in the service of Cromwell and the Reformation. When their cause was successful, Milton wrote Cromwell a collegial caution about the preservation of this freedom:

> Help us to save free conscience from the paw
> Of hireling wolves whose gospel is their maw.

This is the Milton who refused to recant when the Commonwealth later failed; he risked the scaffold but somehow escaped it. Such passionate devotion to the cause one believes in speaks not of resignation, passivity, docility, or loss of energy. Milton's poetry is an example of how tragic experience can be formed by art into a thing of beauty. This outer power in politics as well as the inner power of poetry indicate that Milton had kept very much alive his dialectical relation to his own destiny and thus his experience of authentic freedom.

If Milton had lived in the twentieth century, the same sentiments might have required different expression. Our form of expression might well have been the "rage" Stanley Kunitz holds is the source of the intensity necessary for all poetry.

John Keats had an even more difficult destiny to confront— his own death from tuberculosis, which occurred when he was twenty-five. About his anticipation of this he wrote:

> When I have fears that I may cease to be
> Before my pen has gleaned my teeming brain. . . .

It is fascinating that both Milton and Keats, in the second line of the sonnet of each, are chiefly concerned with the poetry in them that may be forever unwritten. Their chief expression of possibility, their freedom to create, may be taken from them. Keats counts out the different meaningful things he will have to give up in the event of his death,

> When I behold, upon the night's starred face,
>   Huge cloudy symbols of a high romance,
> And think that I may never live to trace
>   Their shadows, with the magic hand of chance;
> And when I feel, fair creature of an hour,
>   That I shall never look upon thee more,
> Never have relish in the faery power
>   Of unreflecting love;—then on the shore
> Of the wide world I stand alone, and think
>   Till love and fame to nothingness do sink.

Let us consider a poet who is not concerned with a physical destiny like blindness or tuberculosis, but considers instead destiny in the form of the complete finitude of human beings—Omar Khayyám. He is generally considered the poet of fatalism. But he can be more fruitfully seen as one who looks without flinching at the brevity of life:

> Into this Universe, and *Why* not knowing
> Nor *Whence*, like Water willy-nilly flowing;
>   And out of it, as Wind along the Waste,
> I know not *Whither*, willy-nilly blowing.

The *Rubáiyát* is often cited as a poem of cynicism. But I wish to present Khayyám as the poet who is unafraid of the glaring light and does not flinch as he looks directly at human destiny:

> Up from Earth's Centre through the Seventh Gate
> I rose, and on the Throne of Saturn sate;
>   And many knots unravel'd by the Road;
> But not the Master-knot of Human Fate.
>   . . .
> The Moving Finger writes; and, having writ,
> Moves on: nor all your Piety nor Wit
>   Shall lure it back to cancel half a line,
> Nor all your Tears wash out a Word of it.

He attacks the false wishes and illusions that we all tend to carry—the hope that somehow we shall escape, through our special piety or our self-pity, the common fate of mankind. We simply do not know the ultimate answers. But despite this fate and the injustice that it implies, we must seize what freedom we can and push on. The mystery will remain a mystery, Omar states; or, as we would put it here, our destiny cannot be unraveled by reason or by wit.

Though often seen as the poet of hedonism, advocating whiling away one's life "under the bough" with poetry, wine, and sex, Omar can more truthfully be read as the poet who pits fortitude against fatalism. He confronts fate without becoming fatalistic. This is the same Omar who, as a boy eight centuries ago, studied Sufism and science and as an adult became known as Persia's outstanding astronomer, who wrote an authoritative text on algebra, who revised the astronomical tables, who persuaded the sultan to reform the calendar, and who in other ways worked diligently in the sultan's government. Hardly a hedonistic loafer!

The embracing of one's fate so directly and so clearly—as well as so blithely and courageously—reduces the negative effect of the piddling worries about destiny, and sets one free inwardly for actualizing one's freedom outwardly. Like Omar, those persons who often seem the most capable of accepting the inevitable are also the most productive and the most capable of pleasure and joy.

We see in these poets that the acceptance of human destiny is the way to put one's feet on solid ground. We then are not the ready prey of hobgoblins—we are no longer fighting battles against figments of our imagination; no boogeyman is lurking in the closet. We are freed from the hundred and one imaginary bonds; we are loosed from the need to beg others to take care of us. Having confronted the worst, we are released to open up to the possibilities of life.

4. *The Uses of Destiny*

Euripides has bequeathed to us some excellent advice:

> Events will take their course, it is no good
> Our being angry at them; he is happiest
> Who wisely turns them to the best account.

How can we "wisely turn them to the best account"? What powers do we have to guide and influence the direction of our destiny? How does one both shape one's destiny and live as an expression of it? Whittier expressed it directly, "This day we fashion Destiny /Our web of fate we spin."

Ludwig van Beethoven was one of these from whom we may learn.

What one individual has done another can aspire to; the destiny that one man has challenged and finally mastered another has it in his power to confront courageously also. In its externals Beethoven's destiny was his own; seen from within it is the destiny of man made manifest in one individual. . . .

He does not fulfill our destiny for us, but he shows us how we in our turn may fulfill it.

Destiny sets limits for us physically, psychologically, culturally, and equips us with certain talents. But we do not simply ask: How do we act *within* those limits or how do we develop those talents? We ask the more crucial question: Does the confronting of these limits itself yield us constructive values?

Can one, in other words, turn misfortune into fortune and keep fortune fortunate, turn handicaps into assets and keep assets from becoming handicaps? Is something taught us by the very process of confronting hardship that yields greater benefits than we gave up in our hardship and greater gifts than we lost? There come to mind hosts of examples of persons who have been burdened with a cruel destiny and have turned it to a constructive use. Epictetus says it powerfully:

I must die. I must be imprisoned. I must suffer exile. But must I die groaning? Must I whine as well? Can anyone hinder me from going into exile with a smile? The master threatens to chain me: what say you?

Chain me? My leg you will chain—yes, but not my will—no, not even Zeus can conquer that.

Spinoza relates freedom to our capacity to be active rather than passive. In this sense let us inquire: What possibilities does our capacity to be active give us in molding our destiny? Which trends in our destiny do we choose to identify with, and which others do we avoid? Do we cringe before our destiny, feeling sorry for ourselves, crying out: If only we could have been such and such? If so we shall go down like cowards or, more likely, robots—mechanical human beings whom the universe erases. Or do we confront destiny directly, using it as a stimulus to call forth our best efforts, our greatest sensitivity, our sharpest creative vision? If so, we then are men and women for whom the future cries.

We can see the vicissitudes of finding and losing, searching for but fleeing from, our personal destiny in noting how other historical figures have dealt with their destiny. Carl Jung tells of his own experience:

From the beginning I had a sense of destiny, as though my life was assigned to me by fate and had to be fulfilled. This gave me an inner security. . . . Often I had the feeling that in all decisive matters I was no longer among men, but was alone with God.

I have offended many people, for as soon as I saw that they did not understand me, that was the end of the matter so far as I was concerned. I had to move on. I had no patience with people—aside from my patients. I had to obey an inner law which was imposed on me and left me no freedom of choice.

Ortega tries to understand Goethe's destiny:

Goethe is the man in whom for the first time there dawned the consciousness that human life is man's struggle with his intimate and individual destiny, that is that human life is made up of the problem itself, that its substance consists not in something that already *is* . . . but in something which has to make itself, which, therefore, is not a *thing* but an absolute and problematical task.

Thus the task is not only to answer "Who am I?" but it goes beyond the problem of identity. For what is this "I," this sense of self, except me-in-relation-to-the-universe? It is more fruitful to ask: To what am I called in this world? What is my vocation?

Goethe himself wrote: "However much a man searches heaven and earth, the present and the future, for his higher destiny, he remains the victim of a perennial vacillation, of an external influence which perpetually troubles him." We may take this as a personal confession from Goethe as well as a statement about all of us. The heroes and heroines in Goethe's works go through life seeking their own destiny, often with the passion of Faust. Meister "goes wandering through the universe without ever finding his own life. . . . What befalls Werther, Faust and Meister is . . . they want to be and they do not know how—that is, they do not know *who* to be."

At forty we find Goethe wandering through Italy asking himself, "Am I poet, artist, or scientist?" The pondering led him to some conclusion, for he then writes from Rome, "For the first time I have found myself and am happily in harmony with myself." Is he in harmony because he has accepted his confused callings, accepted the fact that he is called to a number of tasks at once? When Goethe got back to Weimar, he went into politics, which Ortega thinks separated him from his world and from himself. "He looked so hard for his destiny, his destiny was so little apparent to him, because in looking for it he had already made up his mind to flee from it." To be continually preoccupied with one's destiny is also a way of escaping living it out. A sense of abandon is necessary, a sense of throwing oneself into one's calling.

Also, it is relevant that Goethe, according to Ortega, spent most of his days depressed, a psychological state that can be a symptom of a lack of harmony between oneself and one's way of life, a state opposite to the way Goethe described himself in Rome. In depression one feels on the rack, one struggles against meaninglessness, against the burden of it not being worthwhile to get up in the morning. Goethe's Faust, at the onset of the drama, greets every morning with "bitter weeping." Using the term *vocation* as a calling (the word is cognate of "vocal"), a voice from the universe proclaiming "this is where you belong," Ortega then asks, "Was the man Goethe in the service of his vocation, or was he, rather, a perpetual deserter from his inner destiny?"

It is the genuiuses, the persons of abundant talents, who have the greatest difficulty in seeking and living out their destiny because their gifts continually present them with so many different possibilities. Hence geniuses are more often depressed and anxious than the rest of us, and more often joyful and ecstatic. Life, especially for creative people, is generally anything but simple and harmonious. It is especially hard, admits Ortega, for those with a multiplicity of gifts, which "troubles and disorients the vocation, or at least the man who is its axis." It may well be, I would add, the destiny of persons like Goethe *not* to rest in an unambiguous vocation.

The example *par excellence* of one who struggled to discover and live out his destiny is found in William James, to my mind the greatest psychologist and most original philosopher America ever produced. He embraced many different professions. He first studied art and planned to be an artist; then he shifted back to his childhood interest in science, from which he moved to biology and medicine. "I originally studied medicine in order to be a physiologist," he tells us, "but I drifted into psychology and philosophy from a sort of fatality." Those two words, "drifted" and "fatalism," reveal the paradox he experienced in acknowledging destiny. The psychology and philosophy into which his restless quests drove him were, interestingly enough, subjects in which he had had no academic training. These shifts were by no means dilettantish, but an expression of the earnest seeker who lives perpetually on the razor's edge.

At sixteen we find William James writing passionately to a friend that what gives a person's life importance is its *use*, citing as an example a poet writing a poem. We find our path of greatest use, he wrote, by following our own individual inclinations, and if James had his way, he would simply "take a microscope and go into the field and become a scientist." He was prevented from doing this by his weak eyesight. This conflict of destinies shows us that the point where one's individual inclinations collide head-on with the necessities of life is where we see revealed the deeper density of ourselves.

James tells us also how he struggled with bad health, poor eyesight amounting at times to blindness, disabilities of his back, and his profound and recurrent psychological depression. But James managed to surmount his depression by his belief in freedom. The focus of his depression had been a conflict around the question of whether his actions were caused by prior influences such as childhood conditioning, or did he have some margin of personal freedom of action? He could not prove the latter, and none of his friends could send him proof. No one can prove in positivistic terms the *qualities* of life such as courage, love, beauty, or freedom. Thus began the important work of James on will and belief, illustrated by the title of one of his collections of essays, *The Will to Believe*. *"The first act of freedom is to choose it,"* he wrote. Anyone who has done psychotherapy knows that this would give the person a point outside the depression from which to view it and would provide some rising above the malady.

James is here demonstrating the relation of belief to destiny. Does belief—or faith, as some may put it—change the "track" of destiny? There are many wise persons in the history of the Western world who would answer "yes" to that. They would hold, with Kant, that the state of mind of the beholder influences what he perceives in life, that our minds not only conform to reality but reality also conforms to our minds. Thus, our state of mind influences the reality we experience around us. Karl Pribram's recent experiments on the neurology of the brain and its relation to the world would support this, as would Gregory Bateson's concept that "values are constituted in part by our beliefs." James was apparently stumbling—forced as he was by his own severe depression—upon the same truth.

Out of his problems and his perpetually difficult destiny William James developed a remarkable sense of personal freedom. He was amazingly flexible and broad-minded: he was the living example of freedom from cant and constriction. He not only wrote the classical volume on academic psychology, but books on religion, will, mysticism, and education as well. He insisted everlastingly that in human life there *are* options, however much destiny may limit these options.

Two

Mistaken Paths to Freedom

VII

The New Narcissism

Willy, dear. I can't cry. Why did you do it? I search and search and I
search, and I can't understand it, Willy. I made the last payment on
the house today. Today, dear. And there'll be nobody home. [A sob
rises in her throat] *We're free and clear.* [Sobbing, more fully,
released] *We're free.* [Biff comes slowly toward her] *We're free*
. . . We're free . . .

     —ARTHUR MILLER, *Death of a Salesman*

If we are to understand contemporary narcissism and its relation to freedom, we must look at the cultural crisis out of which
the narcissism was born. The 1960s were marked by pronounced
rejections, especially on the part of young people: the rebellions
against education as a factory, the strident protests of draft-age
persons against the automatic assumption that they could be sent
off to be maimed in the swamps of Vietnam; the fairy-tale "love"
of the flower children; the hippies, who camped together believing they needed nothing more than themselves; the vast number
of young people who severed all ties to their parents and took to
the road.

All of these movements in the 1960s can be seen as endeavors
to gain freedom. Free from the assembly line of education, free
from wars regarded as psychotic, free to make love with no hin-
drance by the mores of the past or vague dreads of the future,
free from the limits of space for those who donned knapsacks and
set out hitchhiking to live "on the road." The faith was that everyone could be born anew in a secular sense. They were all Jay
Gatsbys, not representing but rebelling against the Horatio Alger
myth.

I do not wish to burlesque the decade of the 1960s. Among the good things it did produce were highly valuable gains in race relations, the erasing of some of the barriers between adolescence and adulthood, and the new sharing of responsibility on college boards by students as well as faculty.

But the general feeling with which the decade of the 1960s left us was one of disappointment and disillusionment. Something important had been missing. Was it not that this freedom from past structure brought with it the assumption that all structure could be thrown to the winds? One's own purity of heart would suffice for everything. One's faith would move the mountains even of legislative passivity. The belief was, in Peter Marin's words, that "the individual will is all powerful and totally determines one's fate." There was no sense of responsibility to society, no acceptance of the inevitable, no sense of a human destiny that could not be denied. The American tradition, where, according to Tocqueville, people believe that their whole destiny is in their own hands, was acted out to the extreme in these movements of the 1960s.

Why Americans should believe this is also described by Tocqueville:

Born often under another sky, placed in the middle of an always moving scene, himself driven by the irresistible torrent which draws all about him, the American has no time to tie himself to anything, he grows accustomed only to change, and ends by regarding it as the natural state of man. He feels the need of it, more, he loves it; for the instability, instead of meaning disaster to him, seems to give birth only to miracles all about him.

1. The Threat of Loss of Self

No one can exist long on disillusionment. There soon was visible a different kind of concern among the equivalent groups. The young people of the 1970s turned inward. They asked, logically enough: Is it because of something lacking in ourselves that these movements failed? Since we cannot change the outside world as we wished, can we change the inner world?

Since the extrovert efforts proved more or less bankrupt, they now were replaced by introvert concerns. One felt the question in the 1970s—and we therapists heard it time and again: Can we find ourselves by means of some therapy for the inner person or with some new religion? Can we find our guidance in the East? Can we learn a new kind of yoga or meditation? Many of those who had been leaders in the activist movement went directly into the introvert movements. Of the Chicago Seven, Rennie Davis became one of the devotees of a teenage guru who dominated the news for a while and now is, like so many of them, heard of no more. Jerry Rubin turned to writing introspective, confession-type books, availing himself of that avenue which beckons to all who feel empty—i.e., writing about sex.

It needs to be said, in defense of the new narcissism, that the threat of losing oneself was real—losing oneself to behaviorism, which was indefatigably preached in those years with the dogma that the self did not exist, that all behavior was simply a conglomeration of conditioning, and that freedom was an illusion. The extent of the general culture's acceptance of these ideas, partly to escape the pervasive fears of atomic warfare and internal chaos, was shown in the wide sale of Skinner's *Beyond Freedom and Dignity*. Or losing oneself to a technologized culture that was becoming more computerized by the minute, losing oneself by becoming a mechanical robot of our society. A significant minority retreated—some of them would say "advanced"—to another fort, the fort of oneself, in the hope that behind that stockade they could form the final line in defense not only of freedom but of their existence as human beings. The new narcissism is seen in Nicole's statement concerning sex: "I have a right to do what I wish with my own body."

The songs said it: "I Gotta Be Me," "I Do It My Way," and "My Heart Belongs to Me," the last sung convincingly by Barbra Streisand. Hence, also the great tidal wave of self-awareness books for shoring up the individual's self-esteem: *I'm OK—You're OK, I Just Met Someone I Liked and It's Me, Being Your Own Best Friend*. Even Alan Watts entitled his autobiography *In My Own Way*. One book, written by the same person who produced *Win-*

ning by Intimidation, was entitled *How I Found Freedom in an Unfree World* and includes such monstrous examples of the ultimate in narcissism as "free men in any country have found ways of living their lives freely and happily without feeling a responsibility to be involved." Also, "Of what importance is society if you must give up your happiness for it?" Where did this man learn to speak if not in society? Who protected him as an infant if not the society of his mother? Did he never attend society's schools or the million and one things for which people join in society? That this "me" age is still alive is shown in a full-page advertisement that recently appeared in the *New York Times* for a book entitled *The Sky's the Limit*, which promises "absolute happiness" and to "make you a winner 100% of the time!"

Along with these came the mushrooming of self-help groups and the endeavor to raise consciousness to the point where it would suffice not only to direct ourselves, but to insure that our sense of freedom will not be threatened by the vast mechanical pressures all about us. It is not surprising, then, that many believed "If I am me, I will be free." This is the "new narcissism," as Peter Marin called it, or the "me" decade.

It is significant that in psychotherapy, too, narcissism has become the dominant problem. It is recognized, from Freud on, that the completely narcissistic person is the most difficult to help in psychotherapy because the therapist can achieve no relationship. The client seems unable to break through his own self-enclosing fog.

Christopher Lasch points out that now our whole society partakes of the culture of narcissism. He describes the narcissistic person:

Liberated from the superstitions of the past, he doubts even the reality of his own existence. Superficially relaxed and tolerant, he finds little use for dogmas of racial and ethnic purity but at the same time forfeits the security of group loyalties. . . . His sexual attitudes are permissive rather than puritanical, even though his emancipation from ancient taboos brings him no sexual peace. Fiercely competitive in his demand for approval and acclaim, he distrusts competition because he associates it unconsciously with an unbridled urge to destroy. . . . He extols cooperation and teamwork while harboring deeply antisocial impulses. He praises respect for rules and regulations in the secret belief that they do not apply to himself. Acquisitive in the sense that his cravings have no limits, he does not accumulate goods and provisions against the future, in the manner of the acquisitive individualist of nineteenth-century political economy, but demands immediate gratification and lives in a state of restless, perpetually unsatisfied desire.

Christopher Lasch's book, in my judgment, is a relevant dissection of our culture, and his comments are often piercing. But I wish to comment on its assumptions and statements about psychoanalysis and clinical activity, which is my field. What he fails to see is that psychoanalysis is a *symptom* of the whole development of modern culture, not simply an endeavor to correct its problems. Furthermore, he limits himself to one aspect—orthodox Freudianism—and depends chiefly on two analysts, Otto Kernberg and Heinz Kohut, who have written on modern narcissism. In the index of his book there are not even mentioned the host of other important figures: Erikson, Jung, Rank, Adler, Sullivan, all of whom wrote importantly on narcissism. The great loss in his failure to know more about these tributaries to Freud is, first, that one cannot even understand Freud without understanding why these persons developed their deviations from Freud. One of these deviants, Erich Fromm, Lasch takes to task for being "sermonic." But Harry Stack Sullivan was not given to moralizing and contributed most, in my judgment, to what Lasch is talking about—the problems of character neurosis.

By not looking at these persons who differ with Freud, Lasch repeats a great deal of what was said decades ago. Lasch talks about death. But the existential analysts, for example, have been discussing the fear of death ever since the 1940s, and working directly with it in therapy. (See Yalom's writings and my own.) Lasch talks of modern patients not having "symptoms" but being generally purposeless, aimless, empty, and complaining of boredom and a lack of commitment. This is exactly what I discussed in *Man's Search for Himself* in the 1950s. Lasch speaks of "character problems" as being the chief ones now facing analysts. Wilhelm Reich made this point in his book *Character Analysis* in the late 1920s, and Sullivan has done most of the significant contemporary work on this question. As a matter of fact, the narcissism

Lasch discusses as though it were a relatively new development has been the central concern of existential therapists—and, in different terms, in Sullivan—for over two decades. Thus, Lasch's book seems to me to be valuable as a social critique, but parochial as a psychoanalytic and clinical discourse.

2. "If I Am Me, Will I Be Free?"

In a series of verses written over the past five years, a youngish acquaintance of mine demonstrates the estrangement from community that is part of the new narcissism. She sets out to find "How to set myself / Totally free." A few pages later we come to a verse which states,

> I have no special
> Circle of friends
> Who think the way I do,
>   No rights, no wrongs, no desired ends.

This reveals a world with no structure of human relations and no moral structure—"no rights, no wrongs," no purposes. It is a celebration of isolation and emptiness. No wonder she is driven inside herself, taking refuge in an essentially narcissistic relation with herself:

> The purest form of love
> The warmest kind of love . . .
> The most exciting love
>   Is knowing that these feelings
>   Are not mine for another
>   But mine for me.

But this solipsism, a powerful illustration of the "me" decade, leads her to anxiety, which at this point is a sign of residual health.

> I am just beginning to see
>   how scary it is
> To live first for myself.

Afterward, in the series of verses, there comes a growing degree of resentment and anger when she senses that in her alienation and isolation she has somehow missed the boat. The series ends with a strong attack on the discipline of oneself,

Self-discipline is self mutiny.

These verses are like the cry of Willy Loman's wife at his funeral: "We're free and clear . . . We're free . . . We're free . . . We're free." But there was no genuine freedom at all since the family had been broken up by the fact that Willy had committed suicide.

The main problem in the "if I am me" syndrome, and the reason it so quickly goes bankrupt in the search for personal freedom, is that it omits other people; it fails to enrich our humanity. It does not confront destiny as embodied in the community. It reminds us of the famous statement of Fritz Perls:

I do my thing and you do your thing.
I am not in this world to live up to your expectations,
And you are not in this world to live up to mine.
You are you and I am I;
If by chance we find each other, it's beautiful.
If not, it can't be helped.

This yields the courage—or arrogance, if one wishes to call it that—of one against the world. True, it may be a necessary phase of individuation at certain times in one's history—and I think the past decade has been such a time. But it is a cop-out as a permanent way of life. Tubbs, in "Beyond Perls," is certainly right when he states, "The I detached from a Thou disintegrates." "Narcissism is self-hate disguised as self-love," says Clint Weyand. "It is probably the cruelest and most insidious form of self-deception, because it destroys the healing power of loving relationships. We must now transcend the seduction of the mirror, and replace the ego's image with a moral and political vision which restores our morale and enriches our humanity."

The "I am me" always sooner or later comes to grief because it tries to escape confronting the destiny that limits every expression of freedom. The writer of the verses quoted above and all other devotees of Fritz Perls's dictum could benefit by taking to heart a simple statement made by Angelus Silesius in the seventeenth century:

> Nothing   keeps   you
>   bound
> except your Me—
> until you break
> its chains, its handcuffs,
> and are free.

In our birth, the cutting of the umbilical cord is a first step on the long and tortuous path, fraught with endless difficulties and emblazoned with many joys, becoming autonomous. Obviously, we never fully reach our goals. But we shall never even start on the right track until we become aware that individuation occurs in our confronting, accepting, or engaging in various ways our destiny as social creatures.

If there are no limits in a human relationship, no place in the other where one cannot go, there is then no gratifying relationship from which one can learn. The concept of the unconscious used to provide this, but now, when everyone wears his dreams on his sleeve, it no longer does. Complete self-transparency, not withstanding its value as an ideal aim, is impossible and even undesirable. To keep the secret self—that sanctum sanctorum— is as important as the transparency.

The new narcissism brought with it a distrust of reality, as though we could never be sure anything was real, and we grasped desperately at what was inside ourselves in the hope of finding an anchor. The positive side of this uncertainty about reality is shown in the Zen story of the person asking: Am I a man looking at a butterfly, or am I a butterfly dreaming I am a man? The negative side is shown by a remark of Susan Sontag's: "Reality has come to seem more and more like what we are shown by cameras." There comes to mind the scene from *Apocalypse Now*, where the marine at night is desperately shooting at random not knowing where the enemies' shells are coming from, not knowing where his commander is or even *who* he is or whether he even *has* a commander. It is a Kafkaésque story that we are playing out, except that it is not played out now on a calm scene: it is played with atom bombs and the possibility of annihilated cities and the dreaded prospect of darkness at noon.

It is the uncertainty about the reality of oneself that threatens us. The self becomes increasingly insignificant in our world of technology. The emphasis on living now, with no ability to get solace or renewal from the past or future, the inability to commit oneself because one is not sure there *is* a self, the pervasive sense of purposelessness and vague despondency always threatening to become severe depression—these are all symptoms crying out that something has radically gone wrong with the self in relation to its world. The new narcissism and the "me" decade are symptoms of what has gone wrong with the reality of oneself. We seem to have to question every relationship, and the answers continue to be ambivalent.

Confronted mostly by young people in the 1960s, this unreality of the self has led to a fear of psychosis on a scale broader than ever before. For their elders all these compulsive-obsessional symptoms—the rigidity, the hollowness, the lack of affect—were protections against psychosis. But the young had taken LSD, and the psychoticlike shock to one's consciousness that this produces makes it clear that a similar shock was possible for the whole of society. More and more the question is being asked whether society as a whole is psychotic, and the pause after the question is a sign that the answer could be yes as well as no.

The widespread passion to be "me" with the assumption that then I will be free turns into becoming a candidate for a mental hospital, as seen in Ibsen's fantastic prophecy in 1887. The director of the insane asylum that Peer Gynt visits in Egypt states, in contrast to Peer's expectation that these inmates are there because they cannot be themselves,

> Here we are ourselves with a vengeance;
> Ourselves and nothing whatever but ourselves.
> We go full steam through life under the pressure of self.
> Each one shuts himself up in the cask of self;
> Sinks to the bottom by self-fermentation,
> Seals himself in with the bung of self,
> And seasons in the well of self,
> No one here weeps for the woes of others.
> No one here listens to anyone else's ideas.

There can be no sense of the self without a sense of the destiny of that self. How we respond to the facts of illness, disaster, good fortune, success, renewed life, death ad infinitum is crucial; and the pattern of such response is the self relating to destiny. For the sense of self consists, when all is said and done, in the relationship between the person's freedom and his or her destiny.

So we must conclude that the lack of sense of reality of the self is due to the fact that we have omitted destiny. We secretly tend to believe the advertisements that tell us that we are "unlimited," "the sky's the limit," "we'll be 100-percent winners," "we make our own destiny," and so on and on. And it is this that robs us of the sense of reality—and of adventure also—in our encountering the vicissitudes of human existence. It is certain that the "if I am me, I will be free" is a mistaken path, for it lacks the sense of destiny that gives freedom to reality. Instead of freedom, this path leads to isolation and estrangement.

3. The Myth of Narcissus and Revenge

Most of us remember the myth of Narcissus as the story of a beautiful youth who fell in love with his own image in a pool and pined away because he never could possess it. But the actual myth is a great deal richer.

It begins with Tiresias, the aged prophet, predicting to the river nymph who was Narcissus' mother that her son would live to a ripe old age "provided he never knows himself." This catches us up short. What is the meaning of not knowing oneself? True, the dynamics of narcissism always have as their fulcrum the problem of self-knowledge. But could Tiresias be saying that Narcissus will live long if he avoids the absorption of self-love, the very thing we later call narcissism? Or can he be referring to the literal translation of "know thyself," from the Greek "know that you are only a man," accept your human limits, which Narcissus obviously refused to do?

The second character in the myth, also forgotten by most of us, is Echo, a lovely mountain nymph who falls hopelessly in love with Narcissus and follows him over hill and dale as he hunts for stags. Intending to call his hunting companions, Narcissus cries, "Let us come together here!" Echo responds in the same words and rushes out to embrace Narcissus. But he shakes her off roughly and runs away crying out, "I will die before you ever lie with me!"

Echo then pines away, leaving behind only her melodious voice. Disdaining her supine resignation, the gods condemn her to wander forever in the mountain glens and valleys, where we hear her voice today. But in her need for revenge, she calls upon the gods to punish Narcissus by making him also the victim of unrequited love. It is only then that he falls in love with his own reflection.

At first he tried to embrace and kiss the beautiful boy who confronted him, but presently he recognized himself, and lay gazing enraptured into the pool, hour after hour. How could he endure both to possess and yet not to possess? Grief was destroying him, yet he rejoiced in his torments; knowing at least that his other self would remain true to him, whatever happened.

Echo, although she had not forgiven Narcissus, grieved with him; she sympathetically echoed 'Alas! Alas!' as he plunged a dagger in his breast, and also the final 'Ah, youth, beloved in vain, farewell!" as he expired.

Narcissus' tragic flaw, in the eyes of the gods, is that he could never love anyone else, never love in the sense of giving himself in union with another person. There is no fertility in Narcissus' "love," and none in narcissism—no genuine coupling, no cross-fertilization, no interpersonal relationship. This threatens to be a tragic flaw in our present-day "I am me" effort to escape the paradox: we cannot love without committing ourselves to another person. In grasping for freedom from entanglement with other persons, we come to grief over our failure of compassion and commitment—indeed, the failure to love authentically.

But there is another important insight in this story that will help us understand present-day neo-narcissism and that, to my knowledge, has not yet been mentioned in the literature. It is that *narcissism has its origin in revenge and retaliation.* Echo's plea, answered by Aphrodite, is a gesture of revenge.

And this is also true in our contemporary neo-narcissism: there is in it a strong motive of anger and revenge. This is shown in the above series of verses. "I have . . . no rights, no wrongs" can be translated into the cry "The culture has let us down." What we learned as children turns out to be phony; our parents seemed unable by dint of their confusion to show us any alternative moral guideposts or teach us wisdom; and what we were taught often turns out to be undesirable anyway and promotes counterrebellion.

It is out of revenge upon those in the culture who "betrayed" her that the writer of the verses withdraws into herself and comforts herself with a lonely self-love: "The purest form of love / The warmest . . . / The most exciting love / Is . . . / . . . not mine for another / But mine for me."

In our society we have called this self-love. The phrase "self-love" came into general currency after Erich Fromm's essay "Selfishness and Self-Love." Fromm condemned the first and elevated the second. He did not see the important differences between self-love and love of another. There is a tragic flaw in this self-love, a seductive error that carries over into the masses of self-help books and spreads the havoc that arises from neo-narcissism. What is called love for others and "self-love" are two different things. Love for another person is the urge toward the uniting of two separate entities who invigorate each other, revivify each other, contribute their differences to each other, and combine their different genes in a new and unique being—toward which the sex urge is a powerful motivation. The essence, then, is the combining of two different beings. Nature's obvious purpose in this, in contrast to incest, is the increase of possibilities. The insemination, the combination of two different sets of genes, results in the creation of new forms and original patterns. All of this Narcissus could not or would not do.

The well-worn dogma that you cannot love others if you hate yourself is true. But the converse of that—*that if you love yourself, you will automatically love others—is not true.* Narcissus, in his rejection of Echo, dramatically demonstrates this. Many persons use self-love as a substitute for the more difficult challenge of loving others. What is generally called self-love, then, ought really to be termed self-caring, which includes self-esteem, self-respect, and self-affirmation. This would save us from the confusion of self-caring and love for others, as it is shown so vividly in the myth of Narcissus.

To be free to love other persons requires self-affirmation and, paradoxically, the assertion of oneself. At the same time it requires tenderness, affirmation of the other, relaxing of competition as much as possible, self-abnegation at times in the interests of the loved one, and the age-old virtues of mercy and forgiveness toward each other.

Destiny is the other person in the act of loving. The dialectical poles of self-caring and love for the other fructify and strengthen each other. Fortunately, this paradox can neither be escaped nor solved, but must be lived with.

VIII

Is Sex without Intimacy Freedom?

Cavanaugh . . . bent toward Berliner. "Solly, aren't you jealous when your wife is making it with another guy?"
"Jealous?"
"Yeah, jealous."
"No, man. I'm liberated."
"What the hell does that mean?" I said.
Berliner said, as if it were obvious, "I don't feel anything."
"Liberated means you don't feel anything?"
"Yeah, I'm liberated."
    —LEONARD MICHAELS, *The Men's Club*

At what moment do lovers come into the most complete possession of themselves, *if not when they are* lost *in each other?*
   —PIERRE TEILHARD DE CHARDIN, *The Phenomenon of Man*

At one of the student crusades for freedom in the 1960s at the University of California in Berkeley, handbills were passed out emblazoned with the proposal "Sleep with a stranger tonight." Similarly, on the fringes of the psychotherapeutic movement workshops are offered on the theme "Sex with the Stranger." The logic of these phrases is fairly clear. Is not an essential part of being free the freedom to have sexual intercourse with whomever one wants and whenever one is so inclined? Does this not guarantee spontaneity, self-affirmation, the cleansing out of the last vestiges of culturally inherited guilt, and the opportunity to fling caution to the winds with a vengeance? And is not the best guarantee of this our being able to separate sex from intimacy by having sex with the stranger? Or, as it may be put, "Sex does not involve intimacy."

For the first time in history we have in our day the contraceptive pill, and we are confused about what to do with it. The pill has made possible a new attitude toward sex. But what are the implications for interpersonal relationships? What is the effect on personal freedom of using sex—that most intimate of human physical relationships—in the service of nonintimacy?

Sex without intimacy obviously happens about us all the time. One has only to mention prostitution to demonstrate that. Sex without intimacy does give some "freedom from," which we shall consider presently. But something new has been added in our day. This is the elevation of this form of sex, among sophisticates, into an ideal, a principle, a virtue. I believe that this making sex without intimacy the ideal, something to strive for, is an expression of narcissism, that it also is a rationalization for fear of intimacy and closeness in interpersonal relations, and that it arises from the alienation in our culture and adds to this alienation.

Intimacy is the sharing between two people not only of their bodies, but also of their hopes, fears, anxieties and aspirations. Intimacy is all the little gestures and expressions that endear us to each other. Intimacy is sensation blooming into emotion. As I have said in *Love and Will*, sex consists of stimulus and response, but love is a state of being. That relation is intimate which is enriched by the sharing of one's being with the other, in which one longs to hear the other's fantasies, dreams, and experiences and reciprocates by sharing his own.

But first let us look at the constructive side of sex without intimacy. It is seen in carnivals in Latin countries, in customs like *Fasching* in Germany, and in masked balls. There is a singular attraction in these mysteries, a stimulation in the fact that one does not know who one's partner is. Who among us has not thrilled—at least vicariously—at the new innocence assumed in such balls and carnivals, where responsibility for the moment is checked at the door? These customs are an intentional reversal of the wisdom in the ancient languages of Greek and Hebrew, where the word "know" means also to have sexual intercourse.

This *not* knowing carries a kind of folk wisdom—that the fallible human being, as the Grand Inquisiter said, needs periodic flings and especially a last fling before the long privation of Lent. Having lived for three years in a country in which the carnival season was built into the yearly calendar, I can testify to the great relief and pleasure in attending champagne parties that went on all night long and that ended only when the sun was rising.

For most people the carnival season is a time to dream dreams that may never come into reality. A patient from Germany, a shy man among whose problems was a fear of intimacy, told how he had gone regularly to the masked balls in Berlin after the war, "always hoping to meet some mysterious 'great love.' But, of course, I never found anybody."

1. Freedom from Barriers

Sex without intimacy is sometimes helpful for adolescents, who are stumbling their way into the scary and confusing wilderness of sex and afraid of getting trapped. Yet another use is for divorcees in healing the wounds of separation, abandonment, and rejection. Sex without intimacy is said by some therapists to be a stage in getting emotionally free from the estranged spouse and launching oneself into the stream of life again. Other therapists add that a period of promiscuity can be a way of avoiding marrying on the rebound or getting too deeply involved with a partner before one has lived through the inevitable mourning period of the previous abandonment.

Now we note that each of these is clearly a freedom *from*. Prostitution is allegedly freedom from tension; masked balls are freedom from the perpetual burden of too much consciousness; adolescent sex a freedom from bewilderment; divorcees' promiscuity is a freedom from the pain of wounded self-esteem. If sex without intimacy cannot enhance freedom of being itself, at least it can prepare the ground for later enhancement.

But when sex without intimacy is made into one's overall way of life à la *Playboy* a very different thing occurs. This is a compartmentalization of the self, an amputation of important parts of one's being. In one's fascination with the mystery in masked balls of sex without intimacy, one wakes up, in our twentieth-century "age of no mystery," to find oneself with the mechanical counterpart to the masks, the love machines, literally or in the form simply of feelingless people. As Dorothy Parker once said: "It's so nice to be in love. I'm tired of doing it for my complexion."

We recall that Nicole, in Chapter II, spent the weekend with a man who was almost a stranger and then summed it up to Philip, after restating that sex does not involve intimacy, "Sex bored me." Is not this confession of boredom also a confession of alienation, a cutting off of possibilities, and, therefore, of freedom?

Many therapists are consulted by clients whose aim is to learn how to perform sex with sensation but without emotion. The strange thing is that these clients sometimes come for therapy on the advice of their lovers. A young woman in her first session stated that she was entirely happy with her lover and did not want to have sex outside the relationship, but her lover had persuaded her that something was wrong if she could not go to bed with other men. And this is what she, at his urging, had come to learn to do. Merle Shain, in her book *Some Men Are More Perfect Than Others*, tells of a quarrel she had with her lover in which he expressed his irritation that she confined herself sexually to him. She found herself crying out, "If I want to be faithful to you, what bloody business is it of yours?"

In such men we see the fear of intimacy, often stimulated by their general fear of women. They may be afraid that too much responsibility will be dumped on them by the woman, afraid of enchainment to the woman's emotions, afraid of being encroached upon by the woman's needs.

Obviously, women have similar fears of men: fear that they'll be enveloped by the man, fear that they won't be able to express themselves, that they will lose their autonomy—fears made all the stronger by the cultural emphasis, at least until recently, on the woman's "role" as subordinate to men.

These fears are understandable. Sex involves a degree of intimacy—for the woman the momentous act of opening herself for the male to penetrate and invade her body. And for tens of thousands of years before the last few decades, this has meant the man's leaving his seed inside her with the possibility of her carrying a fetus for nine months and then having another mouth to feed and child to take responsibility for. What arrogance makes us think we can change that cultural inheritance of tens of thousands of years' duration in a couple of decades?

The merging of two bodies in sex is, physiologically, the most intimate of all the relationships to which the human being is heir. It is a uniting of the most sensitive parts of ourselves with an intimacy greater than is possible with any other parts of the body. Sex is the ultimate way we become part of each other; the throb of the other's heart and pulse are then felt as our own.

It is not the fear of intimacy I am questioning—there is no wonder we yearn for freedom from intimacy in carnivals and occasional flings. But I am questioning the rationalization of this fear into a principle that ends up amputating the self.

Another rationalization is the idea that, since sex is at times recreation, it is *nothing but* recreation; and one does not get intimate with one's partner in tennis or bridge. This ignores not only the meaning of sex, but the power of eros. No wonder true eroticism in our society is being steadily replaced by pornography.

The penetrating psychologist and master of words Dostoevsky gives us a vignette of this use of sex. In *The Brothers Karamazov*, the drunken buffoon of a father, coming home from a party one night, accepts the dare of his friends and has intercourse with the idiot woman in the ditch. That copulation spawns the son who later kills his father. Dostoevsky's use of symbols has powerful meaning. This act of sex, which is "sex without intimacy" in the extreme, leads ultimately to one's own death.

2. Sensation without Emotion

Considering the above factors, it will not come as a surprise when I state that, on the basis of my psychotherapeutic experiences, the people who can best function in a system of sex without intimacy are those who have little capacity for feeling in the first place. It is the persons who are compulsive and mechanical in their reactions, untrammeled by emotions, the persons who cannot experience intimacy anyway—in short the ones who operate like nonsentient motors—that can most easily carry on a pattern of sex without intimacy. One of the saddest things about our culture is that this nonloving, compulsive-obsessional type seems to be the "fruit" of the widespread mechanistic training in our schools and life, the type our culture cultivates. The danger is that these detached persons who are afraid of intimacy will move toward a robotlike existence, heralded by the drying up of their emotions not only on sexual levels, but on all levels, supported by the motto "Sex does not involve intimacy anyway." Little wonder, then, that in the story which cites what the women of different nationalities say after sexual intercourse, the American woman is portrayed as saying "What is your name, darling?"

I have noticed that in detached relationships with women, some male patients, not uncommonly intellectuals, are sexually very competent. They not only exemplify sex without intimacy, but they also think and live without intimacy; and their yearnings, hopes, fears have been so strait-jacketed as to be almost extinct. Then in therapy they begin to make progress. Suddenly they find themselves impotent. This troubles them greatly, and they often cannot understand why I regard it as a gain that they have become aware of some sensibilities within themselves and can no longer direct their sexual organs on command as one would a computor. They are beginning to distinguish the times when they really *want* to make love and the times they don't. This impotence is the beginning of a genuine experience of sex *with* intimacy. Now their sexual life ideally can be built on a new foundation of relationship; now they can be lovers rather than sexual machines.

Christopher Lasch rightly points out that the new "narcissist is permissive about sex," but this has given him "no sexual peace." What happens is that a premium is placed upon not feeling. Susan Stern, in describing how she gravitated toward the Weathermen, confesses an "inability to feel anything. I grew more frozen inside, more animated outside."

We recall that Nicole had adjured Philip to "hang loose" with other women. She had added that she would be hurt only if he felt too much—i.e., developed some intimacy with the other woman along with the sex. This puts a premium on *not feeling*, and the ideal then becomes the mechanized person who has sensations but no emotions. This is our situation in the latter half of the twentieth century. As in a Kafka novel, everything is waiting for us, but we ourselves—the feeling persons with their own emotions—do not appear. With the frankness that characterizes modern artists, Andy Warhol in his autobiography epitomizes this modern attitude: "Brigitte Bardot was one of the first women to be really modern and treat men like love objects, buying them and discarding them. I like that." Many others treat men and women like love objects, but cover it up under such principles as sex without intimacy.

The sex-without-intimacy trend in our culture goes hand in hand with the loss of the capacity to feel. This is a trend I saw developing in patients in therapy as early as the 1950s. Lasch now also sees this. Speaking of some new movements in our culture he says they arise "out of a pervasive dissatisfaction with the quality of personal relations." This teaches "people not to make too large an investment in love and friendship, to avoid excessive dependence on others, and to live for the moment—the very conditions that created the crisis of personal relations in the first place." Lasch also states:

Our society . . . has made deep and lasting friendships, love affairs, and marriages increasingly difficult to achieve. . . . Some of the new therapies dignify this combat as "assertiveness" and "fighting fair in love and marriage." Others celebrate impermanent attachments under such formulas as "open marriage" and "open-ended commitments." Thus they intensify the disease they pretend to cure.

3. The Lost Power of Eros

Gay Talese's book *Thy Neighbor's Wife* appeals to the voyeurism of large numbers of people because it is a record of what "real people do in real bedrooms." If it were just that, however, we could write it off as simply another example—perhaps the best written and most readable—of how eros is being eroded by pornography in our day. The sexual descriptions in this book are interspersed with references to contemporary writers—say, at Sandstone—who are quoted and misquoted, cited and miscited. The painter Hieronymus Bosch, with his paintings of hell, and John Smith, the founder of Mormonism, are cited by Talese as leaders in new trends in sexuality in ways that would have horrified them. Talese talks continually of his people, whom he describes in every kind of group sex and wife and lover exchanging, as being "freed," "liberated," and maintains that this is the way to "liberation" from the "suffocating bonds of traditional marriage." One reviewer said that the theme of the book is that "a freer fuck means a freer world." Hence, it will be helpful to examine this book to inquire further into the relation between sex and freedom.

The first seventeen pages of the book describe a young man who masturbates with a photograph of a sexy young woman propped up before him in bed. Indeed, an aura of masturbation hangs over the whole book: solitary sensation without emotion, sex without any real relationship to another person, sex without involvement. This is so whether Talese is talking about massage parlors, where actual masturbation is practiced, or the sexual circus of Sandstone, where people have sex in which the mood is masturbatory. The children, with whom some of the couples happen to be blessed, are mentioned only vaguely, and then as being shunted around among baby-sitters.

Talese tells us about Bullaro, the second most important character in the book, turning out in the end to have lost his wife, his children, and his job, and reports it as though he were commenting on the weather. Bullaro is "alone, jobless without a sense of hope." The "months that had seemed so exhilarating and liberating now loomed as a preamble to destruction and chaos." But what does this imply about the vaunted "liberation"? Freedom for destruction and chaos?

On almost every page there is some reference to freedom from Puritan repression. But in the process of beating this dead horse again and again, the book reveals no awareness that the more urgent danger is that in freeing ourselves we lose our humanity as well.

One of the aims of Williamson, the chief character in this book and the founder of Sandstone, is freeing lovers and their partners from all sexual possessiveness. The ideal is to have sex with "thy neighbor's wife" or lover and he with yours without any spark of jealousy. It is surprising, then, to read that Williamson, originally confident to the point of authoritarianism, had brooded in his bedroom "when a woman he had gotten attached to left him, and [he] had barely spoken to anyone at Sandstone for nearly two months."

We are given a detailed account of Hugh Hefner's parlaying his original hunches into the vast financial empire of *Playboy*, with all its available bunnies, where freedom from possessiveness would assumedly be the *sine qua non*. Again, it is amazing to read the dreary catalogue of Hugh Hefner's pursuing Karen Christy around Chicago, during which pursuit the guards he brought along, with walky-talkies, searched the rooms of Karen's friend, "in her closets, under her bed. Hefner looked haggard and desolate, his hair blown wild, his Pepsi bottle empty." Karen had explained that she had to get away from "faithless Hefner," whom she "had overheard . . . in the next room talking on the telephone with Barbi [Benton] in Los Angeles, reaffirming his love and even making arrangements to join her for a week-end. . . . Obviously Karen concluded, Hefner was deceiving her."

I mention these uninspiring items in order to ask the question: Why is it so hard for people like these two men to see that if one really cares about some other person, there will be some attachment, some normal jealousy and one will be vulnerable to pain; and that the aim with jealousy is not to exorcise it entirely, but to realize it is a problem only when it reaches neurotic proportions? *The awareness of normal jealousy is the one corrective to the growth of neurotic jealousy*, the dreary picture of which we have seen in these vignettes.

Freud gives us some hints as to one of the causes of our present preoccupation with sex:

In times in which there were no difficulties standing in the way of sexual satisfaction, such as perhaps during the decline of the ancient civilizations, love became worthless and life empty, and strong reaction-formations were required to restore indispensable affective values . . . the ascetic current in Christianity created psychical values for love which pagan antiquity was never able to confer on it.

In the judgment of many of us, our great preoccupation in America with sex, like "the decline of the ancient civilizations," when "love became worthless and life empty," is related to the disintegration of our mores and culture. Roman society was the only other historical society that was as preoccupied with sex as we are—with sex not only in our bedrooms but in our advertising, our literature, our movies, our TV, and heaven knows what else. It is said that when the Goths were outside the walls, the Romans masturbated in order to drown their anxiety. For sex is a very effective antidote against anxiety; the neurological pathway that carries the sexual stimulation cuts off that pathway which transmits anxiety. In our own concern with the innumerable problems in our society that we cannot solve, it is understandable that we turn to preoccupation with sex. But we should avoid making principles out of our own abnormal state.

Joseph Adelson, reviewing two books in the *New York Times*, remarks that "the books are alike in that they reflect and act upon the moral vacuousness that has become so commonplace as to be nearly normative in recent writing about sex." Is not this moral vacuity one explanation for the fact that, while we never had more talk and workshops and public-school teaching on sexual practices and contraception, the rate of venereal disease, teenage pregnancies and abortions are rising dramatically?

Sex and the intimacy that goes with it are so basic a part of human existence that one cannot separate them from one's values. To treat sex and values as totally divorced from each other is not only to block the development of one's freedom, but also to make the cultural problem of sex simply insoluble. Moral concern in sex hinges on the acceptance of one's responsibility for the other as well as for oneself. Other people do matter; and the celebration of this gives sexual intercourse its ecstasy, its meaning, and its capacity to shake us to our depths.

Benjamin De Mott remarks that Talese escapes moral vacuity because he is a good reporter. But this does not solve our overall cultural problem. De Mott also believes that writing like that in

Talese's book will self-destruct. The statement we have heard above, "sex is boring," is perhaps the beginning of such a self-destruct.

Sex without intimacy, when made into the be-all and end-all of sexuality, is an expression of narcissism. It is a refusal to love, a running from the beautiful Echo as Narcissus did in the myth. Sex as solitary stimuli, carried on in the absence of sharing, whether in masturbation or with a partner in sex without intimacy, is an overpowering concern with one's own stimuli, a peering endlessly at oneself, as Narcissus peered into the pool.

As a way of life, sex without intimacy is motivated by resentment and vengeance, like Echo's in the myth. Narcissus self-destructs by stabbing himself, but we self-destruct by a long, drawn-out amputation of vital parts of ourselves. Our contemporaries seem not to be vengeful because some specific person won't love them now (as was the case with Echo), but they seem to carry a vengeance from infancy, an experience of not having been loved, that they have never come to terms with. They have never accepted, as one must accept, their destiny, with all its cruel and its beneficent strains. Nor have they accepted the fate that no one ever gets enough love. This yearning for love makes us human. Having accepted that aspect of destiny, perhaps then we can join the human race.

What the proponents of the ideal of sex without intimacy as the way to genuine freedom have grossly overlooked is that freedom in sex is like freedom in every other realm of life: one is free only as one recognizes one's limits—i.e., one's destiny. The structure, the design, of the sexual function in life needs to be seen steadily and whole. In human relations responsibility comes out of ever-present loneliness and our inescapable need for others, which is dramatically true in sexuality; and without this sense of responsibility there is no authentic freedom. Our freedom in sex then grows in proportion to the parallel growth of our sensitivity to the needs, desires, wishes of the other. These needs, desires, and wishes of the other are the givens. The fact that sexual stimuli can blossom into authentic intimacy and into love is one of the mysteries of life which can give us a lasting solace and joy.

As in all aspects of confronting destiny, there is a risk. If you have feelings, you are bound to be vulnerable and to hurt. And sometimes the pain and ache and even agony of miscarried love is almost more than we can bear. But accepting this risk is the price of freedom, and especially the freedom to love authentically. Who wishes to trade these for existence as a zombie?

Three

Characteristics of Freedom

IX

The Significance of the Pause

*I don't think I handle the notes much differently from other pianists.
But the pauses between the notes—ah, there is where the artistry lies!*
—ARTUR SACHNABEL'S answer to reporters who inquired
about the secret of his genius.

*The goal of fasting is inner unity. This means hearing but not with
the ear; hearing, but not with the understanding; it is hearing with
the spirit, with your whole being. The hearing that is only in the ears
is one thing. The hearing of the understanding is another. But the
hearing of the spirit is not limited to any one faculty, to the ear, or to
the mind. Hence, it demands the emptiness of all the faculties. And
when the faculties are empty, then the whole being listens. There is
then a direct grasp of what is right before you that can never be heard
with the ear or understood with the mind. Fasting of the heart empties
the faculties, frees you from limitations and from preoccupations.*
—THOMAS MERTON, *The Living Bread*

In a previous chapter we defined freedom as the capacity to
pause in the midst of stimuli from all directions, and in this pause
to throw our weight toward this response rather than that one.
The crucial term, and in some ways the most interesting, is that
little word *pause*. It may seem strange that this word is the important one rather than terms like *liberty, independence, spontaneity*.
And it seems especially strange that a word merely signifying a
lack of something, an absence, a hiatus, a vacancy, should carry
so much weight. In America especially, the word "pause" refers

to a gap, a space yet unfilled, a nothing—or, better yet, a "no thing."

The pause is especially important for the freedom of being, what I have called essential freedom. For it is in the pause that we experience the context out of which freedom comes. In the pause we wonder, reflect, sense awe, and conceive of eternity. The pause is when we open ourselves for the moment to the concepts of both freedom and destiny.

The word *pause*, like the word *freedom*, seems essentially to signify what something is *not* rather than what it is. We have seen that freedom is defined almost universally by what it is not—or, in a sentence definition, "Freedom is when you are anchored to nobody or nothing." Similarly, the pause is a time when no thing is happening. Can the word *pause* give us an answer not only as to why *freedom* is a negative word, but is also loved as the most affirmative term in our language? It was, notes the anthropologist Dorothy Lee, "this conception of *nothingness* as *somethingness* that enabled the philosophers of India to perceive the integrity of non-being, to name the free space and give us the zero."

One version of a famous question is "How many Zen Buddhists does it take to screw in a light bulb?" The answer is two: one to screw it in and one *not* to screw it in. And the latter is as important as the former, for emptiness is something in Eastern thought.

It should not surprise us that this contribution to our thinking and experience comes mainly from the East, especially from India, China, and Japan. In our crisis of thought and religion in the West, the wisdom of the East emerges as a corrective. This wisdom recalls us to truths in our own mystic tradition that we had forgotten, such as contemplation, meditation, and especially the significance of the pause.

Freedom is experienced in our world in an infinite number of pauses, which turn out not to be negative but to be the most affirmative condition possible. *The ultimate paradox is that negation becomes affirmation.* Thus, *freedom* remains the most loved word, the word that thrills us most readily, the condition most desired because it calls forth continuous, unrealized possibilities. And it is so with the "pause." The "no thing" turns out to bespeak a reality that is most clearly something. It is paradoxical that in our lives empty can be full, negative can be affirmative, the void can be where most happens. In the *Tao Teh Ching*, for example, Lao Tzu says,

> We put thirty spokes to make a wheel:
> But it is on the hole in the center that the use of the cart hinges.
>
> We make a vessel from a lump of clay;
> But it is the empty space within the vessel that makes it useful.
>
> We make doors and windows for a room;
> But it is the empty spaces that make the room livable.
>
> Thus, while existence has advantages,
> It is the emptiness that makes it useful.

1. The Language of Silence

This conception of the pause gives us a whole new world. It is in the pause that people learn to *listen to silence*. We can hear an infinite number of sounds that we normally never hear at all—the unending hum and buzz of insects in a quiet summer field, a breeze blowing lightly through the golden hay, a thrush singing in the low bushes beyond the meadow. And we suddenly realize that this is *something*—the world of "silence" is populated by a myriad of creatures and a myriad of sounds.

Luther Standing Bear, describing his childhood as an Oglala Dakotan in the 1870s, wrote that children "were taught to sit still and enjoy [the silence]. They were taught to use their organs of smell, to look when apparently there was nothing to see, and to listen intently when all seemingly was quiet." And Modupe, writing of his so-so childhood in French Guinea, says, "We learned that silences as well as sounds are significant in the forest, and [we learned] how to listen to the silences. . . . Deeply felt silences might be said to be the core of our Kofon religion. During these times, *the nature within ourselves found unity with the nature of the earth*."

In Japan, free time and space—what we call pauses—are perceived as *ma*, the valid interval or meaningful pause. Such perception is basic to all experience and specifically to what constitutes creativity and freedom. This perception persists in spite of the adoption of Western culture and science. Even in 1958, Misako Miyamoto wrote of the Nō plays, "The audience watches the play and catches the feeling through not only the action and words but also the *intervals of the period of pauses. . . .* There is a free creation in each person's mind . . . ; and the audience relates to this situation with free thinking." Of silent intervals in speech, she says, "Especially [in] the pauses in a tone of voice, I can feel the person's unique personality and his joy, sorrow or other complicated feelings." On listening to a robin in early spring, "It sang with pauses, . . . I could have time to think about the bird [in] the silent moment between one voice and others, . . . The pauses produced the effect of the relation between the bird and me."

Lest these examples seduce us into assuming that this valuing of the pause is chiefly in Oriental and esoteric cultures, let me point out that the phenomenon is just as clear, though not as frequent, in our own modern culture. John Cage, a composer noted for his originality, gave a concert in New York which consisted of his coming out on the stage, sitting down at the keyboard for a period of time, and not playing a note. His aim, as he explained to a less-than-pleased audience, was to give them an opportunity to listen to the silence. His recorded music shows precisely this—many pauses are interspersed with heterogeneous notes. Cage sharpens our awareness, makes our senses keener, and renders us alive to ourselves and our surroundings. Listening is our most neglected sense.

The very essence of jazz is in the space between notes, called the afterbeat. The leader of a band in which I once played used to sing out "um-BAH," the "Bah"—or the note—coming always between the beats. This syncopation is a basis of jazz. Duke Ellington, for example, keeps the audience tantalized, on edge, expectant—we *have* to dance to work out the emotion building up within us. On an immediate level this expectancy has a similarity to the exquisite levels of feeling before orgasm. Hence, some musicians, can simulate the process of sexual intercourse in the tantalizing beat of their songs. In the ever-changing jazz group at Preservation Hall in New Orleans, this infinite variety, with each person improvising, produces each time a piece of music never before played and never to be played again. This is freedom *par excellence.*

There seems to be no pause in technology. Or when there is, it is called a "depression" and is denied and feared. But pure science is a different matter. We find Einstein remarking that "the intervals between the events are more significant than the events themselves."

The significance of the pause is that the rigid chain of cause and effect is broken. The pause momentarily suspends the billiard-ball system of Pavlov. In the person's life response no longer blindly follows stimulus. There intervenes between the two our human imaginings, reflections, considerations, ponderings. Pause is the prerequisite for wonder. When we don't pause, when we are perpetually hurrying from one appointment to another, from one "planned activity" to another, we sacrifice the richness of wonder. And we lose communication with our destiny.

2. Time and the Pause

The length of time of the pause is, in principle, irrelevant. When we look at what actually happens in people's experience, we note that some pauses can be infinitesimally small. When I am giving a lecture, for example, I select one word rather than another in a pause that lasts for only a millisecond. In this pause a number of possible terms flash before my mind's eye. If I want to say the noise was "loud," I may consider in this fraction of a second such words as "deafening," "startling," or "overwhelming." Out of these I select one. All this happens so rapidly—strictly speaking, on the preconscious level—that I am aware of it only when I stop to think about it afterward.

Note in this last sentence I say "stop to think." This habitual phrase is another proof of the importance of the pause. Hannah Arendt remarks in *Thinking* (volume 2 of *The Life of the Mind*) on the necessity of "stopping" to think—i.e., pausing as essential to the process of reflection.

But something else, even more interesting, occurs in those small, multitudinous pauses as one speaks. This is the time when

I "listen" to the audience, when the audience influences me, when I "hear" its reaction and ask silently, What connotations are they taking from my words? For any experienced lecturer the blank spaces that constitute the pauses between the words and sentences is the time of openness to the audience. At such times I find myself noting: There someone seems puzzled; here someone listens by tipping his head to one side so as not to miss any word; there in the back row—what every speaker dreads to see—is someone nodding in sleep. Every experienced speaker that I know is greatly helped by the cultivation of his awareness of facial expressions and other subtle aspects of unspoken communication from the audience.

Walt Whitman once remarked that "the audience writes the poetry," and in an even clearer sense the audience gives the lecture. Hence, a lecture delivered from the same notes, say once to a social club and then again to graduate students at a large university, will often seem to be two entirely different speeches.

The pause for milliseconds while one speaks is *the locus of the speaker's freedom*. The speaker may mold his speech this way or that, he may tell a joke to relax the audience, or—in a thrilling moment of which there cannot be too many in a lecturer's career—he may even be aware of a brand new idea coming to him from heaven knows where in the audience.

Cassandra, we are told in Aeschylus' drama, foretold the doom of Mycenae. A prophetess, she was sensitive to communications on many different levels of which the average person is unaware. This sensitivity caused her much pain, and she would gladly have given up her role if she could have. She was "doomed," or destined to listen on these different levels; she could not escape hearing the messages coming in her pauses. Quite apart from the roles of prophetess or mystic—which we see also in Tiresias and Jeremiah and Isaiah—it would seem that multitudes of us have such capacities, but we train ourselves (a process abetted by much contemporary education) to suppress this sensitivity to the pauses. And we may do this in the hope of avoiding the pain. The difference between the charlatan and the genuine prophet may well be the sense of pain the latter experiences in his or her prophecies.

The pauses may be longer, for instance, when one is answering questions after a lecture. In response to a question, I may silently hem and haw for a moment while different possible answers flash through my mind. At that time I do not usually think of Kierkegaard's proclamation "Freedom is possibility," but that is what I am living out in those moments of pause. The thrilling thing is that at such a time a new answer that I have never thought of may suddenly emerge. It is often said that intellectually creative people—like John Dewey, for example—are a strain to listen to and are not good public speakers, because the time they pause to consider different possibilities requires a capacity to wait that most people find tedious.

One's freedom may involve still larger pauses. "Let me sleep on it" is a not infrequent remark when one is making an important decision like buying a house. These are the situations in which a longer interval between stimuli is desired; there may be many different houses available, or one can decide not to buy any at all. The decision then requires complex consideration, pondering, setting up possibilities for choice, and playing "as if" games with oneself to assess various factors like view and design and so on. My point is simply that freedom consists of these possibilities. The pauses are the exercise of one's freedom to choose among them.

We recall that Jesus and Buddha, each following his own inner guidance, went off into his separate wilderness to engage in his quest. Both "paused" for forty days, if the records are to be believed. These were assumedly times for each of intense concentration, times of considering possibilities, of listening to whatever voices were available on deeper levels within themselves, voices from nature, voices from what we now term archetypal experiences, voices from what Jesus called God and Buddha called Atman and I would call Being. These assumedly were periods in which they experienced their visions and integrated themselves around their messages.

But students tell me that they have professors who *pause permanently.* These teachers make a career out of pausing. The pause is then not a preparation for action but an excuse for never acting at all. It has been remarked that the academic profession is the only one in which you can make your living by questioning things. How much it is still true in academia that persons substitute talking for decision or rationalize lack of commitment by calling it "judicious pausing" I do not know. Nevertheless this is a tendency that confronts us all: to use pausing as a substitute for committed action. In our action-oriented life in America this misuse of pausing is a not infrequently found neurotic reaction. But this dilemma is not overcome by acting blindly, without consciousness and without reason. To be free obviously requires the courage to act when it is necessary to act if one's freedom is to be actualized at all.

A person may ponder for months and years or all life long, never finding satisfactory answers. This occurs particularly with the question of death. Hamlet spoke for many of us when he stated his concern with what might happen beyond death,

> When we have shuffled off this mortal coil,
> [It] must give us pause.

But our personal freedom can be actualized regardless of whether we find satisfactory answers or not, or even if there are no answers at all. We can exercise our freedom even against destiny. Indeed, in the long run to "know that he dies," as Pascal said, is the most essential and triumphant experience of freedom possible for a human being.

3. Creativity and the Symbol

The relation between creativity and the pause is as close as it is startling. Not only does one get one's original ideas in the pause—Einstein got his while shaving; Poincaré got his while walking by the sea; others get theirs in dreams at night—but the capacity to pause is woven all through the creative production itself. The pause is an active, nimble, often intense state, as when an Olympic diver pauses at the end of the diving board until that precise hundredth of a second when every muscle is tensed in harmony. And at that instant he dives. The creative person stands in a state of openness, heightened sensitivity, incubating the creative idea, with a sharpened readiness to grasp the creative impulse when it is born. The phrase "inviting the Muses," which is part of the occupation in the "pause," is an active yearning, an imploring, the authenticity of which is demonstrated by the hours of hard work the creative person puts in before and after the insight.

While writing this chapter, I went to the nearby coast one Sunday hoping to do a sketch. Afterward, I wrote some notes about the experience:

I walk about on the shore in a mood of readiness, openness, asking myself, Where is the scene that grasps me? This red cliff with that water behind it or that boulder with the other rocks in front of the ocean? I continue looking until I have the special feeling that a particular scene seizes me. I *see* it; and though I don't think of this consciously, I see it in a way that no one has ever seen it before. I think only: "This I like, this turns me on."

When I start painting:

The colors flow into each other . . . my muscles react . . . I make this line going off in that direction, another great rock on the paper . . . the colors form almost as though they had their own plan in mind . . . the world is born anew in the painting. Not only did no one ever see this scene before as I do now [everyone sees every scene differently] but I find a new picture coming to birth, new to *me* as well as others, in the flowing of the colors into each other, new in that the combination makes a different effect from what I had expected.

We see how important are such terms as "readiness," "openness." In these active pauses, we see the work of destiny expressed in my feeling grasped, seized, and a "new picture" is born in the unpredictable flowing of the colors.

Hence so much of creativity seems accidental. But the artist, whether he be scientific inventor or painter or writer or what not, is the one who can most often put himself in *readiness for* the "accident." True, the picture comes out differently from what one expects. But knowing he can never predict for certain how a picture will turn out, the artist can hold himself open for the "lucky accident." This means that "accident" is not the right term: rather, a myriad of different possibilities exist, and out of these one is born.

Our *capacity to appreciate* is already a kind of creativity which shows the activity in the pause. Our appreciative listening to Mozart of Bach, our concerned reading of Aeschylus, is our creative contribution. The listening and the seeing are what is important; hence, Frederick Franck in his book on Zen painting entitled it, very rightly, *The Zen of Seeing.* Indeed, it takes listeners, actual or imaginary, for a musician to compose a sonata. The audience is necessary and partakes of the creative act by virtue of the fact that writing poetry or prose or music or dramas would not be possible without a real or imagined audience, whether an author writes for people of his own century (like most of us) or for later centuries (like Kierkegaard).

The presence of the pause is very clear in Matisse's paintings in his use of space—which is a synonym for pause. Ben Shahn tells, in his description of creativity, of one day taking his daughter out to his studio with him to make a mock-up book out of papier-mâché for a friend. His daughter watched him as he tried one color, rejected it, pondered another, put it aside, and so on for half an hour. When they came back into the house, the little girl asked her mother, "Why can't Daddy make up his mind?" Shahn goes on to explain that the artist is the one who has the courage to pause, to be suspended for a certain duration in midair. And even though in our technological culture such doubts may appear on the surface to imply weakness, this pausing is really a sign of an inner richness of discriminatory powers.

There is a phrase among artists, "negative space," which stands for space not noticed by the usual viewer. On a Rorschach record "negative space" is the white area surrounding the black or colored. Many people who take the Rorschach never notice or remark on the white space—it is simply "surroundings." Those who do, who see many white spaces may be adjudged "stubborn" on the test because they are preoccupied with the opposite to what most people point out. This is an interesting commentary on the conformist tendencies in our culture to see artists and musicians as a bit strange and to see the pause as an anomaly.

I want to make clear that the common misconception that the creative person is passive is just that—a misconception. The creative person is *receptive.* I agree entirely with Archibald MacLeish when he quotes a Chinese poet, "We poets struggle with Non-being to force it to yield Being. We knock upon silence for an answering music." MacLeish continues, "The 'Being' which the poem is to contain derives from 'Non-being,' not from the poet. And the 'music' which the poem is to own comes not from us who make the poem but from the silence; comes in *answer* to our knock."

The creative act has always been a paradox, and it probably will always be one. Practically everybody trying to explain it, especially the psychoanalysts who propose that creativity is "regression in the service of the ego," find they crash upon the rocks of their inability to distinguish between passivity and receptivity. The creative persons are the latter; they are certainly not the former.

We do not know from what combination in the brain cells and synapses the creative ideas spring. But we do know that creativity requires freedom, and the pause is the way to give that creative combination the chance to work. Pausing is wondering, and wonder is first cousin to creativity.

"Poetry for me," writes a poet friend, "is the space between the words. A poet is a poet when he or she can create that tension between words—a tension created by spaces—that lifts the reader outside the piece of paper." Lifts the poet into an experience, I would add, of intense or mild ecstasy—standing mentally outside oneself. These new experiences of splendor or wonder or just plain insight have their start in the poem, but they leap out into the reader's conception of his own private world. Creativity comes not only out of our moments or hours or weeks of effort; it requires—and this is essential—the moments or hours or weeks of pause between the effort.

The pause is that situation in which symbols are formed. The intensity of handling all the stimuli that come at us requires the symbol. How are we to assess these stimuli, how are we to judge them, to weight them—all of which must be done before one can throw one's strength toward this response rather than that one, to employ our simplest paradigm of freedom?

The term *symbol* comes from two Greek words, *sym* meaning "with" and *bollein* meaning "to throw." The symbol is, thus, that which throws or brings together these antimonies into one image, one form. The vitality of the situation is preserved for as long as the symbol continues to exist.

We surely cannot handle all these stimuli by computor; we cannot add and subtract and in other mathematical ways try to fashion them into a decision. In a technological problem one can do this. But when one tries to turn human decisions—such as whom shall I marry—over to the machine and tries to abstract oneself out of the picture, one becomes more and more mechanical, less and less personal and human. Lo and behold, the warmth has gone out of the situation, the vitality lost, the personal characteristics fled, and the person talking to you experiences you as less and less a person and more and more a machine. This is similar to talking with brain-injured patients in a mental hospital: they understand all the words you use, but cannot go behind the words to understand you as the *person* speaking. A human being in normal communication speaks in symbols, and if these are not grasped—and they are not by the brain-injured—the person is not understood. All vital words carry some residue of their origin as symbols.

In a human problem, the *pattern* is all-important and personal likes and dislikes are crucial. The response, to which you throw your weight, will not be only a conclusion, but will also be a commitment with its own power. Many factors need to be taken into consideration, some of which are only partially conscious. In such personal questions there is no decision which is "right," but only approximately so. We have to keep the different factors all alive, like a juggler with a dozen balls in the air; we cannot avoid some factors without doing damage to the totality. What ideally happens is that these stimuli begin to fit into a pattern, a whole, a totality, a form that preserves the kernel and the value of each one. *This is the symbol.*

Take, for example, the apparently simply stimuli that arise around the concept of patriotism. There is the call of one's homeland; the fact that our forefathers fought in 1776 to construct this nation; the feeling of comradeship with people who speak the same language; and a million and one other facts and memories acting as stimuli. You hit upon a banner, and you call it a flag. The flag does not leave out any of the above meanings; it expresses the multitude of meanings in a compact, dynamic symbol.

The elements that are forged and united into symbol in this pause which we have made the center of freedom come from many sources. They are from past and present, individual and group, consciousness and unconsciousness, and they are both rational and irrational. All of these antimonies are brought together in the pattern which is the symbol. The symbol keeps them alive and vital.

4. Leisure and the Pause

That form of the pause which we call leisure is also, curiously enough, both desired and feared. Unbounded leisure can turn people's lives into chaos, which those people can then blame on "excessive freedom." Persons who despair about such problems as delinquency, truancy, alcoholism, drugs, often point to "too much leisure" as the villain of the piece. These people believe that the devil indeed has work for idle hands. The word "leisure" can be read as "freedom" or "pausing." Dorothy Lee suggests:

This is why American leisure has to be filled with named games, organized recreation, labelled hobbies, planned activities. And this is why the *have to* is often paradoxically freeing.

Observing the sharp dilemma people are thrown into by leisure time, we ask: What is this apparent fear of leisure? In America we have traditionally associated freedom, especially in the form of leisure, with *space*. There was always some new, unexplored space to go to. Land was free. Although this is not true in a literal sense nearly as much as it used to be, the concept is still very much a part of our American myths. The Native Americans were never considered as owning the space or the land. Freedom of the land was recognized as the fundamental freedom, from which other freedom was derived. We expressed our freedom of the body by moving to a new space. So we remained extroverts, concerned with our muscles. Hence, the great outcry, and near panic, with the gasoline shortage. People interpreted it as having their freedom to travel, to move, taken away from them, thus enslaving them.

In Europe, on the contrary, all space has been explored for a long time, and is now apportioned out and owned by somebody. So the Europeans' emphasis has been on *time*. Europeans cultivated the introvert side, turned inward, free in their imaginations and thought to travel all over the world. Freedom meant freedom of the mind in contrast to the body.

But in America this leaves us with a problem. We no longer can simply pack up and move to another house, typically farther west. When our freedom essentially means what we do with our leisure, freedom then turns out to be a vacuum. There is no being in it; it is a "no thing." This becomes clear in psychoanalysis. Horney has written about the "Sunday neuroses," the anxiety that subtly eats away at businessmen on Sunday when nothing is planned, nothing scheduled. These businessmen are filled with anxiety and stoically endure the passage of time until Monday morning when they can go back to work and again become occupied. (What a graphic phrase, "become occupied," implying that something outside ourselves takes over and occupies us!)

Dorothy Lee raises the question, "Does this version of freedom, with its dependence on the pre-planned and its main emphasis on the capacity of the self, engender creativity, originality, spontaneity? My own opinion is that it does not; that indefiniteness and randomness, the recognition of the *pauses* are all essential to creativity." I enthusiastically agree. Randomness, the recognition of the pauses, and the confronting of leisure rather than destroying it by excessive planning are essential if the person is to be open to his creative impulses. The pause is the essence of creativity, let alone of originality and spontaneity. One cannot avail oneself of the richness of preconsciousness or unconsciousness unless one can let oneself periodically relax, be relieved of tension. It is then that the person lets the silences speak.

Frieda Fromm-Reichman, the psychiatrist about whose work,

I Never Promised You a Rose Garden, was written, used to talk to her classes about the value to the analyst when a patient missed an hour. "If the analyst is the creative type," she put it, "this empty hour is of the essence."

True. Unstructured freedom is difficult for most people to confront for long periods. But there are happy mediums, and the use of leisure falls in that category. The constructive limits to our freedom are given by what we are committed to and by the myths we live by. Then there can be meaning to leisure. We can use it for random thinking, reverie, or for simply wandering around a new city for a time. Yes, the time may be wasted. But who is to say that this "wasted" time may not bring us our most important ideas or new experiences, new visions, that are invaluable? The "letting be" and "letting happen" may turn out to be the most significant thing one can do.

5. The Psyche and the Ego

A friend responded to my question as to how he was with these words: "I've got a cold, I didn't sleep much last night, everything is going wrong. By rights I ought to feel terrible. But actually I am quite good." My friend went on: "The people who argue that the psyche and the ego are identical are wrong. My ego is in bad shape; my psyche is fine."

All through history human beings have wrestled with the fact that each of us experiences two aspects of selfhood which are never fully separated from each other. One of these aspects is the ego-self. This has the functions Freud rightly assigned to it: beleaguered monarch though it is, it keeps, as best it can, some harmony in the different sections of its kingdom. It judges the demands of reality, balances preconscious ideas, and sifts out unacceptable unconscious impulses so that the person can live with some unity. The ego-self is related to the instincts and bodily well-being. A number (though not all) of the concerns about wounded prestige, suffering slights, I would assign to this ego-self. The ego-self's question is some form of "Do I get what I want?" Hence, its association with the term *egocentricity*.

The other aspect is the psyche-self, which seeks to "see life steadily and see it whole." The psyche-self is concerned with the *context* of freedom. The "heightened consciousness" of which we speak from time to time is a function of the psyche-self. It is the aspect that scans the various possibilities of the self; it is the locus of what we call essential freedom. When Christopher Burney, during five years in solitary confinement in Germany in World War II, set himself to review everything he had been taught in school in order to keep from going psychotic, he was using not the ego-self, but the source of purpose that transcends the ego, which is the psyche-self. The ego-self is correlated with freedom of doing, the psyche-self with freedom of being.

When Kierkegaard points out again and again that "freedom depends on how the self relates itself to itself at every moment," he is speaking of the psyche-self in relation to the ego. The self relating to itself was the aspect of selfhood that Freud never understood. About his therapeutic practice we find Freud writing, "analysis does not set out to make pathological reactions impossible, but to give the patient's ego *freedom* to choose one way or the other." This refers to freedom, but it omits the function most concerned with this freedom—namely, the self relating to itself.

There is a curious phenomenon in human selfhood that I have noticed in my clients and in myself that I call the "automatic pilot." The automatic pilot is the device on passenger planes to which the pilot can shift the directing of the plane when, on a long flight, he needs to rest. A client, for example, will be intensely anxious about a confrontation he must have with some other person or about a difficult phone call he must make. Finally, he gets his courage up and goes ahead to do these anxiety-laden acts. He is surprised to discover that they turn out much better than he had anticipated. There seems to be some unexpected aid, some power that he did not know he had. From a Freudian point of view, it would be asserted that the help of which he was not aware comes from the client's preconscious; and in Jungianism, it would probably be interpreted as a voice from the unconscious. I call such aid a function of the psyche-self. The implication is that we, whether we are patients in therapy or not, can rightfully trust ourselves on those deeper dimensions which I have called the psyche-self. In the welter of self-distrust in which we generally find ourselves these days (covered up as it is by neonarcisscism, techniques of "assertiveness," and advice to "stand up for yourself"), we can bank on more power, more capacity than most of us give ourselves credit for.

This upsurging of strength and energy which we did not know we had is an example of the working of destiny through the psyche-self. But it is required at the same time that we confront our despair and our anxiety rather than suppressing them; otherwise the despair and anxiety will take over in the moment when we need their opposites.

The automatic pilot is partially an influence from Eastern mysticism, particularly Zen Buddhism and its offshoots. It is the phenomena of "letting go" and "letting be."

The awareness of the duality of selfhood enables us to correct a radical misunderstanding of Zen Buddhism and other Oriental psychoreligions with regard to transcending the self. There is a passion among some groups in America to lose oneself, to escape from oneself, to get "free" of oneself. It is significant that this passion came along with, or followed closely, the age of narcissism and the preoccupation with self-sentiments. The "me" decade followed hard upon the Zen decade. These two phases sound contradictory—and they are on paper. But their proximity shows that they had in common the same longing to escape from oneself. Students in search of a drug would ask a friend, "Do you have any uppers?" or, if the answer was no, "Do you have any downers?" It didn't matter whether the result one got was elation or depression. At least one got free of oneself.

The rushing after Zen and the narcissism was thus often to be found in the same person. There was no distinction between the constructive self-concern of a person and the self-concern of one who leaps after one gimmick one weekend and after another gimmick the next weekend. This leaping often leads not only to temporary elation, but to eventual confusion and despair.

The "loss of the self," I believe, is a misnomer. The misunderstanding of the Zen Buddhist goal of freedom from the self actually leads to a more subtle kind of narcissism. One's own pushiness, one's demands, one's egocentricity may still be present;

only the person now rationalizes them in terms of "nonselfullness." We cannot help noting that the exemplars of Zen Buddhism and TM and other forms of psychoreligion are not without any self; the idea is absurd. They are relieved of one phase of the self—namely, what I have called the ego-self. But they seek to discover in the psyche-self a new clarity, a freshness, a sense of immediacy and of eternity.

The self we transcend in Zen Buddhism and meditation is the ego-self. The ecstasy we experience is the freedom from the concerns of the ego-self, a process of dumping the "garbage" of the self, followed by the pre-eminent presence, however temporary, of the psyche-self.

6. *Meditation and the Holy Void*

Most of us are so preoccupied with the noise, the uproar, the cacophony of the modern world that we have no energy left for constructive living. We long to pause, to absorb into our day-to-day existence, some calmness, some inner order in which we can call our soul our own, in which we take time to experience some beauty, to know and enjoy our friends, and to let whatever creative impulses or visions we have be heard, listened to, have their moment. This pressing need coincides with the influx of Oriental influence, especially among the young people in this country, shown by the wide sale of books on Oriental religion, the endless listening to gurus, the renunciation of all worldly possessions to join an ashram. There can be no doubt of the depth and urgency of the hunger for some psychoreligious center of life.

Meditation is a way, available for most of us without a radical changing of our vocation, by which we can put meaningful content into the pause. No matter what form or stripe this meditation may take—yoga of the physical or mental variety, Zen Buddhism, Tao, Transcendental Meditation, Christian Contemplation, Concentration—they all have in common the aim of providing channels to deeper levels of experience by means of the pause.

When I, for one example, am overburdened with fatigue or

gloom or the distress of problems and the sleeplessness that goes with these things, I may pause temporarily to withdraw myself from the ego-self. I cannot do this by the head-on force of thinking. But it can be done, sometimes with the help of a mantra, or through relaxation, or pausing and "letting be." I seek to move into the psyche-self, in which I see things *sub specie aeternitatis*, in which I no longer feel the pains described above—the ego-self that feels them is temporarily transcended. The fatigue, the distress, the gloom all seem to vanish. The psyche-self, freed from the groveling kind of pain, freed from the narcissism, freed from ego-centered misery, can be a channel to awareness of infinite possibilities. This state is what the Zen Buddhists mean when they advise withdrawal and compassion.

Meditation is, *par excellence*, a concentration of the void, the pause, the "no thing." It is a freeing of the self from the clutter of life, giving one a pleasantly dizzy and mildly ecstatic experience. This dizziness is an attractive state that one likes to come back to, at least in memory, in moments throughout the day. In this sense meditation is a relief and a freedom from our buying and selling, our technological culture. Meditation seems "magical" and curative because it opens one's vision and being to a new world, a brightly colored world, conducive to calmness and peacefulness. In general it seems to be a less intense form of the world than the mystics describe, but in quality the same, a world which has within it sweetness, overflowing love, beauty now all about.

This is the common denominator of the many diverse methods of meditation. They seem to have in common (1) stopping the machinery, the noise, the pressure, the haste, the compulsive driveness, and (2) a higher level of consciousness, what was called "oceanic" by Freud and Einstein. One experiences being absorbed into the universe and the universe being temporarily absorbed into one's self. These aims are summed up in the words of the Taoist Chuang-tzu, as translated by the Trappist Thomas Merton,

> No drives, no compulsions
> No needs, no attractions:
> Then your affairs are under control.
> *You are a free man.*

There is always the danger that descriptions of such events will be too flowery, too separate from the reality of most people's experience. Let us keep in mind that meditation occurs in all gradations, from a chance insight on a crowded elevator to the conscious cultivation of the sense of peace to the regular discipline of meditating for short periods several times a day. There are also dangers in becoming isolated from the world of social action by meditating too much, which, as I have pointed out in *The Courage to Create*, can be a detriment to one's own creativity. We never wholly leave the ego-self behind, and we still live in the real world with its rationality and irrationality, and with our responsibility toward this world. But it is precisely in this ever-present world that meditation can give meaning to our pauses.

All forms of meditation seek to change the character of the self, a change that involves a new relationship with the void. Many people will be familiar with at least the beginning stages of the void by their practice of meditation.

I speak of the "holy" void because holy, coming from the root *whole*, refers to the mystical experience of grasping the wholeness of the universe in one's meditation. "The feeling of the world as a bounded whole," writes Ludwig Wittgenstein, "is the mystical." The holy void is the pause appearing in imaginary spatial form. This is one reason the mystics are so often shepherds since they look out continuously on the endless desert. One has this experience of the void in looking steadily out over the sea, an experience rightly termed "oceanic" since it gives one the feeling of infinity. Being in the desert or at the ocean where our vision can seemingly go on for ever can give us acute anxiety, since the eye has no boundaries with which to orient us; or it can give us a sense of profundity, of eternity, or of infinity, all of which are pleasurable. This is why floating in a stimulus-free tank, where we are insulated from every sound and every glimmer of light, can bring either intense anxiety or a transcendent, holy experience.

In the void the experience of nothingness occurs, and in this one's spiritual inspirations are called forth and one's deepest thoughts are made manifest. Wittgenstein helps us here again,

There are, indeed, things that cannot be put into words. They *make themselves manifest*. They are what is mystical.

In the experience of nothingness, we find ourselves cleansed of the chatter and the clatter of a "world which is too much with us," to borrow Wordsworth's words. Wordsworth goes on in that peom to say,

> Great God!
> I'd rather be a Pagan, suckled in a creed outworn;
> So might I, standing on this pleasant lea,
> Have glimpses that would make me less forlorn,
> Have sight of Proteus rising from the sea;
> Or hear old Triton blow his wreathèd horn.

It is not by accident that Wordsworth goes back to the Greek myths in searching for ways these things can be said, for mythic language is one of the ways such truths can be made manifest.

In the holy void the nothingness that we experience gives our deeper thoughts room to make themselves manifest, and the otherwise silent inner voice can be heard. This is the equivalent of the listening to the silence we referred to earlier. One method of meditation, that of Aurobindo, consists of continuously clearing the mind of all content until God—or being, as I would prefer—can speak to us out of the void. The nothingness then becomes a something; a something that comes, the mystics would say, from the depths of our soul.

The void is the dimension of eternity. "If we take eternity to mean not infinite temporal duration but timelessness, then eternal life belongs to those who live in the present," writes Wittgenstein. Our human hope in these experiences of timelessness—such as when we see something breathtakingly beautiful or hear a piece of music that seems to raise us into eternity—is to hang on to the experience forever. Edna St. Vincent Millay shows this in the sonnet "On Hearing a Symphony of Beethoven":

> Sweet sounds, oh, beautiful music, do not cease!
> Reject me not into the world again.

And again in "God's world":

> O world, I cannot hold thee close enough!
> . . . Lord, I do fear
> Thou'st made the world too beautiful this year;
> My soul is all but out of me,—let fall
> No burning leaf; prithee, let no bird call.

The void may seem to be contact with pure being, but I prefer a more modest judgment, that one gets glimpses of being, awareness that there *is* a beckoning path to pure being even though none of us gets very far on it. The concentration on the spaces between words, the intervals, the pauses in life—these yield the touch of ecstasy. But the moment formulation in words occurs, the "no thing" becomes a something. Obviously, one listens with care to any message that may be formulated in moments like these, and one need not worry too much about its origin. It may be interpreted as coming from one's deeper self, or from the various autosuggestions that occur, or from contact with the being of the universe. The last may be experienced as a glimpse of God— assuming that God is conceived as the ground of being and meaning in the universe. At this point I feel, as I often have in this section, the caution of Wittgenstein: "What we cannot speak about, we must pass over in silence."

X

The Dizziness of Freedom

I tell you one must harbor chaos if one would give birth to a dancing star.
— FRIEDRICH NIETZSCHE, Thus Spake Zarathustra

Eternal anxiety is the lot of the free man.
— JAMES TRUSLOW ADAMS

Anxiety is the dizziness of freedom.
— SÖREN KIERKEGAARD

Since personal freedom is a venture down paths we have never traversed before, we can never know ahead of time how the venture will turn out. We leap into the future. Where will we land? With freedom one experiences a dizziness, a feeling of giddiness, a sense of vertigo and dread. The dizziness involves the whole body, not just one's mind; one can feel it in the stomach and limbs as well. We recall that dizziness can be both pleasurable, as when one is being whirled around on a roller coaster, as well as painful, as it is in the first stages of panic. All of these feelings—dizziness, vertigo, giddiness, dread—are expressions of the anxiety that accompanies freedom like its shadow.

Sometimes a patient in therapy will wryly smile and say, "When I am mad at you, I think I was better off when I was neurotic—then I could go along in only one groove." I say "wryly" because if he really believed this, he wouldn't be in therapy in the first place since the purpose of therapy is precisely to take one out of the rigid grooves, the narrow, compulsive trends, which are blocks to freedom. This gives the person a sense of release. But it is a freedom that brings anxiety.

Anxiety is potentially present whenever we are free; freedom is oriented toward anxiety and anxiety toward freedom. "Anxiety is the reality of freedom as a potentiality before this freedom has materialized," Kierkegaard put it. For freedom is possibility, and who is to forecast what the end result of any possibility may be?

Dostoevsky's Grand Inquisitor saw this clearly: "Nothing has ever been more insupportable for a man and a human society than freedom. Man is tormented by no greater anxiety than to find someone quickly to whom he can hand over that gift of freedom with which the ill-fated creature is born." Freedom is a burden because it brings anxiety in its wake; and the Grand Inquisitor sought to shield people from the paralyzing aspects of anxiety by robbing them of its positive aspects—chiefly, freedom. Requiring the surrender of their freedom, he removed the stimulus to invent new forms, new styles, new ideas—in short, new possibilities. Now, as he insisted, men and women are "vile, weak creatures," "slaves by nature," "base creatures." He is surely logical: if you take away freedom, you make people into the base, weak, vile slaves the Grand Inquisitor describes.

It is helpful to keep in mind that anxiety, like dizziness, can be both constructive and destructive. The constructive aspect is stimulating and gives one energy and zest; anxiety is a teacher that, since we carry it inwardly, can never be avoided. Anxiety illuminates experiences that we would otherwise run away from. Alfred Adler used to say that civilization is the result of anxiety in that cavemen were forced to invent thinking in order to cope with the saber-toothed tiger and the bison and other animals, which were stronger in tooth and nail and would have exterminated the human race.

The anxiety that comes with excessive freedom can also be destructive in that it can paralyze us, isolate us, send us into panic; and when repressed, it may lead to cardiac ailments and other psychosomatic illnesses. These two aspects of anxiety are parallel to what Hans Selye calls constructive and destructive stress. Every person must bear constructive stress if he lives with any sense of adventure; but destructive stress is the excessive tension we see on the modern assembly lines which can tear the human being to pieces. This is why personal freedom is fascinating and the most prized of all human conditions. But because it is inseparable from anxiety, it is dangerous and understandably dreaded at the same time.

1. Anxiety and the Pause

In the previous chapter we found the specter of anxiety forcing its way into the picture time and time again. The pause is the moment when a person is most vulnerable to anxiety. It is the tremulous moment when we balance possible decisions, when we look forward with wonder and awe or with dread or fear of failure. The pause is the moment when we open ourselves, and the opening is our vulnerability to anxiety.

When we spoke about "listening to the silence," we noted that many people flee from silence because of the anxiety the silence brings. They perpetually seek the company of some noise from TV or radio even to the extent of carrying blaring portable sets with them on the streets or in the erstwhile "peace" of the parks. John Lilly found in his experiments in which people floated in his stimulus-free tank that silence, with its complete freedom, brings to many people more anxiety than they can bear. Who knows what devil may emerge out of the complete silence? Where are our familiar boundaries? The members of John Cage's audience at his famous "concert of silence" were required to absorb their own anxiety. There was no music to do it for them. People shrink from the "quiet desperation" that confronts them in periods of complete silence, fearing they will lose all ways of orienting themselves.

In our technological society, we are moving toward periods of greater and greater leisure—in earlier retirement, for example— and superficially we welcome this prospective leisure. But we find within ourselves a curious gnawing fear of something missing. What will we do with all this unfilled free time, this unplanned, unscheduled empty space? Does it not hang before us—O paradox of paradoxes!—like a great threat, the threat of emptiness, rather than the great boon we were seeking? Will our capacities, lying fallow, evaporate? Will we lose our abilities?

Will we be blotted out in sleep for a half century like Rip Van Winkle? Will we lose our consciousness if there is nobody knocking at the door? Secretly, many of us interpret freedom as becoming nothing. And will we, in our now unhampered possibility, become simply "no thing"?

This is a real and immediate source of anxiety, covered up and unadmitted though it generally is. Formless freedom, unstructured freedom without the limits of destiny, leaves human beings inert. At such times the "pause" takes over. People do not know what to do, and they cry out for someone or something to organize them. Hence, *organized* play and *planned* leisure—which are really contradictions in terms. Thrown on their own resources, people may find themselves bankrupt since they have long gotten into the habit of ignoring their pauses.

Let us consider again the illustration in the last chapter of the speaker receiving promptings and directions from his audience. Suppose, in his millisecond pauses, no such prompting comes. In anxiety over this possibility, some speakers choose to write out their lectures word for word, and then they can fall back on the printed page regardless of the promptings or lack thereof from the audience. But in reading his speech the speaker has surrendered his opportunity for freedom, for the discovery of new ideas, for the adventure of exploring new frontiers, for the heady thrill of uncertainty. Thus, one chooses security over freedom, as the Grand Inquisitor so passionately adjured. But such a choice exacts a serious price in self-consciousness, tension, and the loss of freedom.

Sometimes the anxiety that accompanies freedom is intermixed and confused with excitement. Once, while waiting (which is a form of pausing) at an airport for a person whom I knew only slightly and who was going to be my guest at my country farm for three days, I felt the excitement that always comes with the anticipation of meeting a new person. But this excitement merged back and forth into the anxiety that came as I asked myself in fantasy: What will two people do cooped up in a little house for so long? Will the intimacy become boring or scary? So I jotted down the following notes:

When does excitement—i.e., the constructive side of anxiety, which keeps life from being boring, keeps us spontaneous, stimulated, and alive—lead into destructive anxiety, which shuts out spontaneity, paralyzes, and blocks our freedom? Excitement, the risking of which is pleasurable, gives us the spirit of the chase, keeps us growing. This has a clear survival value. It remains excitement so long as I feel I can cope; I can retain a sense of some autonomy. It becomes destructive when I cannot do this. Thus as long as we can experience "I can" and "I will," we remain open, we experience our freedom, we preserve the power to experience new possibilities.

Does this anxiety always occur in the exercise of freedom? The answer to that depends on how one views life. If we follow Martin Heidegger and Paul Tillich, who conceive of life as a continuous dialectical tension between being and nonbeing, each of us engaged in every breath in preserving our own being against the threat of nonbeing, then we must answer "Yes." In any case I prefer to keep the question on the level of consciousness. This would mean stating that while there is always some accompaniment of dizziness with freedom, we, as human beings, may not be aware of it since we have different points where we block it off, where we repress the dizziness temporarily or deny it altogether.

2. Anxiety and Discovery

We also recall that I described, in Chapter V, the anxiety which engulfed me like a tidal wave when I exercised my freedom in achieving the insight that determinism gives birth to freedom and vice versa. The anxiety came in the person of this figure whom I identified as my "enemy-friend," a kind of figurative devil. It is the anxiety that comes, in varying intensity, whenever one leaps into the field of new possibilities, whenever one moves into the area of new ideas or new compositions in music or a new style in art. It comes after such subconscious thoughts as "Ah, there is a new vision—nobody ever painted a scene like this before." Then there comes the feeling "Do I want to venture out so far?" And I remind myself of all the dangers in venturing into that no man's land. In such situations the person finds himself adjuring himself to calm down, not to get too excited, when getting excited in the sense of becoming inspired is exactly what, on the deepest level, he wants.

Freedom and anxiety are two sides of the coin—there is never one without the other. The anxiety is part and parcel of the excitement and enthusiasm that accompany the birth of a new vision or an idea that, in the particular form it comes to us, no one *has* ever thought of before. This anxiety—or "dread," if we wish to use Lowrie's translation of *angst*—is a function of the freedom of imagination we must exercise in order to get any idea of significance. The dread comes with the new possibility and the risk that this leap requires.

We might, like the scientists who split the atom, break through into a new land, where the usual mooring places by which we have oriented ourselves no longer even exist. Hence, the sense of alienation and bewilderment—and even the experience of intense human aloneness—that such a breakthrough brings in its train. I am told that when the scientists stood behind their glass barrier near Los Alamos and saw the first atomic explosion, the faces of a number of them turned white. One cried aloud, "My God, what have we done?"

There is a rational explanation for this anxiety. We must keep in mind that the anxiety comes not from the possibility that the new idea or discovery might be wrong and useless (then it can simply be discarded), but from the possibility that it might be *true*, as it was, for example, with atomic fission or with Beethoven's new ideas about musical harmonies. Then one's colleagues, the professors at one's university, will be jolted, will be required to change their viewpoints, and even, God willing, to rewrite their lecture notes. This causes upset, which was very great indeed with the splitting of the atom. Or if one is a Copernicus with the new theory that the earth moves around the sun, or a Karl Marx with a radically new approach to the economic life of humankind, the uproar that accompanies the shaking of the foundations will be that much more catastrophic.

Although the examples above are of great men, we are illustrating something that we all experience, though to a lesser degree. Every human being experiences this anxiety when he or she exercises the freedom to move out into the no man's land of possibility. We can escape the anxiety only by not venturing—that is, by surrendering our freedom. I am convinced that many people never become aware of their most creative ideas since their inspirations are blocked off by this anxiety before the ideas even reach the level of consciousness.

A pressure toward conformism infuses every society. One function of any group or social system, as Hannah Arendt has pointed out, is to preserve homeostasis, to keep people in their usual positions. The danger of freedom to the group lies exactly at that point: that the nonconformist will upset the homeostasis, will use his or her freedom to destroy the tried and true ways. Socrates was condemned to drink hmlock because, so the good citizens of Athens believed, he taught false *"daimones"* to the youth of Athens. Jesus was crucified because he upset the accepted religion of his day. Joan of Arc heard voices and was burned at the stake. These extreme examples are of persons whose ideas later became the cornerstones of our civilization. But that fact only confirms my point. The persons whose insights are too disturbing, who bring too much of the anxiety that accompanies freedom, are put to death by their own generation, which suffers the threat caused by the earthquake of the new ideas. But they are worshiped by subsequent generations, when their ideas are crystallized into the dogma of the new age and there is no chance of the dead figures rising from their silent graves to disturb the peace anew.

The prototype of the person who produces something new is found in Prometheus, who created fire—or, as the myth presents it, stole it from the gods—and gave it to mankind as the beginning of human civilization. No one envies his punishment in being chained to a mountainside, where an eagle would eat away at his liver all day. At night, the liver would grow back, and the same grisly process would begin all over again the next day. This agony may be pictured as the severe form of the anxiety that accompanies his great act of defiance, which was one aspect of Prometheus' personal freedom.

The denying of the dizziness of freedom is shown in the phrase "pure spontaneity." For no one can seek that without succumbing to the dreadful implications of freedom. Even John Lilly, in his experiencing "pure spontaneity" in his stimulus-free tank, describes the great dangers therein, and his own great anxiety in his experience hovering on the edge of nonbeing, death. One may envy one's colleagues who claim to exist in pure spontaneity and who seem to be on a perpetual "high." Yes, we may envy them, but we do not love them for that. We love them for their vulnerability—which means their accepting and owning the dizziness of their freedom, their destiny which always stalks their freedom.

The legend of Icarus presents a picture of a young man refusing to accept the dizziness, or the anxiety, of freedom. Icarus that day must have felt a sense of great adventure—to be the first person who could sail "high" and taste the ecstasy, the sheer freedom from the bonds of the earth, with no limits at all. For this one afternoon he was completely *subject*, not limited even by the distant reaches of the sky. He could order his universe as he wished, could live out his whim and desire born in his own imagination. Here, indeed, was "pure spontaneity." No longer part of the world, no longer subject to the laws of earth or its destiny or the requirements of community. What exhilaration there must have been in the young man's breast! A great dream comes true, an experience of complete freedom, pure spontaneity at last. One needs only the self-preoccupation, the refusal to consider compromise. He is like the humanists of previous decades who insisted that there was no evil they need bother to consider. Mankind had done such great things in the past; why could we not overcome any and all difficulties in the future? Icarus remained as spontaneous as a child and burst into the sea to drown not as a young man, but as a child.

3. The Anxious Prophet

The authentic prophet experiences the anxiety that comes with his freedom to see into the future, to see beyond the usual limits in which other people see. Thus, Tiresias cries out to Oedipus:

> "How terrible it is to know . . .
> Where no good comes from knowing!
> . . . my say, in any sort,
> I will not say, lest I display my sorrow.

And again:

> I will not bring remorse upon myself
> And upon you. Why do you search these matters?

We recall also that the prophetess Cassandra, in ancient Mycenae, hated her role as a medium and hated to prophesy. One way to distinguish between the authentic prophet or saint from the fanatic or charlatan is this: the authentic prophet feels anxiety about his role and the charlatan does not. Like the prophets in the Old Testament, the authentic ones do not want to be prophets; they do their best to decline the role. They would escape if they could because of the dizziness and dread such great freedom entails. Jonah even fled from Nineveh and had to be brought back by a whale to give his prophecies.

The common ways of denying the anxiety of freedom include, in our society, alcohol and drugs. When Peer Gynt, in Ibsen's play, hears the passing people talking and laughing at him as he hides behind the bushes, he comforts himself:

> If only I had a dram of something strong,
> Or could go unnoticed. If only they didn't know me.
> A drink would be best. Then the laughter doesn't bite.

True, it does not bite so much when one has recourse to a dram of Scotch; this is the dominant way of escaping anxiety in our culture. Harry Stack Sullivan once remarked that liquor was a necessity in a technological civilization like ours to relax people after a compulsive-obsessional day in the office. Whatever truth there may be in that statement, probably made by Sullivan with tongue in cheek, it is obvious that alcohol drunk to avoid anxiety may ease the mind and dull the sensitivities. But the drinking to escape anxiety puts one on a treadmill: the next day, when the anxiety increases, the drinking must increase also, and so on, until Alcoholics Anonymous has a new member. Overuse of alcohol erodes our freedom to imagine, to reflect, to discover some possibility that would have helped us cope with the anxiety in the first place.

During a recent year there were 50 million prescriptions written in the United States for Valium—one for every five persons in the country. In addition there are Librium, Equanil, Miltown, and a long list of similar drugs whose main purpose is to block off feelings of anxiety and consequent depression. These drugs obviously have their constructive uses, especially with people whose anxiety rises to paralyzing heights and who cannot then communicate fruitfully with others or a therapist. In this limited sense the tranquilizing drugs may temporarily promote freedom. They can relieve the anxiety long enough so that the person can then see some real possibilities in his life.

But used as a crutch, the drugs, like alcohol, can be a way of blocking off freedom and possibility, a way of becoming an unfeeling robot, avoiding the sensitivity necessary to be open to possibilities. Personal freedom thus evaporates. One gives up the sharp play of imagination; one surrenders the inspiration that comes from the interplay of exhilaration and sadness, ecstasy and grief, "joy and woe" in Blake's terms. The human being then approximates the non-sentient computor which simply recites its pre-programmed responses.

4. Dogmatism Is Fear of Freedom

Since I will be attacking some so-called scientific forms of psychology in this section, I want to make it clear at the outset that I am by no means antiscientific. I ask the reader's permission to quote from a book published by the distinguished research professor of psychology at Yale University, Irvin Child:

. . . Consider, for instance, two books by psychologists which have recently been best sellers with the American public: Rollo May's *Love and Will* and B. F. Skinner's *Beyond Freedom and Dignity*. People who have studied psychology, I suspect, place Skinner's book very decidedly in the scientific tradition in psychology, and May's hardly at all.

Yet Skinner's book seems to me to be connected with the scientific tradition only in a personal sense, having been written by a psychologist who is a most distinguished leader of the experimental analysis of animal behavior. What Skinner's book has to say about human beings—and they are the subject of the book—seems to me to be in the philosophical or religious tradition rather than the scientific. It appears to me an expression of the author's personal values and beliefs, stated with papal confidence and buttressed principally by wild extrapolations from rats and pigeons to man, making almost no contact whatever with the great body of psychological research on man, which might be drawn on to present a very different picture from that drawn by Skinner.

May's book, on the other hand, grows out of his years of clinical experience with patients, and that of many other psychologists and psychiatrists. It draws on the interaction of hypothesis and observation, displays humility about the author's wisdom, and looks toward future modification of knowledge. All this seems to me very much in keeping with the spirit of science, and with one reasonable opinion about what methods are at present most useful in scientific inquiry into human psychology.

The prototype of the tendency in psychology to deny its own limits, became, in the last two decades, B. F. Skinner. I count Fred Skinner as a friend, but this does not hinder me from emphatically opposing his viewpoint in the debates we have had over the air and before college audiences. Skinner has made many constructive contributions to animal psychology and to educational theory which we all prize. But he has refused to admit the limits of psychology, which means, in my terms, destiny; and he has stretched his theory to include, among other disciplines, philosophy, sociology, criminology, and mental health. His work is an amazing example of hubris in psychology (we have defined hubris as the refusal to acknowledge destiny). Indeed, in Skinner's view it seems psychology has no limits at all.

The popularity of his book *Beyond Freedom and Dignity* testifies to the vast number of people who are crying to be told that freedom is an illusion and they need worry about it no longer. Skinner capitalizes with a vengeance on the widespread feelings of powerlessness and helplessness, which are the underlying anxiety of our time; and he reassures people that personal responsibility is *démodé* and that they do not need to trouble their consciences— if they have any left—about it. We need to look once again into the phenomenon of that book to find several hitherto unexamined problems about personal freedom.

Skinner argues that we must develop a technology of behavior, but that our belief in freedom and human dignity stands in the way. This new technology, he writes,

will not solve our problems, however, until it replaces traditional pre-scientific views, and these are strongly entrenched. Freedom and dignity illustrate the difficulty. They are the possessions of the autonomous man of traditional theory, and they are essential to practices in which a person is held responsible for his conduct and given credit for his achievements. A scientific analysis shifts both the responsibility and the achievement to the environment.

We would be the last to argue that the environment does not influence—to a considerable extent—the development of the person. Indeed, I would argue that the environment has an even more varied effect than Skinner argues: anyone in psychoanalysis knows that the environment is important even on unconscious levels and in dreams. Any viewpoint that leaves out the environment—like the extreme forms of the human-potential movement, where it is argued that *only* the inner potentials are significant—is equally wrong. But there are other points related to responsibility and freedom in Skinner's system that concern us here.

Again and again Skinner attacks the traditional belief that a man "can be held responsible for what he does." "A scientific analysis shifts the credit as well as the blame to the environment." The "literature of freedom and dignity"—whatever that means— cannot "accept the fact that all control is exerted by the environment and proceed to the design of better environments rather than of better men."

Now we would all agree that ideally all citizens should strive—I would use Skinner's prohibited word and say it is their *responsibility*—to correct the flaws in the environment, say, of school children (on which Skinner has helped us greatly), the poverty-stricken, the lame, etc. Indeed, I believe—apparently contrary to Skinner—that there are times we should "proceed to the design of better environments" by outright rebellion against the cruel and unfair laws in our society.

But what, pray tell, is the environment composed of except other human beings like you and me? And how can an environment be "responsible"? True, when a society is formed, there develops a group force which makes for conformism; to keep people in line is one of the functions of the group, as we have said. But if we surrender our individual responsibility, what leverage, what power, do we have against this force of the group? One gets the feeling, when reading Skinner, that the environment is some holy form made in heaven and superimposed by some god or demigod upon us mortals. Completely absent is the wisdom in Pogo's remark, "We have met the enemy and he is us."

Skinner heaps scorn on the mythic "autonomous man," who "possesses miraculous powers."

A scientific analysis of behavior dispossesses autonomous man and turns the control he has been said to exert over to the environment. . . . He is henceforth to be controlled by the world around him, and in large part by other men.

Again, what kind of psychoengineering is this which "turns the control . . . over to the environment," holds that the world around us does the controlling, and this consists "largely of other men"? This seems to me to lack the logic that we have a right to expect of "engineers of behavior," which Skinner aspires to be. It sounds like the following lines from Goethe:

> . . . for each, incompetent to rule
> His own internal self, is all too fain to sway
> His neighbor's will, even as his haughty mind inclines . . .

Skinner's statement also betrays the fundamental confusion of values in his system: toward *whose* values is the environment going to be changed? Who are the "other men" who will do the controlling? Perhaps Skinner himself?

The problem is that either alternative—to blame the environment for everything or to locate everything within oneself as the human-potential movement used to do—is wrong. Both deny freedom. But human beings have a third possibility: *they can choose when and whether they are to be acted upon or are to do the acting.* When I fly in a plane, I let myself be acted upon. I nap a little; I look out the window and daydream. The pilot entirely controls the success or failure of my flight. When I get off the plane, however, to make a speech at a college or university, I choose the opposite alternative. I seek to persuade the audience; I want to get my viewpoint across. I am now assumedly the controller. What is important is that when I move between being controlled and controller, I am on a deeper level of freedom—the freedom of being. So far as we know, this choice between controlling or being controlled is not present for pigeons or rats, which comprise the basis of Skinner's studies.

It would not matter if these ideas of Skinner's only slightly confused people about psychology and the state of being human. "One of the saddest things about psychology today is that so many of its better minds are forced to cope with the cant, error and falsehood generated by the discipline itself," writes Joseph Adelson, professor of psychology at the University of Michigan. The problem is that so many people are on the edge of panic these days and yearn for some rationalization for dumping their responsibility someplace outside themselves. Such a simplistic gospel as Skinner's greatly appeals to them since it promises a way out and reinforces their desire to escape from a world that so baffles them. The gospel is especially seductive since Skinner is against sin: he opposes the things that ought to be opposed, such as aversive control and destructive punishment. *Thus, people "dump" on their environment the very responsibility that would be needed if they are effectively to influence their environment.*

What about the high-school student who finds looming up before him problems that he cannot possibly solve in the political and economic world, who is struggling with drugs and alcoholism and all the conflicts that occur in adolescence? Then he hears that he has no responsibility, that the environment will take over, that an impersonal science of engineering should take the blame and the credit. How is he going to experience himself and his life? One does not need to blame Skinner for the problems of juvenile delinquency like drugs, crime, violence. No single man can be expected to answer for the exigencies of history, to state the obvious. But young people are scarcely going to take responsibility for their actions or lives if they are continually told that they are powerless and all the influence is exercised by the environment. Is it surprising, then, that they resign from life, become "the uncommitted," go to such films as *A Clockwork Orange*, mumbling the while a paraphrase from Shakespeare: Oh brave new world that has such robots in it?

When I was reading Skinner, I had a flash, unmistakable and demanding, of *déjà vu*. Then it struck me: the Grand Inquisitor! How alike the statements of these two men are. The Inquisitor says: "For now, for the first time, it has become possible to think of the happiness of man," and "we shall plan the happiness of universal man." Skinner likewise proposes his system for the sake of mankind. When Skinner talks about his "cultural technology," he also talks about the greater happiness of mankind as the goal of his engineering. The parallel is amazing.

The Grand Inquisitor states: "Turn [these stones] into bread and mankind will run after thee like a flock, grateful and obedient, though forever trembling, lest Thou withdraw thy hand and deny them Thy bread." Skinner does this with candy and other forms of reinforcement, but the same reward is immediately present. The Inquisitor states: "There is no crime, and therefore no sin." Skinner, as we have seen, argues that responsibility be shifted to the environment; people do not need incarceration, but rather treatment, rehabilitation. Both men emphasize *obedience* as a cardinal virtue. The Inquisitor states that "man seeks not so much God as the miraculous," and comes forth with his triumvirate, "miracle, mystery and authority." Skinner likewise presents the miracle and authority of psychology and the concepts of science, arguing that these are rational and clear. He seems unaware that scientific concepts are the most miraculous and mysterious of all the concepts in our age.

But the greatest similarity of Skinner and the Grand Inquisitor is that both regard freedom as the central enemy. The only difference is that Skinner goes further than the Inquisitor: he holds that freedom does not exist at all, whereas the Inquisitor grants the reality of freedom but regards it as dangerous for people at large. The Inquisitor seems to be aware of his fear of free-dom; hence, he has Jesus, who he knows would preach freedom, locked up in jail. Skinner not only does not give any room to freedom, but he is dogmatic in his "papal" insistence that the individual's responsibility—and, hence, his freedom—is non-existent. This dogmatism of Skinner's is an expression of the *fear of freedom*, which the Inquisitor is aware of but Skinner is not. Skinner's ideas are the concerted endeavor to flee from freedom and to rationalize and justify that flight.

At a recent conference on behaviorism and human ethics, one of the speakers, representing Skinnerian behaviorism, stated at the beginning of his presentation that he never read any philoso-phy and was not going to speak in that field. He then proclaimed that freedom is an illusion. However much our actions might seem to be freely chosen and performed, he could easily demon-strate that all our behavior was the result of previous condition-ing. He went on to point out that behaviorism already had control of 80 percent of all the Psychology Departments in the country and would soon have control of all of them. The rest of us, he was good enough to advise, had better get on the behaviorist band wagon since what we had to teach was irrelevant anyway. Oth-erwise we would be buried and forgotten.

Some of us immediately pointed out to him that the statement "Freedom is an illusion" is a philosophical statement, not a psy-chological one. It seemed to us frightening that he should brag about never reading any philosophy if he was going to talk phi-losophy. None of us denied determinism in its rightful place.

But the real puzzle is: Why is it that behaviorism, almost alone among the many forms of psychology, is so dogmatic, so certain it has the whole truth? Especially since at the present time, five years after that conference, behaviorism is *not* the form of psychology to which most concern is given. Cognitive psy-chology has replaced it. We who are not behaviorists have almost universally smarted under such belittling as the above words. This strange dogmatism, as Child pointed out above, is charac-teristic of Skinner, and apparently explains why he subsumes under his psychology the many other disciplines of sociology, philosophy, religion, and mental health.

This dogmatism is now even recognized and admitted by some erstwhile Skinnerians as they look back on the past four or five decades. One behaviorist, Roger Ulrich, writes of that period, "there was nothing we could not do if we just put our behavior to it . . . science and the scientist-priests could do anything and everything." He continues, "our leader [Skinner] let us know that we could go even further and control the whole world."

All this obviously takes away the freedom of the individual. It is not by accident that Skinner and his cohorts argued so determinedly that freedom is an illusion since they had given up their own freedom in their very dogmatism.

What accounts for such hubris in a discipline in which the members pride themselves on being scientific? Psychoanalytically, dogmatism is interpreted as being a symptom of the fact that the person really doubts in his unconscious the truth he externally espouses so strongly. A person becomes more dogmatic—like Paul on the Damascus Road—the more he doubts his own "truth" and gets closer to the point of collapse. Thus, despite Skinner's insistence that what goes on between the ears is irrelevant, the kind of psychology that has superseded behaviorism is cognitive psychology, the psychology of what occurs in the mind.

But we wish to suggest a reason for the dogmatism of behaviorism on a different level from the psychoanalytic one. We propose that this dogmatic behaviorism is itself a flight from destiny and an escape from the dizziness of anxiety in freedom. It cannot be by accident that behaviorism dominated the half century (from the 1920s to the 1970s) that has faced vast social problems such as nuclear fission, concentration camps, the aftermath of one world war and the agonizing endurance of the second, the period that includes the "age of anxiety," when inflation and unemployment occur simultaneously, when there is an energy crisis, and so on endlessly. This distraught age was offered a simple gospel, promising escape from responsibility, from confusion, and especially from such difficult problems as freedom. Certainty was in the saddle, even though it was a false certainty. In such behaviorism there is no sense of the freedom of uncertainty.

This alone can explain why there was such a great segment of our population who not only succumbed to the behaviorist view-point, but showed the telltale symptom at the same time—namely, its dogmatism. I believe that this flight from destiny includes a frank refusal to let oneself see any of the aspects of life—such as responsibility, limits in science, and so on—that require us to understand our destiny.

A vicious circle gets started in dogmatism of any sort. The person's security is bolstered by the dogmatism, and the dogma-tism is, in turn, reinforced by the security.

True, anxiety can be avoided by such dogmatism, but there are clear penalties. The person reinforces the stockade around him-self and his ideas; he blocks out the anxiety by cutting off his possibility and his maneuverability. The anxiety is escaped, but the person is a prisoner in his own stockade. This, by definition, is the loss of freedom. And the constant expansion that character-izes freedom is blocked. If we were to peel off the defensive cover of the dogmatist, we would almost always find a trembling person imprisoned within the walls he himself has created.

Whether scientist or religious, the dogmatic person is one who fears secretly that he must crystallize his beliefs or they will evap-orate. He is afraid that any pause, as we used the term in the last chapter, would result in his losing his "truth" suddenly, and then he would be thrown into panic. He fears that his truth will dis-appear unless he puts a firm stockade around it.

Yeats's remark that "some truths we *embody* and do not *know*," which covers a great deal of experience, is totally ignored by our dogmatist. He *knows* everything, has an answer for everything; no question can make him ponder. Such persons are boring to others precisely because there is no freedom in what they are saying or standing for. In extreme forms and in clinical terms such a person becomes the compulsive-obsessional.

All this has great bearing upon freedom. For freedom is release from dogma. Freedom is the capacity to increase our the-ories, to look about ourselves to find more possibilities. Freedom means that we can see many different forms of truth, some from the West and others from the East, some from technology and others from intuition. The very existence of theories and our dependence upon them are on the side of freedom. Then we achieve the mark of the mature intelligence, as Alfred North Whitehead is reputed to have said, that is, we can hold in the mind two opposing thoughts without undermining either one of them. So the inescapable uncertainty of human life is accepted as our destiny from which we do not flee.

The shadows cast upon the wall in Plato's myth of the cave are one degree removed from reality. But if we *know* they are shadows, we are saved from the shackles of dogmatism. And knowing we live in a cave can also turn our imaginations loose in new freedom. This confrontation with destiny releases us to experience a sea change in the realm of possibility. We can find new forms, new ways of relating to each other, new styles of life.

XI

Freedom and Destiny in Illness and Health

My very chains and I grew friends,
So much a long communion tends
To make us what we are:—even I
Regain'd my freedom with a sigh.
—GEORGE GORDON, LORD BYRON, "The Prisoner of Chillon"

But we have understood nothing about illness so long as we have not
recognized its odd resemblance to war and to love, its compromises, its
feints, its exactions, that strange and unique amalgam produced by the
mixture of a temperament and a malady.
—MARGUERITE YOURCENAR, Memoirs of Hadrian

Most people assume that their illnesses and diseases are almost
wholly under the command of destiny. An ailment is accepted at
best as "bad luck" and a disease as "irrevocable fate." Our very
language expresses this attitude. We "fall" ill, as though the process were as fateful as gravity. We "catch" a germ as though it
were an accident. We are the "victims" of cancer. We "get" sick
(instead of "sicken"), and we go to the doctor to "get cured." And
all we can do is be "patient" while the doctor treats us. All these
words and phrases are in the passive voice. We assume that we
are under the command of some fate and we can do nothing about
it. The good patient is considered docile and cooperative, one
who puts himself completely in the hands of the physician. Our
conscious selves seem outside, standing there like slaves on the
block while their fate is decided by forces greater than they.

This attitude toward illness reminds us of the statement made
by the Grand Inquisitor that "man is tormented by no greater

anxiety than to find someone quickly to whom he can hand over that gift of freedom with which the ill-fated creature is born." This attitude is unfortunately furthered by some misguided physicians under the illusion that it makes their role easier. Even in psychotherapy this occurs. The following is an actual verbatim exchange of a doctor with a patient who had come to a clinic suffering from depression:

PATIENT: *What will I do about my problems?*

DOCTOR: *Don't inquire into the source of your trouble. Leave this to us doctors. We will steer and pilot you through the crisis. . . . Whatever the pathological process . . . we will cure you.*

I believe this attitude works against health rather than for it. My belief is expressed on one hand by Professor Eli Ginzberg, "No improvement in the health care system will be efficacious unless the citizen assumes responsibility for his own well-being." Dr. René Dubos agrees: "Recovery depends upon the mobilization of the patient's own mechanisms of resistance to disease." Dubos emphasizes time and again the *"vis medicatrix naturae,"* the healing power of nature. That is to say, far from robbing us of our total freedom, destiny expresses itself through nature with a constructive force which is available to us only when we assert our freedom in engaging it.

1. Western Medicine and the Great Revolution

Of the countless empirical studies which bear this out, I will cite an article from the *Journal of the American Medical Association,* which was reported in the daily press under the caption "Nice Patients Die Faster." This was a study of how two groups of women dealt with terminal breast cancer. "Feisty, combative women survived longer than trusting, complacent women" was the conclusion. The women who survived longest were, as a group, more anxious, depressed, hostile, and alienated about their illness than those who succumbed faster. The "feisty" women seemed to maintain a combative posture rather than being hopeless victims. "They were going down fighting!" wrote Dr. Derogatis, the pyschologist who made the study. "The women

who survived longer had mechanisms of externalizing their conflicts, fears and angers about the disease. They were more
demanding of physicians, less satisfied with treatment and were
rated as less well adjusted. By contrast, the other women—who
died sooner—felt less anxious and more positive towards their
doctors, and rated themselves as more content on a self-evalua-
tion. I believe they had *divested themselves of the responsibility* of
fighting the disease."

Now breast cancer does indeed seem to be a blow of fate. Yet
the women who could assert their freedom and take responsibility
for the illness—and thus for fighting it—have a better chance of
living. I do not wish my emphasis on responsibility to be confused with that of est. "You are the sole source of your own experience, and thus totally responsibile for everything you
experience" is the message of est training. Is the unborn baby the
cause of its brain defect because of its mother's malnutrition? To
hold that we are responsible for everything that happens to us is
to show to what absurdities we go when we have no understanding of destiny. Our freedom—and, therefore, our sense of
responsibility—exists only as we acknowledge and engage our
destiny.

Norman Cousins's book *Anatomy of an Illness* excellently
describes his own encounter with a vital problem of health. Cousins was pronounced incurably ill of a rare disease of the collagen
tissues which he had developed in Russia. Possessing a remark-
ably strong will to live, he asked himself the question: "If negative
emotions produce negative chemical changes in the body,
wouldn't the positive emotions produce positive chemical
changes? Is it possible that love, hope, faith, laughter, confidence, and the will to live have therapeutic value?" He tells us
how, when the specialists pronounced him doomed, he sum-
moned his own concern with the problem and his will to health.
He moved out of the inhospitable hospital and into a hospitable
hotel and began a new regimen, in consultation with his own
physician. He went on a program consisting of large quantities of
vitamin C and equally large amounts of health-giving laughter.
His story is the documentation of how one individual asserted his
limited freedom and his responsibility for confronting his own

destiny, cruel and unfair as that destiny was. When asked by a friend whether he had not been terribly discouraged, Cousins answered that he was, "especially at the start when I expected my doctor to fix my body as though it were an automobile engine that needed mechanical repair, like cleaning out the carburetor, or reconnecting the fuel pump."

When he was a healthy man again, Cousins met one of the specialists who had stated that his disease was incurable, and told him that his cure began "when I decided that some experts don't really know enough to make a pronouncement of doom on a human being. And I said I hoped they would be careful about what they said to others; they might be believed and that could be the beginning of the end."

When one discusses the need for the individual to take responsibility for his own health, the tendency of listeners is to interpret the discussion as an attack on modern medicine. An address of mine, "Personal Freedom and Caring," before the convention of the American Occupational Therapy Association was reported in a newspaper under the caption "Caring Physicians Rob Patients of Their Freedom, Responsibility." This was, if anything, directly opposite to the meaning of my address. I was not attacking medicine as such. None of us can escape marveling at and valuing the tremendous progress of modern medicine in the development of medical technology and the new drugs. Among my friends who are advocates of holistic medicine, my task is to caution against viewing the medical profession as the enemy. "Talk of enemies does not sit well," Norman Cousins says, "in a movement in which spiritual factors are no less vital than practical ones."

It does no good, furthermore, to refuse on principle to take a prescribed drug because one wants to preserve one's "freedom," nor to refuse to go to a doctor when such is indicated. We cannot withdraw from the contemporary world, hermitlike, to contemplate our own navels. Furthermore, such revolt smacks too much of the Luddites, eighteenth-century workers who, realizing the threat to their livelihood in the industrial revolution, armed themselves with crowbars and pickaxes and attacked the machines. This rebellion does no good beyond the self-righteous feelings it gives the rebels themselves. In a given illness I believe one's responsibility to oneself is to get the best medical advice available.

But the very progress of modern medicine makes our emphasis here all the more necessary, since this progress increases the mystification and authoritarianism that people have thrust upon the medical profession and the medical profession has assumed all too readily. When I lived in a large metropolis, I found myself, when I needed medical service, phoning my own physician to find out which specialist I should go to. The "laying on of hands," which has classically been central in the healing profession, has now become all too often the laying on of techniques.

Since assuming the role of the priest, as doctors began to do as early as Paracelsus in the sixteenth century, the tendency has been for people to see in the physician the god who has power over life and death. But as long as physicians are made god on people's conscious level, they will also be made the devil on an unconscious level. The rash of malpractice suits in the last twenty years shows the disillusionment and rage that people feel as this belief in the "devil" begins to surface.

When I told my present physician of my intention to work also with an acupuncturist on the problem of tachycardia, he well remarked, "Western medicine is on the verge of a great revolution." He did not mean in the sense of new discoveries in techniques. He meant, rather, a revolutionary change in the philosophical and ethical basis of medicine, a change in the cultural context in which doctors operate. This revolution is seen most dramatically in the incursion of Oriental insights into Western medical treatment.

2. Acupuncture and the Oriental Influence in Western Medicine

Let us single out one aspect of that revolution, acupuncture, as represented by Dr. Harold Bailen, a doctor of Western cardiology who later became an acupuncturist. His shift to acupuncture occurred because of his growing conviction that the model of Western medicine was at best incomplete and at worst simply wrong. The sickness itself is not the enemy. Rather the wrong way of life is. Western medicine, being disease-oriented, blocks off the symptom with which patients come to the doctor, whereas Eastern medicine, with a tradition of thousands of years behind it, asks: What is the symptom trying to tell us?

The symptom is the right-brain language—in its pain, ache, or other discomfort—saying that something is amiss. Dr. Bailen often remarks to patients, "Isn't it marvelous that your body is so bright that it can speak to you in that language?" In contrast to the left brain, from which language, logic, and rationality largely spring, the right-brain is the side that communicates in fantasies, dreams, intuition—and symptoms. The symptom is a red warning light. Right-brain language cannot be attacked from a purely rational, left-brain point of view. Acupuncture enhances communication between the right and left brain, states Dr. Bailen. It synthesizes this information, something like an altered state of consciousness.

The aim of acupuncture is to stimulate, through the use of the needles, the energy circuits of the body so that the body will be energized to cure itself. These circuits, called meridians, are not synonymous with the neural pathways of the body. The most accepted theory these days is that acupuncture activates endorphins, a morphinelike hormonal substance in the body. Dr. René Dubos, who is not an acupuncturist, describes this well:

Acupuncture can trigger the release of pituitary endorphin which, somehow, gains access to the cells of the spinal cord and can thus exert an opiate-like effect on the perception of pain. It is not too far-fetched to assume that, as in the case of other hormones, mental attitudes can affect the secretion of endorphin and thereby the patient's perception of disease.

Dubos goes on to say that endorphin acts not only on the mechanisms of pain itself, but also inhibits the emotional response to pain and, therefore, to suffering. Hence, the demonstrated anti-pain effect of acupuncture as used by a number of dentists in their work.

Acupuncture requires that the person being treated not simply be a "patient," but that his body and his consciousness—

meaning his whole self—be an integral part of the treatment. It is not simply done *to* a patient, but requires the patient's awareness of his freedom and responsibility at every point. If the patient gets this message loudly and clearly, Dr. Bailen states, he is confronted with a "choice point." This may take the form of a question to himself: "Oh, my God. Do I *want* to get rid of this?" Occasionally patients (generally arthritics) become better, get the insight, and then stop the treatment with the conclusion "It's easier for me to bear the pain than to make the change." They had become so rigid, so bound by habit, and had gotten so much secondary gain, such as being taken care of, out of the ailment that they chose not to change their way of life. This is a conscious, responsible choice. The person is no longer in his "victim" role.

This is very much like the goal of psychotherapy, in my judgment. The purpose of psychotherapy is not to "cure" the clients in the conventional sense, but to help them become aware of what they are doing and to get them out of the victim role. Its purpose is to help the disturbed one get to the stage where he is free to choose his own way of life, as far as that is realistically possible, and to accept his situation in life, as far as that is unavoidable.

To illustrate the "choice point," I will cite an experience of my own. The problem—or the symptom—with which I went to Dr. Bailen for treatment was tachycardia, which I had had since I was four years old. Though it had not handicapped me seriously as an adolescent, during the last years it had gotten severe enough to cause fainting and even more dangerous symptoms. I had been put on Inderal, one of the drugs which controls the beat of the heart. When I began I was on six Inderal (each one 10 mg.) a day. This, indeed, did control my heartbeat, but at the price of shutting off my brain. I felt like a zombie.

The following are notes I made at the time of my acupuncture.

This past Monday I felt very good after the acupuncture treatment, and my mood continued to be excellent on the morning of Tuesday. I was already down to one Inderal a day after several months of treatment. I decided then to cut the Inderal out entirely. But by noon, when I was feeling high because of the possibility of curing the tachycardia entirely,

I began to get a strange feeling of deep and pervasive loneliness. I paced back and forth in my office trying to figure out what this might be. There was no particular reason why I should be lonely. But I continued to feel as though I were in a foreign land where I could not speak the language, in a world in which I was lost and unable to communicate with anyone. I had also the strange feeling that I had lost myself; I had only half an identity.

In the middle of the afternoon it occurred to me that this loneliness had come out of my fantasy that the tachycardia could be cured entirely and I would be free of it. Yes! an important part of how I had experienced my identity in the past would be gone. I had grown accustomed to this image, this myth of myself, that I was this man with this particular ailment, namely tachycardia. The ailment seemed to be my friend; it had stood by me faithfully when I was under too much stress and needed some withdrawal from the active world. Like the prisoner of Chillon I had become friends with my very chains.

That night I dreamed that I was dying. My friends were gathered together and I was going around the circle saying good-bye to them. I was crying in the dream and felt that I was saying good-bye to this world.

The following night I dreamt that I was having a brain operation and part of my hair had been cut away in order for the surgeons to get to the part of my skull that was going to be cut out. The chief surgeon was a tall, thin man [Dr. Bailen is tall and thin]. I ran out of the operating room.

When I woke up the next morning [Wednesday] my tachycardia had returned in full force; my heart was pounding at the rate of 150 a minute. The tachycardia continued to trouble me all morning.

I was glad to get to Dr. Bailen's office that afternoon; for I knew that the dreams and behavior had been a very clear, if strident, cry that I was not yet ready to give up this ailment. The loneliness, and the first dream, were saying that to give up my symptom of tachycardia would be tantamount to dying, and also surrendering the identity by which I had known myself and survived since I was a child of four. The second dream makes an even more explicit cry about parting from the tachycardia: "Not yet!" it was shouting. Dr. Bailen laughingly agreed with my interpretation that I would need another month or so before making the drastic change completely.

The hanging on to illnesses, or the difficulty in asserting one's freedom and responsibility toward illnesses, has been well known through history and literature. Jean-Jacques Rousseau remarks about the tendency of human beings "to run to meet their chains thinking they secured their freedom." Even in the Declaration of Independence our forefathers recognized this truth: "All experience hath shown that man-kind are more disposed to suffer, while evils are sufferable, than to right themselves by abolishing the forms to which they are accustomed."

Thomas Mann shows in one of his stories how we make a way of life out of our own or others' sickness. In "Tobias Mindernickel," he pictures the dog as overly independent, a loner and not very friendly toward its master. In an accident the dog breaks its two front legs. The man then puts it in bed beside him and nurses it through the illness. Finally, when the dog recovers and is able to run around as used to be its wont, the man no longer has the animal to care for nor the animal's friendliness and dependency upon him. He is beside himself. Unable to stand his present isolation, the man takes a hammer and breaks the dogs legs all over again.

The moral of this story is applicable to the multitude of relationships in our world in which marriages, friendships, dependencies of various sorts are kept together essentially by the need to be cared for on the part of one member and the need to take care of on the part of the other. On the healthy side this is the comradeship we experience in comforting each other as we embrace cold and lonely destinies we cannot change. On the unhealthy side, it is the self-limitations built into the world by persons who have suffered illness and are loathe to give up their dependency when the possibility of freedom does open up again.

3. The Balance between Illness and Health

We need to understand the function of illness and health in a culture. The disease itself, as Harold Bailen puts it, is not the ultimate enemy. It may actually be a blessing in disguise in that it forces the person, as my tuberculosis did me, to take stock of his life and to reform his style of work and play. I wish to quote here two paragraphs which I wrote in the *Meaning of Anxiety:*

Having a disease is one way of resolving a conflict situation. Disease is a method of shrinking one's world so that, with lessened responsibilities and concerns, the person has a better chance of coping successfully. Health, on the contrary, is a freeing of the organism to realize its capacities.

I believe that people utilize disease in the same way older generations used the devil—as an object on which to project their hated experiences in order to avoid having to take responsibility for them. But beyond giving a temporary sense of freedom from guilt feeling, these delusions do not help. Health and disease are part and parcel of our continuous process throughout life of making ourselves adequate to our world and our world adequate to ourselves.

Nor is pain the ultimate enemy. As Norman Cousins writes: "Americans are probably the most pain-conscious people on the face of the earth. For years we have had it drummed into us—in print, on radio, over television, in everyday conversation—that any hint of pain is to be banished as though it were the ultimate evil." He goes on a show how leprosy is such a dreaded disease because of the fact that the affected person has lost the sense of pain and has no signal to tell him how and when to take care of the infected parts. We consume in this country a fabulous number of tranquilizers in the process of blocking out pain.

The interplay of pain and pleasure, and the dependence of one on the other, was seen by Plato:

How strange would appear to be this thing that men call pleasure! And how curiously it is related to what is thought to be its opposite, pain! The two will never be found *together* in a man, and yet if you seek the one and obtain it, you are almost bound always to get the other as well, just as though they were both attached to one and the same head. . . . Wherever the one is found, the other follows up behind. So, in my case, since I had pain in my leg as a result of the fetters, pleasure seems to have come to follow it up.

Pain is a sensitizer in life. In running away from pain we lose our vitality, our capacity genuinely to feel and even to love. I am not saying that pain is a good thing in itself. I am saying that pain and the relief from pain paradoxically go together. They are the bow and the string of Heraclitus. Without pain we would become a nation of zombies. Some critics believe we already have arrived at that state.

There is a common illusion that medical technology is wiping out one disease after another—such original lethal scourges as tuberculosis and infantile paralysis being among the recent examples—that we need only to wait, hoping we live long enough until medicine vanquishes all diseases. But this illusion rests on a serious misunderstanding of the functions of illness and health in any human society. "Physicians must resist the idea that technology will some day abolish disease," states Dr. Robert Rynearson in the *Journal of Clinical Psychiatry*. "As long as humans feel threatened and helpless, they will seek the sanctuary that illness provides. The distinguished scientist and humanitarian, Jacob Bronowski, cautioned us in this regard: 'We have to cure ourselves of the itch for absolute knowledge and power. We have to close the distance between the push-button order and the human act. We have to touch people.' "

Not only do physicians need to resist this illusion, but even more do lay people, to whom the idea that medical technology will ultimately save them is the most powerful rationalization for evading their own responsibility for their health. For human beings live—it is their destiny to do so—delicately balanced between health and illness, and *this balance is what is important.* There is no doubt that we, as a race, are getting healthier. But will I be misunderstood when I affirm that the possibilities of illness get proportionately greater at the same time? Certainly, there is just as much consulting with doctors as there was fifty years ago. What seems to be occurring is the shift in the kinds of illness from infectious diseases—which attack the person from the outside—to internal diseases like heart attacks, hypertension, and strokes—which are intimately related to anxiety and stress. The latter are the greatest killers of our day.

Illness and health are complexly balanced in each of us, and taking responsibility, so far as we can, gives us some possibility of restoring the balance when it goes awry. It is not by accident that so many of our greatest persons have struggled with disease all their lives. Noting the large number of important creative human beings who have had tuberculosis, a physician some years ago wrote a book entitled *Tuberculosis and Genius* in which he argued that the tubercular bacilli must eject some serum into the blood to produce the genius. This explanation seems to me absurd. It makes much more sense to hold that the way of life of the genius—intensive work, unquenchable enthusiasm, the fire in the brain—puts too much of a strain on the balance, and hence the individual becomes ill as a necessary way of withdrawing into himself for a time.

The struggle between health and illness is part of the source of creativity. British doctor George Pickering gathered data which he put into a book entitled *Creative Malady* and subtitled *Illness in the Lives and Minds of Charles Darwin, Florence Nightingale, Mary Baker Eddy, Sigmund Freud, Marcel Proust and Elizabeth Barrett Browning.* Each one, he points out, suffered severe illness and met it constructively. Pickering speaks of his own osteroarthritic hips as "an ally," which he puts to bed when they get painful; and in bed he cannot attend committee meetings or see patients or entertain visitors. "These are the ideal conditions for creative work: freedom from intrusion, freedom from the ordinary chores of life."

Dr. O. Carl Simonton has pioneered in the treatment of cancer by having the patient himself take responsibility through meditation on the cure. He teaches the person with cancer to become aware that a fight is going on and to meditate for two ten-minute periods each day on the white corpuscles killing the cancer cells. When we look at the drawings of the fantasies of these people of their meditation, we see pictures of warfare, of rats and tigers, of the white corpuscles as soldiers. A be-all and end-all struggle in occurring, and the consciousness of the person is the chief participant in the struggle. The old ways of being "patient" and handing the responsibility for one's illness over to the doctor are simply not relevant any more.

The art of wellness is described by Hadrian in his facing his illness:

I was better, but in order to contrive with my body, to impose my wishes upon it or to cede prudently to its will, I devoted as much art as I had formerly employed in regulating and enlarging my world, in building the being who I am, and in embellishing my life.

Four

The Fruits of Freedom

XII

The Renewal of Life

At an Independence Day celebration in Norway, Henrik Ibsen recited a poem on freedom that he had written expressly for this festival. In this poem Ibsen notes how broadly and meaninglessly the word *freedom* is bandied about, "with salutes and holiday flags," and how the crowds are "inspired by a pretty word / Which the eye deadens and thought enfeebles." "What is Freedom then?" Obviously not merely "To send men to parliament every three years— / To sit there dully, wings of thought clipped / Like inert prisoners behind a sea of prejudices."

Freedom, rather, is "life's finest treasure."

Only he is free who boldly aspires forward,
Whose deepest craving is the deed, whose goal is an heroic act of the
    spirit. . . .

And is it anything more than words and sound,
If we hail the rosy dawn of freedom,
And not understand that its finest fruit
Can ripen only in the *light of the spirit?*

1. Freedom and the Human Spirit

Freedom can "ripen only in the light of the spirit," as Ibsen says. But it is just as true that the human spirit is made possible only by freedom. Without freedom, there is no spirit; and without spirit, no freedom; and without freedom, no self.

"Man is spirit," proclaims Ibsen's fellow Scandinavian, Sören Kierkegaard. "But what is spirit? Spirit is the self. But what is the self. . . . The self is a relation which relates itself to its own self. . . . Man is a synthesis of the infinite and the finite, of the temperal and the eternal, of freedom and necessity."

In our day the word *spirit* has become less respectable because of its association with ghosts, apparitions, specters, fairies, and other forms of "spiritualism." "I have the spirit" is the prelude to speaking in tongues and other practices in fundamentalist churches. It is significant that all of these are endeavors to leave behind our humdrum existence and get "free" by leaping immediately into a spiritual existence. Paul Tillich has stated that crossing the boundaries from material to spiritual existence so easily was a sign of magic rather than spirit. Whatever one may think of these apparitions, I am not talking of this usage of *spirit*.

I use the word *spirit* in its etymological sense of the nonmaterial, animating principle of human life. Its root is *spirare*, which also means "breath" and is the root of *aspire, aspiration, inspire,* and *inspiration.* Thus, spirit is the breath of life. God breathes the spirit into Adam, as the creation myth puts it, and from then on Adam shares this capacity to pass on the life-giving principle to his own descendants in ways that are still a mystery to us.

Spirit is that which gives vivacity, energy, liveliness, courage, and ardor to life. We speak of the Spartans fighting at Thermopylae "with great spirit." When one is "high-spirited," one is lively, active in the sense that Spinoza meant when he described the free person as active and not passive. Or one has "lost all spirit," meaning that the person is in deep despondency and at the point of giving up life entirely. We borrow from the French the phrase "esprit de corps," implying the confidence that comes from participating in the spirit of everyone else in one's group.

Spirit increases as it is shared, and decreases as one's freedom is blocked off. Spirit has its psychological roots in each individual's inner freedom. Rousseau sees this identity between freedom and spirit when he writes,

Nature commands every animal, and the beast obeys. Man feels the same impetus, but he realizes he is free to acquiesce or resist; it is above all in the consciousness of this freedom that the spirituality of the soul is shown.

Spirit can be powerful—indeed, so powerful that it can transcend natural law. Goethe says of Faust,

> For fate has put a spirit in his breast
> That drives him madly on without a pause,
> And whose precipitate and rash behest
> O'erleaps the joys of earth and natural laws.

The spirit here is described as part of fate, of destiny—or, as we would say in contemporary language, it is both born in us and developed as our culture influences us from birth. Goethe's description can be seen in our day in the patients who come for psychotherapy who are workaholics, driven by ambition, who not only push themselves into a heart attack, but also miss what Goethe calls the "joys of earth" en route.

Spirit is also an epistemological capacity: one can see into things, get insights, perceive things that were covered before. This capacity is partially intuition, again as Spinoza sees intuition. Spirit is a special perspicacity, a keenness, a lucidity. One seems to exist on a higher level; one transcends the mundane and the boundaries of the mundane.

The language of spirit is image, symbol, metaphor, myth; and these also comprise the language of freedom. This is a language that points toward wholeness; a half image, for example, is still a whole image. Each one of these terms, whether it be *image, symbol, metaphor,* or *myth,* deals with the "whole circuit," as Bateson would phrase it. The terms point toward the totality of the event. Hence, these terms in the language of spirit deal with quality, which by its very nature is a wholeness, rather than quantity, which by its very nature is partial. We speak, for example, of a painting as being sensitive, powerful, communicating a richness of color to us—all terms that deal with qualities. The quantity of a painting or piece of music—say, the size of the canvas of a Picasso or the number of notes in a concerto—is silly when we are talking of works of art.

This "whole circuit" is Bateson's way of pointing out that logical, left-brain thinking deals in "arcs"—i.e., parts of the circuit rather than the whole. One is thus confined, limited, unfree as one sees only part of the reality one is looking at. This confinement is, of course, necessary in empirical thinking. But when freedom and the spirit enter our discourse, we find ourselves bursting out of these limits and dealing with a symbol of the whole, the universality of a myth, or a metaphor which stands for the totality.

This is why Bateson insists on the inclusion of right-brain thinking as part of any description and why he puts so much emphasis on the *contexts* in which one does one's thinking. He writes:

Mere purposive rationality unaided by such phenomena as art, religion, dream, and the like, is necessarily pathogenic and destructive of life; and its virulence springs specifically from the circumstances that life depends upon interlocking circuits of contingency, while consciousness can see only such short arcs of such circuits as human purpose may direct. . . . That is the sort of world we live in—a world of circuit structures—and love can survive only if wisdom [i.e., a sense of recognition of the fact of circuitry] has an effective voice.

2. The Authentic Mystics

Mystics, such as Meister Eckhart and Jacob Boehme, use the language of the spirit with a greater insight than the rest of us. Such mystics, as Wittgenstein has told us, "make things manifest." A German contemporary of Dante, Meister Eckhart describes his own experience when he says that "the human spirit . . . can never be satisfied with what light it has but storms the firmament and scales the heavens to discover the spirit by which the heavens are driven in revolutions and by which everything on the earth grows and flourishes." Though he taught in the fourteenth century, his words have a contemporary ring when he states that

the spirit, in knowing, has no use for number, for numbers are of use only within time, in this defective world. No one can strike his roots into eternity without being rid [of the concept] of number. The human spirit must go beyond all number-ideas, must break past and away from ideas of quantity and then he will be broken into by God. . . . God leads the human spirit into the desert, into his own unity. . . . Here the spirit achieves unity and freedom.

Freedom turns out to be central in the concepts of the mystics, probably because they exercise their own freedom so intensively in achieving their inspirations. Arguing that God does not constrain the will, Eckhart says, "Rather, he sets it free, so that it may *choose* him, that is to say, freedom. The spirit of man may not will otherwise than what God wills, but that is no lack of freedom. It is true freedom itself." This sentence expresses the curious union of destiny and freedom that characterizes the great religions. In them freedom and necessity, or freedom and bondage, are ultimately identical. Eckhart makes it a condition of those who wish to understand him that "your intentions are right and your will is free."

An uneducated cobbler, Boehme spoke with such an amazing degree of insight that half a dozen books are necessary to contain his wisdom. Though he had never read Heraclitus or any of the Greek philosophers or had any systematic schooling, Böhme spoke of God being a fire. "For Boehme, existence is a stream of fire. All life is fire. The fire is will." "According to Boehme, will—freedom—is the principle of all things." "Freedom is deeper than and prior to all nature." "Boehme, first in the history of human thought, has made freedom the first foundation of being, freedom is to him deeper and more primary than all being, deeper and more primary than God himself." The wrath of God is necessary if the love of God is to have any meaning. With respect to the question of where his wisdom came from, he tells us, "By my own powers I am as blind as the next man, but through the spirit of God, my own inborn spirit pierces all things."

Evelyn Underhill speaks of Boehme as "the inspired shoemaker" and "one of the giants of mysticism." Nikolai Berdyayev writes in his introduction to one of the books by Boehme: "We must salute Boehme as the founder of the philosophy of freedom that represents the true Christian philosophy."

It is important to recall that both of these mystics were condemned as heretics by the institutional church, and their writings were viewed as dangerous to the ecclesiastical establishment. The Grand Inquisitor's statement that since the eighth century the Church had given up following Christ is not entirely a figment of the imagination. Perhaps another characteristic of the authentic mystics is that their insistence on freedom of religion cannot be stomached by the ecclesiastical organization.

However one judges them, such authentic mystics have a source of wisdom that cannot come from learning (because they often have so little learning), but must come from insights that spring out of an immediate participation in the universe in ways we cannot understand but surely can admire. It recalls to mind the "participation mystique" that French anthropologist Lévy-Bruhl has found in primitive tribes around the world. The mystics' wisdom seems to be a combination of empathy, telepathy, intuition. This shows how far off the mark are those who criticize such things as acupuncture, and placebos of many sorts from a purely left-brain, rationalistic point of view. Such things as placebos may simply represent tangible patterns that act as foci on which a person may project the insights and intuitions that come from different sources.

We have said that human freedom gives birth to the human spirit and that spirit is necessary if there is to be freedom. But are not human spirit and freedom also the sources of evil? What did Böhme mean when he proclaimed that the wrath of God is necessary if there is to be any love of God?

3. Compassion and the Meaning of Evil

In the course of my therapeutic experience I have met and talked with a number of parents whose son or daughter happened to be in treatment with me. When the parents let their hair down, their attitudes varied from tearful regrets on the part of a clergyman high up in the ecclesiastical hierarchy about his son's depression to the genuine, if sad, puzzlement of a mother whose psychotic episode when her daughter was born had a good deal to do with the latter's present promiscuity to the boisterous instructions of a Wall Street executive who adjured me to hurry and get his son to shape up. The boisterousness of the executive only served to emphasize his subconscious realization that his authoritarianism had a good deal to do with his son's perpetual failures in everything he tried. If these parents could have spoken out of the depths of their feeling, each one of them—even the Wall Street executive—would have cried out, "Why do I harm the very person I love?"

Scarcely any of us can remain unaffected when we see the evil we do, mostly unintentionally, to those in our own family and to people we love by our inability to understand what is going on in the other's thoughts. Oscar Wilde's line "Yet each man kills the thing he loves" may relieve us to some extent in that it presents the universal quality of the problem of evil; we are not alone in the harm we partly cause. But Wilde also makes it impossible for us to forget that each of us participates in the inhumanity to other human beings.

The inevitability of evil is the price we pay for freedom. And the denial of evil is also the denial of freedom, as Berdyayev states in his interpretation of the sayings of Jacob Boehme. Since we have some margin of freedom, we have to make some choices; and this means the chance of making the wrong choice as well as the right one. Freedom and evil presuppose each other, whether we accept responsibility for our freedom and evil or not. Possibility is possibility for evil as well as good. We can pretend innocence, but such retreating to childhood ignorance does not help anyone.

There is an inescapable egocentricity in all of us, leading to the absolutizing of our own perceptions, which then become destructive to those closest to us. Schelling was right when he spoke of "the tendency in each one of us to be absolute in one's self." Each of us is bound up in his or her own skin, each of us sees life through his or her own eyes, and none of us can escape doing some violence to those we long most to understand. "The good that I would I do not, and the evil that I would not do, that I do" was Saint Paul's classic statement of the problem. There is no evading this dilemma. Indeed, Kierkegaard interpreted this as original sin: each of us speaks out of his separate individuality and thus inexorably runs roughshod over yearnings and perceptions that are precious to people we love. And if one tries very hard not to do this, if one makes every effort to do "good," one succeeds only in adding an element of self-righteousness to the ways one confronts one's fellows.

The problem of evil has been a stumbling block for philosophers and theologians for millennia. Those who represent the rational approach to evil, from Aristotle through Aquinas to the rational philosophers of today, hold that the more we solve our problems, the less evil will exist. Evil is thus a lack of goodness. The more our science progresses, the argument goes, the more the mysteries of life and nature are solved, and the less evil there is in the world. I believe this point of view is wrong. I heard this judgment much more in my earlier days before the advent of Hitler, before the Second World War with all its newly technologized ways of killing, before the use of concentration camps as an accepted political arm of government, and before the hydrogen bomb, with its unutterably cruel mass maiming and slaying. This depressing list should make clear the fact that the progress of science and technology has not resulted in our being less evil. Human cruelty and capacity for evil increases neck and neck with human technological progress. Our ways of killing are made more efficient as well as our ways of living.

The main example of the evil that is present in technology along with the good is, of course, nuclear power. If we had any doubts about the dangers to health and even life itself in radiation, nuclear residue, as well as the nuclear bombs per se, we have only to listen to the Union of Concerned Scientists to shock us out of our delusions. Not only can nuclear fission destroy the world population many times over, but there is evidence that radiation and strontium 90 may already be seeping into the bodies of an unknown number of us. In any case, we walk a razor's edge in dealing with nuclear fission. Science and technology deal with the *how* of life, and not the *why* or *what for*—which truth reputable scientists by the score tell us. Science increases the possibilities for good *and* the possibilities for evil, which many esteemed scientists have been shouting to us from the housetops.

There is also another group of philosophers and theologians who take a different approach. This group includes Heraclitus, who said "war is both king of all and father of all," through Socrates, Augustine, Pascal, Boehme, and down to Kierkegaard and Bateson. These thinkers directly face the fact that freedom makes evil inevitable. As long as there is freedom, there will be mistaken choices, some of them catastrophic. But to relinquish the capacity to make choices in favor of the dictatorial segment of us called our reason is to surrender what makes us human in the first place.

The modern form of the Grand Inquisitor's plan leads people to hand over their responsibility to the scientist in the white coat or to the psychotherapist in the comforting office or to the priest in the church or to the anonymous environment all about us. If we could do these things, we would have the temporary facsimile of evading evil. But while we are no longer committing evil, we also are no longer commiting goodness; and the age of the robot will be upon us.

The ultimate error is the refusal to look evil in the face. This denial of evil—and freedom along with it—is the most destructive approach of all. To take refuge with the Moonies, or with Jonestown, or any others of the hundreds of cults, most of which seem to spring up in California, is to find a haven where our choices will be made for us. We surrender freedom because of our inability to tolerate moral ambiguity, and we escape the threat that one might make the wrong choice. The mass suicides at Jonestown seem to me to be the terrible, if brilliant, demonstration of the ultimate outworking of the attitudes with which the adherents joined in the first place. They committed spiritual suicide in surrendering their freedom to evade the partial evil of life, and they end up demonstrating to the world in their own mass suicides the final evil.

Religious people have for millennia fervently asked, "How could a God of love permit evil?" An answer is given by that tributary of Christianity, Gnosticism:

God allowed evil to exist, woven into the texture of the world, in order to increase man's freedom and his will to prove his moral strength in overcoming it.

But the question the religious people above ask is simplistic. Let us recall the words of Boehme, above, that God is a fire and it is necessary to confront the wrath of God if the love of God is to have any reality. A Hassidic saying points toward the same thing:

> God is not nice, God is no uncle.
> God is an earthquake.

We note that some saints through history have spoken of themselves as the "chief of sinners." Obviously, this cannot mean sinner in the sense of committing overt, objective crimes. But it can mean that the saints, being more highly developed spiritually than ordinary people, have a correspondingly deeper awareness of their pride, vanity, hardness of heart, and obtuseness of understanding. If we look at sin from the inside, we see that there is indeed, sound meaning to their claim. Paul Tillich, in his reminding us that it is impossible to have a sensitive conscience and a good conscience at the same time, points out that if one has a sensitive conscience he will be aware of the evils of the world in which we as human beings participate. Hence, there is no clear, good conscience, but an active concern about the evils.

It is not at all surprising, then, that in the Garden of Eden myth, the knowledge of good and evil comes by virtue of the evil of rebellion against God. If Adam and Eve are to have any freedom, any true autonomy or true independence, they must defy the orders of God; and whether Yahweh is benevolent or destructive does not at that moment matter. This defying of the orders of God is essential for this development of their own consciousness. Otherwise they will forever be the inert appendages of God. Is this alienating? Anxiety-creating? Guilt-producing? Of course. But what becomes available with these "curses" are the blessings of love, responsibility, and the passion and power to create.

4. Forgiveness and Mercy

What, then, shall we do? The only answer is: Be compassionate. The universality of evil makes human compassion necessary. I often remark to the parents who are sad about the part they've played in the problems of their children, "You and I—all of us who are human—are in the same boat." Platitude though this is, it often helps relieve them of the solitary, pariahlike quality that makes them feel they are alone in their mistakes and solitary in their evil.

In his poem "A Dialogue of Self and Soul," W. B. Yeats, describes the confrontation between these two, and has the soul assert that mere rationalism can never solve the problems of life:

> For intellect no longer knows
> *Is* from the *ought*, or *Known* from the *Known*—
> That is to say, ascents to Heaven;
> Only the dead can be forgiven;
> But when I think of that my tongue's a stone.

And the poem finally concludes in an act of harmony between the two,

> I am content to follow to its source
> Every event in action or in thought;
> Measure the lot; forgive myself the lot!
> When such as I cast out remorse
> So great a sweetness flows into the breast
> We must laugh and we must sing,
> We are blest by everything,
> Everything we look upon is blest.

The last five lines are an exquisite description of what happens in the deeper sense of forgiveness toward oneself.

The forgiveness extends, in the case of parents and children, to the sons and daughters as well; for the regrets are often bound up with what seems to be their opposite, resentment on the part of the parents at the son or daughter for causing him or her such perplexity and suffering. Thus forgiveness of oneself permits one to forgive others. Forgiveness, which is one phase of compassion, puts the deeper meaning into our human comedies, and enables us to get insight from our tragedies so that they become bearable. Forgiveness means to overcome the resentment—to "cast out remorse"—which is the curse that accumulates in most human relationships. Forgiving ourselves as well as others may be the only way of transcending this resentment. The health-enhancing aspect of the forgiving of others is that it helps wipe away the resentment toward oneself at the same time.

Compassion—the capacity to have passion *with* another—implies empathy, the ability to see the world as the other person sees it. Compassion gives us fresh perspective on what it means to be human, and helps us judge less harshly ourselves as well as the persons who impinge upon us. Paradoxical as it sounds, this gives us a point outside our remorse from which we can do more to correct it. We stop, then, condemning ourselves for being human, and we can at the same time stop condemning others for the same condition. "This means," as Don Michael puts it, "that everybody needs all the clarity they can muster regarding their ignorance and finiteness, and all the support they can obtain in order to face the upsetting implications of what their clarity reveals to them. A compassionate person is one who, by virtue of accepting this situation, can provide others as well as self with such support."

Freedom without compassion is demoniacal. Without compassion, freedom can be self-righteous, inhuman, self-centered, and cruel. Anatole France's remark about freedom—that the poor man and rich man are both equally free to sleep under the bridges of Paris at night—illustrates how freedom can turn into cruelty toward the underdog. Many of the crusades under the banner of freedom—and not merely the ones we read about in history books—have consisted of requiring the other person to accept one's own concept of freedom. Thus, they have turned out to be tyrannical.

This can be seen in some experiences of psychotherapy. The therapist may be convinced that his own form of freedom is the only thing that is good for the client, which then makes for coldness, rigidity, inhumanness in the therapist even though what he does may be technically correct.

I once supervised a psychiatrist whose patient, a young woman of nineteen, was giving him a good deal of trouble. The patient was constantly being irritated, changing the subject, and in general angry and petulant. I remarked in the supervisory hour that the young woman might be trying to get some sign of affection from the therapist. The psychiatrist in the next session, when the young woman was playing out her petulant drama, interrupted her with "You know, I like you." The patient stopped talking, paused a moment and then said, "I guess that's what it's all about." When the therapist reported this to me, I asked, "*Do* you like her?" And he answered, "No, I really don't." There flashed before my mind a glimpse of the whole treatment collapsing, for there is no doubt that patients in therapy can sense this presence or lack of compassion, despite all pretenses. Surely enough, she broke off the therapy after a couple of sessions.

Compassion on the part of the therapist is the essence of any psychotherapy which deserves the name. Patients will see through any pretense when the level is as basic as compassion, even though they may not speak of it, since they are taught in our culture to pretend that they don't see such negative things.

A therapist colleague of mine was seeing regularly a patient whose manner was generally bombastic and insolent. One day the therapist's daughter had been seriously hurt. Nothing was said by the therapist in the session about the accident, but the patient that day, as we heard on the tape, was tender, kind, and completely without his usual bombast, as though he were aware of the therapist's tragedy—which he could not have known. Does this presuppose some degree of mental telepathy in therapy or some capacity to pick up the tiny cues such as the sound of one's voice? I believe both are probably true. Freud was right, in my judgment, in his "moral" theory of telepathy, stating that he had learned not to lie in therapy because he had often enough experienced the fact that the patient would see through the lie no matter how hard Freud tried to cover it up.

Alfred Adler said time and again, "The technique of treatment must be in yourself," and went on to point out that the best therapist was one who had problems himself but was aware of them and was working on them. In psychotherapy one cannot have compassion for another if one never has experienced psychological problems of one's own. Note that I do not say the *same* psychological problems as the clients—that is not necessary. But the therapist must know what the struggle between "self and soul," to borrow Yeats's terms, really feels like through his own experience.

This is why, in interviewing and selecting candidates for two different psychoanalytic training institutes, I would never consider the candidate who was "well adjusted" and who had not endured the wrestling with his or her own destiny. I assumed— and I believe rightly so—that such persons would not empathize with and feel compassion for the patient or client. The two greatest therapists I ever knew personally, Frieda Fromm-Reichmann and Harry Stack Sullivan, had, individually, almost every problem in the book, and both had fantastic insight into the problems of their patients and corresponding compassion. One of the obvious and central functions of the didactic therapy that the trainee is required to go through is to sensitize oneself to the problems within oneself in order to have compassion for the other persons one is to work with.

Gregory Bateson would have said that the person who lacks compassion does not grasp the "whole circuit" in his human relationships. Speaking of the importance of art, poetry, religion, and other "right-brain" functions, Bateson writes:

Unaided consciousness must always tend toward hate; not only because it is good common sense to exterminate the other fellow, but for the more profound reason that, seeing only arcs of circuits, the individual is continually surprised and necessarily angered when his hardheaded policies return to plague the inventor.

One of Bateson's heros, Blaise Pascal, likewise points out the inadequacy of a solely rational point of view, for reason is "pliable to every sense," and in practice reason is often a matter of "Truth on this side of the Pyrenees, error on that."

It is our destiny to live always in some form of community. Even the frontiersman who counted it a matter of pride that all of twenty miles separated him from his nearest neighbor was still bound to that neighbor by language no matter how rarely he spoke it, by his memory, by every thought, ad infinitum. The "wolf child" is an anomoly and, indeed, is a proof of what I am saying in that he became "human" only when he exhibited a communal morality. The fact that we belong to a community as well as being individual persons requires that we acknowledge this destiny and relate to each other with compassion. Compassion limits our freedom, but it renders freedom human at the same time.

As we have seen in the chapter on narcissism, the refusal to admit destiny is to cut ourselves off from others. And now we can see its cruelty. Surely it is relevant: "If I don't take care of myself, who else will?" But if one takes care only of oneself, one's freedom can become cruelty to others. Love, of which compassion is the first step, keeps freedom from becoming tyrannical.

The universality of evil also makes necessary human mercy, the "gentle" virtue, as Shakespeare, in *The Merchant of Venice*, rightly insisted. Mercy not only drops like a soft Spring rain, but it is like forgiveness in that it blesses him who gives and him who takes. Mercy is

> The attribute to awe and majesty,
> Wherein doth sit the dread and fear of kings;
> But mercy is above this sceptred sway,
> It is enthroned in the hearts of kings,
> It is an attribute to God himself,
> And earthly power doth then show likest God's
> When mercy seasons justice. . . .

Evil will not disappear or shrink away during the night. We will never wake up in the morning to find that evil has vanished from the face of the earth. The purpose of human life is not to avoid mistakes, nor to show an unblemished escutcheon, but to rise to meet the challenges as our destiny reveals itself and to search out in freedom the challenges we wish to engage. As I read the human tragicomedy, we will go on struggling, avoiding complete nuclear catastrophe by the skin of our teeth, trying to become aware of the pitfalls in ourselves and our society, so that we can make constructive choices whenever possible. In this tragicomedy forgiveness and mercy will season justice and make life bearable with the presence of beauty, the emotion of love, and the occasional experience of joy.

XIII

Despair and Joy

Beethoven did not turn away from life toward some mystical Nirvana. He forgot none of the joy, the effort, or the pain. He abandoned nothing. What he achieved was something much more wonderful than an old man's serenity. "I will take fate by the throat," Beethoven cries in a letter. "It shall not wholly overcome me. Oh, it is so beautiful to live—to live a thousand times!"

—J. W. N. SULLIVAN, *Beethoven: His Spiritual Development*

One of the reasons we are so reluctant to confront the aspect of destiny called fate is that we are afraid it will lead us into despair. We Americans are taught always to wear a garment of optimism, and we believe that with despair all hope is lost. So we cling to any false hope we can conjure up to serve as a bulwark against despair, unaware that a hope that has to be striven for is no hope at all. No wonder T. S. Eliot writes "wait without hope / For hope would be hope for the wrong things." This begging for some hope opens us to exploitation by any psychoreligious charlatan who appears on the horizon. All to escape the demon despair!

But suppose that despair were basically a constructive emotion? Suppose despair is often a necessary prelude to the greatest achievement? Virgil wrote in the *Aeneid*, when telling of the voyage of Aeneas and his men, that darkness was "our guide and our leader was Despair." What if Homer were right when, in the *Iliad*, he pointed out that a similar "strength is felt from hope and from despair"?

Let us look again at Philip's experience in his last therapeutic session, as related in Chapter II. He came in feeling sad, hopeless, lonely, lost. He felt everybody had died—his mother, his sister Maude—and the relation with Nicole was nearly dead, and now, at the end of therapy, the relation with the therapist was dying. He was in clear, unadulterated despair. But halfway through the session he began his recovery.

1. The Values of Despair

The despair was essential in bringing Philip to the point where he could give up his previous neurotic ways of behaving in his overwork and in his failure to have full relationships with other people. This experience when he had been a young man had been one turning point in his life, just as he and I believed this therapy, then concluding, would be a turning point in his overcoming his love bind with Nicole.

Thus, despair can lead to highly constructive action. It can be a flushing out of the Augean stables. Despair can be a "giving up" and a "letting go" of neurotic problems that had been solidifying since one was an infant. In this sense despair plays the constructive role reserved for it in every psychotherapy.

I am speaking of despair not as a "cosmic pout" nor as any kind of intellectual posture. If it is a mood put on to impress somebody or to express resentment toward anybody, it is not genuine despair.

Authentic despair is that emotion which forces one to come to terms with one's destiny. It is the great enemy of pretense, the foe of playing ostrich. It is a demand to face the reality of one's life. The "letting go" that we noted in despair is a letting go of false hopes, of pretended loves, of infantilizing dependency, of empty conformism which serves only to make one behave like sheep huddling in a flock because they fear the wolves outside the circle. Despair is the smelting furnace which melts out the impurities in the ore. Despair is not freedom itself, but is a necessary preparation for freedom. The Grand Inquisitor is right: we would not choose to go into despair if we consulted only our rational choices. But there is no denying destiny or fate, and reality comes marching up to require that we drop all halfway measures and temporary exigencies and ways of being dishonest with ourselves and confront our naked lives.

It is well known that Alcoholics Anonymous, that organization which is far and away the most effective in curing alcoholics, states frankly that the alcoholic cannot be cured until he or she is in complete despair. It is only then that the alcoholic can give up the need for alcohol as a solace for his or her forlorn hopes or to bolster his or her false expectations. Those who have been through AA and then work to help new members simply laugh outright at the predespair alcoholic's grandiosity, his pompous I-am-the-master-of-my-fate-attitude, his vain resolutions to control his drinking by his own will power. This is a beautiful example of T. S. Eliot's line of "hope for the wrong things." Hopes themselves can become the most seductive of delusions.

When a person has "hit bottom"—i.e., when he has reached ultimate despair—he then can surrender to eternal forces; this is the dynamic in all authentic conversions. I would describe this process as giving up the delusion of false hopes and, thus, acknowledging fully the facts of destiny. Then and only then can this person begin to rebuild himself. It is a superb demonstration of the hypothesis that freedom begins only when we confront destiny.

The same was true of Synanon before its deterioration. It is also true of the group called Delancey Street in San Francisco, a community of young people who have come out of lives of crime, drug addiction, alcoholism. The object in Delancey Street is to bring the new member to despair—the accomplishment of which is done by energetically attacking his rationalizations, his pretenses, his pompousness, until he is down to the bare bones of his existence. Only then, the leaders of Delancey Street believe, will the person give up the illusionary hopes that block his transformation into a person of authentic freedom.

2. Despair in Therapy

We know in psychotherapy that often despair is essential to the discovery on the part of the client of his or her hidden capacities and basic assets. The function of despair is to wipe away our superficial ideas, our delusionary hopes, our simplistic morality. There are some misguided therapists who feel that they must reassure the patient at every point of despair. But if the client never feels despair, it is doubtful whether he ever will feel any profound emotion. Apropos of considering Voltaire's remark "Despair has often gained battles," a friend wrote this limerick:

> There once was a man named Voltaire
> Who found his best hope in despair.
> If that sounds perverse,
> It could have been worse.
> Voltaire could declare, "I don't care."

There is surely value in the client's experience that he has nothing more to lose anyway so he may as well take whatever leap life requires of him. I suggest that this is what is meant by that sentence in folklore "Despair and confidence both banish fear." It is important to remind ourselves of these points since there are a number of signs that we in America may be on the threshold of a period as a nation when we shall no longer be able to camouflage or repress our despair.

Those who can feel healthy despair are often those who also can at the same time experience the most intense pleasure and joy. Sartre was talking about a life-enhancing despair when, in his play *The Flies*, after Zeus has pointed out all the despair Orestes will face, Orestes asserts against Zeus, "Human life begins on the far side of despair!" He could as well have said that human freedom and human joy also begin on the far side of despair. This is why we believe more firmly in the dignity and the nobility of being human after seeing a performance of tragedy rather than comedy: the characters and the tragic downfall of Hamlet, Macbeth, Lear, or even of Harry in *The Iceman Cometh* give us a conviction of the significance of life. As we leave the theater, we are not only relieved, we are inspired. The despair we have felt in the drama highlights its opposite, the nobility of life.

Despair is a desperate refusal to be oneself. Kierkegaard puts it well, citing the different levels of "despair at not willing to be one's self, or still lower, despair at not willing to be a self; or

lowest of all, despair at willing to be another than himself."
Despair is a failure of spirit, a spiritlessness. "Man when he is
characterized as spirit-less has become a talking-machine, and
there is nothing to prevent him from learning a philosophical rig-
marole just as easily as a confession of faith and a political recita-
tive repeated by rote." Again: "Despair is a qualification of spirit,
it is related to the eternal in man. . . . *In unconsciousness of being in
despair a man is furthest from being conscious of himself as spirit.*"

This "thing of despairing is inherent in man himself; but if he
were not a synthesis he could not despair." Kierkegaard holds
that human beings are a synthesis of finite and infinite, and this
is what makes despair possible. He also emphasizes that the worst
condition of all is to boast about never having been in despair, for
that means that the person has never been authentically conscious
of himself.

3. The Link between Despair and Joy

This link between despair and joy is so important that the
ancient Greeks devoted one of their central myths to it, that of
Persephone and Demeter. Persephone was picking flowers with
her friends one day when Hades, god of the underworld, saw her
and was stricken with love. He seized her and carried her off to
his underworld. When her mother, Demeter, goddess of fruit and
grain and other produce of the fields, heard Persephone's cries,
she rushed around the world trying to find her. Learning that
Hades had carried her off to the underworld with Zeus' conni-
vance, Demeter was filled with a terrible and savage grief.

Demeter left Olympus and wandered about the earth incog-
nito. Meeting two young women who sympathized with her
story that she had been captured by pirates and had escaped,
Demeter was taken to their home to meet their mother, Metaneira. Demeter continued to be so sad that "a long time she sat
upon the stool without speaking, never smiling, because of her
sorrow . . . tasting neither food nor drink, because she pined for
her deep-bosomed daughter."

Metaneira and her daughters proclaimed to Demeter,

"Mother, what the gods send us, we mortals bear perforce though we suffer." What an acknowledgment of destiny, an adjuring of Demeter to accept fate! Its importance is shown in the fact that it is repeated later to make sure we have heard it. Metaneira then asked Demeter to be nurse to her newborn son. Demeter came to life and bestowed love upon the infant, who then grew amazingly.

Meanwhile, in her grief and rage Demeter had caused the land to bear no more fruit and grain, and a cruel famine covered the earth. Zeus finally was moved to command Hades to let Persephone return to earth, though Hades fed "his shy mate" a pomegranate seed.

Persephone returned to Demeter who welcomed her with great joy. When Persephone confessed she had unbeknownst eaten a pomegranate seed, Demeter knew that her daughter would have to return to Hades for one-third of each year—the winter—but could remain on earth the rest of the time.

But this small flaw was quickly drowned in their joyousness. "So did they then, with hearts at one, greatly cheer each other's soul and spirit with many an embrace; their hearts had relief from their griefs while each took and gave back joyousness. . . . And straightway made fruit to spring up from the rich lands, so that the whole earth was laden with leaves and flowers."

Demeter's great grief, to the extent of speaking to no one, refusing all comfort and all food and drink, pining with longing for her daughter, amounts to a profound despair. It was a despair which carried over to mankind in the cruel famine on earth. But Demeter's despair soon became a creative state, shown in her love for Metaneira's infant son and his amazing growth.

Demeter's suffering is followed by this intense joy, which is *stronger than she would have felt had the sorrow not preceded it.* In other words, despair is a prerequisite to the birth of joy. Persephone's fearful descent into the underworld is followed not only by joyful ascension, but the "earth's period of barrenness is followed by an eruption of fruit and flowers." The myth shows "pain followed by joy, separation followed by reunion, death followed by renewal, winter followed by spring."

Winter—the part of the year Persephone must go back to the underground—is often considered the dreaded part of the year, the time when despair would be most prevalent. But winter is the "purifier," as the Magee Indians call it. The snow and the ice purify the ground. They cover over the myriad creatures from insects to deer who have lived out their span of life; and the ground, being enriched, springs forth with new life after the purification. This is the gestation before creativity. Nietzsche seemed to have been writing (and beautifully) about the end of this experience:

> Out of such abysses, from such severe sickness one returns newborn, having shed one's skin, more ticklish and malicious, with a more delicate taste for joy, with a more tender tongue for all good things, with merrier senses, with a second dangerous innocence in joy, more childhood and yet a hundred times subtler than one has ever seen before.

A similar linking of despair and joy is the death and resurrection in Christian theology—and all resurrections, seen in the prototype of the resurrection of flowers and leaves on the trees in the spring. This pattern runs through all of life. It is destiny, the design of the universe, the form in which all of existence is encompassed. In Europe at Easter time, people turn out *en masse* for the sacrament of Good Friday, since they want to make sure Jesus is dead. The celebration of his death is a necessary precursor to any rising from the tomb. The renewal requires the death beforehand. That Christ has risen has meaning only if he has been really dead. In America there is scant attendance on Good Friday, but the churches are filled to capacity on Easter. This is indicative of our lack of belief in tragedy in this country. It is a demonstration of our endeavor to overlook the death that must occur before the resurrection, the suffering that precedes joy, the tragedy that precedes achievment, the conflict that precedes creativity. Henry Miller refers to the same thing in terms of emotional death and resurrection when he writes "those who are dead may be restored to life." For Miller this occurs in the emotional release, after despair, of the creative process.

Despair before joy is the meaning of the "dark night of the soul" of which the mystic Saint John of the Cross writes. Or, as

John Bunyan metaphorically puts it, the slough of despond must be gone through before we can arrive at the gates of the Celestial City. Joseph Campbell informs us in his *Hero with a Thousand Faces* that the hero must be willing to endure trial and dismemberment, even a species of death, if he is to achieve the Holy Grail. Those who claim to live in a perpetual state of ecstasy or in a never-interrupted state of love are either deluding themselves or settling for a mediocre state of existence.

In mystic tradition the state of ecstasy is only the second stage and by no means the goal. Persons of lesser devotion or commitment often want to slide back into this second stage and have to be cautioned against selling the mystic experience short. Gethsemane is not at all an admission of failure on the part of the ministry of Jesus, but a necessary stage that cannot be avoided. It turns out not to be possible to "let this cup pass from me." Without the despair, no resurrection. One of the mystics of history encourages would-be explorers of the mystic path to "endure the pains and the discomfort. For behind this nothingness, behind this dark and formless shape of evil is Jesus hid in His joy."

4. The Nature of Joy

In his description of his "fabulous summer," we may recall that Philip used the word *joy* not *happiness*. What can be the distinction?

Happiness is a fulfillment of the past patterns, hopes, aims; but those are exactly what Philip had had to give up. Happiness is mediated, so far as we can tell, by the parasympathetic nervous system, which has to do with eating, contentment, resting, placidity. Joy is mediated by the opposing system, the sympathetic, which does not make one want to eat, but stimulates one for exploration. Happiness relaxes one; joy challenges one with new levels of experience. Happiness depends generally on one's outer state; joy is an overflowing of inner energies and leads to awe and wonderment. Joy is a release, an opening up; it is what comes when one is able genuinely to "let go." Happiness is associated with contentment; joy with freedom and an abundance of human spirit. In sexual love joy is the thrill of the two persons moving together toward orgasm; happiness is the contentment when one relaxes after orgasm. Joy is new possibilities; it points toward the future. Joy is living on the razor's edge; happiness promises satisfaction of one's present state, a fulfillment of old longings. Joy is the thrill of new continents to explore; it is an unfolding of life.

Happiness is related to security, to being reassured, to doing things as one is used to and as our fathers did them. Joy is a revelation of what was unknown before. Happiness often ends up in a placidity on the edge of boredom. Happiness is success. But joy is stimulating, it is the discovery of new continents emerging within oneself.

Happiness is the absence of discord; joy is the welcoming of discord as the basis of higher harmonies. Happiness is finding a system of rules which solves our problems; joy is taking the risk that is necessary to break new frontiers. Tennyson protrays Ulysses from the point of view of joy; he sees the old man scorning "to rust unburnished, not to shine in use!"

The good life, obviously, includes both joy and happiness at different times. What I am emphasizing is the joy that follows rightly confronted despair. Joy is the experience of possibility, the consciousness of one's freedom as one confronts one's destiny. In this sense despair, when it is directly faced, can lead to joy. After despair, the one thing left is possibility.

We all stand on the edge of life, each moment comprising that edge. Before us is only possibility. This means the future is open—as open as it was for Adam and Eve, Milton tells us in *Paradise Lost*, after their great despair at the rebuke given them by Yaweh. Despair, yes. But it is the beginning of human consciousness and all of the joys that that opens to us.

> Some natural tears they dropped, but wiped them soon;
> The world was all before them, where to choose
> Their place of rest, and Providence their guide.
> They, hand in hand, with wandering steps and slow,
> Through Eden took their solitary way.

Acknowledgment

I wish to express my gratitude to Don Michael, a man who knows the joy of thinking, with whom I spent many evenings before the fireplace discussing these questions. Also, my thanks to Susan Osborn, who served as my research assistant during my work on this book.

Notes

I. The Present Crisis of Freedom

4   "To accept the principle . . . to be free."
Cited by Noam Chomsky, *For Reasons of State* (New York: Vintage, 1973), pp. 392–93.

4   "The whole knowledge . . . prove freedom."
As Schelling also says: "The thought of making freedom the sum and substance of philosophy . . . has given science in all its parts a more powerful reorientation than any earlier revolution" (cited by Chomsky, *op. cit.*, p. 388).

5   "Almost every moralist . . . has praised freedom."
Isaiah Berlin, *Four Essays on Liberty* (New York: Oxford University Press, 1969), p. 121.

5   "It is the . . . to determine itself."
Ruth Nanda Anshen, *Freedom, Its Meaning* (New York: Harcourt, Brace, 1940), p. 123

6   "For love can . . . anything for him."
Jacques Ellul, *The Ethics of Freedom* (Grand Rapids, Mich.: Eerdmans, 1976), p. 200.

7   Statistical studies of Rokeach
Milton Rokeach, *Beliefs, Attitudes and Values* (San Francisco: Jossey-Bass, 1968). Rokeach summarizes many rankings of values by different groups in the country, and therefore his summary can be considered as true for a cross section of the people of the United States. If we consider only the black minority, who has reason to be cynical about freedom, the ranking is highest for "equality," and "freedom" is ranked tenth. Unemployed whites ranked "freedom" third and "equality" ninth.

7   Ancient Greece and Rome
There are a few notable exceptions, like Epictetus, who began as a slave and was later given his freedom, and whose beliefs were as autonomous in the former state as in the latter.

page

7   "marvels done . . . against oppression."
     Quoted by Chomsky, *op. cit.*, p. 392.

8   "In the act . . . to be one's self."
     Kurt F. Reinhardt, *The Existential Revolt* (Milwaukee: Bruce, 1952), pp. 181–83.

8   "Freedom . . . at the expense of society."
     Translated by Dorothy Atkinson. Solzhenitsyn's speech on receiving the American Friendship Award from the Freedoms Foundation, Stanford University, June 1, 1976.

9   "I have felt . . . befits that dignity."
     Quoted by Chomsky, *op. cit.*, p. 397.

10   "Freedom is . . . individual initiative."
     Bronislaw Malinowski, *Freedom and Civilization* (New York: Roy, 1944), p. 242.

10   "I dwell . . . of the Sky."
     Emily Dickinson, Poem 657, in *The Complete Poems of Emily Dickinson*, ed. Thomas H. Johnson (Boston: Little, Brown, 1890), p. 327.

10   "unbearable tensions . . . tears your insides out."
     Irving Janis and Leon Mann, *Decision Making* (New York: The Free Press, 1977), p. 47.

11   "Total war . . . unto his brethren."
     James Farmer, *Freedom—When?* (New York: Random House, 1965), p. 53.

13   "he is . . . settled in freedom."
     Cited by Alan Wolfe, "The Myth of the Free Scholar," in *Toward Social Change*, ed. Robert Buckout *et al.* (New York: Harper & Row, 1971), p. 64.

13   "United States . . . unrecognized."
     Eugene McCarthy, "The 1980 Campaign: Politics as Entropy," *Christianity and Crisis*, 18 Aug. 1980.

13   "repudiation . . . center of allegiance."
     R. H. Tawney, *The Acquisitive Society* (New York: Harcourt, Brace, 1920), p. 47.

14   William O. Douglas
     Douglas continues, in *Of Men and Mountains:* "We can keep our freedom through the increasing crises of history only if we are self-reliant enough to be free. . . . We need a faith that dedicates us to something bigger and more important than ourselves." From Ramsey Clark, "William O. Douglas: Daring to Live Free," *Progressive* 40 (January 1976):7–9.

14   "Freedom involves . . . personal freedom."
     Irwin Edman, *Fountainheads of Freedom* (New York: Reynal, 1941), p. 7.

14   "Like the good Germans . . . of American liberty."
     Editorial, *Progressive* 40 (January 1976):5–6.

page

14   Henry Steele Commager
      Henry Steele Commager, "Is Freedom Dying?" *Look.*

17   "their whole destiny . . . to himself."
      Alexis de Tocqueville, *Democracy in America* (New York: Knopf, 1951), p. 299.

17   "I know of no country . . . America."
      Alexis de Tocqueville, *Democracy in America*, ed. and abridged Richard D. Heffner (New York: Mentor, 1956), p. 117.

17   "There the body . . . to scorn you."
      Ibid., p. 118.

18   "The mental health movement . . . the tranquilizer by physicians."
      Nicholas Cummings, "Turning Bread into Stones," *American Psychologist* 34, no. 12 (December 1979):1119.

20   Psychological problem
      Rollo May, *The Meaning of Anxiety* (New York: Norton, 1977), p. xiv.

21   Freedom and neurosis and psychosis
      See the parable "The Man Who Was Put in a Cage," in Rollo May, *Psychology and the Human Dilemma* (New York: Norton, 1979), pp. 161–68.

II. One Man's Passage

page

34   "the way in which . . . under the heading of imprinting."
      John Bowlby, *Attachment*, vol. 1 of Attachment and Loss series (New York: Basic Books, 1969), p. 223.

36   "Such freedom . . . a creative product."
      Jerome Kagan, ed., *Creativity and Learning* (Boston: Houghton-Mifflin, 1967), p. 27.

36   "Many of our most valuable people . . . traumatic childhoods."
      Richard Farson, *Birthrights* (Baltimore, Md.: Penguin, 1974), pp. 29–30.

III. The Dynamics of Freedom

page

53   "freedom . . . after we have lost it."
      Bronislaw Malinowski, *Freedom and Civilization* (New York: Roy, 1944), p. 74.

page

53 Definitions of freedom
Isaiah Berlin even saw fit in his book on the subject to state two separate
categories, "negative" and "positive" freedoms. See Isaiah Berlin, *Four Essays
on Liberty* (New York: Oxford University Press, 1969).

58 "In the concept of freedom . . . explanation for both."
Friedrich Wilhelm Joseph von Schelling, *Works*, I, xxxvii. Italics mine.

61 "In the very act . . . of his self."
James Farmer, *Freedom—When?* (New York: Random House, 1965), pp. 17–
18.

62 "The free play . . . a significant freedom."
Rollo May, *Psychology and the Human Dilemma* (New York: Norton, 1979),
p. 21.

64 "The arm of art . . . in the world."
Albert Camus, "The Unbeliever and the Christians," in *Resistance, Rebellion,
and Death*, trans. J. O'Brien (New York: Knopf, 1963).

IV. The Paradoxes of Freedom

page

67 People "do not understand . . . and the lyre."
Kathleen Freeman, *Ancilla to the Pre-Socratic Philosophers* (Cambridge, Mass.:
Harvard University Press, 1948), p. 29. Heraclitus also stated, "That which
is in opposition is in concert, and from things that differ comes the most
beautiful harmony" (p. 25).

72 On rebellion
Like the psychologist B. F. Skinner, who cannot admit any profound rebellious quality in human beings and who attacks Dostoevsky as a writer for
"neurotics." In *Notes from the Underground*, Dostoevsky describes at length
this obstinacy, stubbornness, and sheer cussedness which are part of the
destiny of human beings: "Out of sheer ingratitude, man will play you a
dirty trick, just to prove that men are still men and not the keys of a piano.
. . . And even if you could prove that a man is only a piano key, he would
still do something out of sheer perversity—he would create destruction and
chaos—just to gain his point. . . . And if all this could in turn be analyzed
and prevented by predicting that it would occur, then man would deliber-
ately go mad to prove his point."
Skinner, quoting the above, then adds: "This is a conceivable neurotic
reaction. . . . A few men may have shown it, and many have enjoyed Dostoevsky's statement because they tend to show it. But that such perversity is
a fundamental reaction of the human organism to controlling conditions is
sheer nonsense."

Skinner's work has been chiefly with rats and pigeons, and it may be that for them it *is* "sheer nonsense." But I, speaking out of a lifetime of work with human beings as a therapist, say that nothing is more true about human beings than this rebelliousness, this stubbornness, this obstinacy, to show that one is "still a man." Far from being neurotic, it is the central criterion of the psychologically healthy person as well as the fundamental source of human dignity.

74 Frantz Fanon
The Wretched of the Earth (New York: Grove, 1965) and *Black Skin, White Masks* (New York: Grove, 1967).

74 "Freedom . . . remains a slave."
Nikos Kazantzakis, *Freedom or Death* (New York: Simon and Schuster), p. 278.

75 "The way of non-violence . . . more redemptive."
John Ehle, *The Free Men* (New York: Harper & Row, 1965), pp. 81–82.

76 "Something happens . . . their consciences."
Ibid., p. 86.

76 "refused to be victimized . . . *is not yet free.*"
Farmer, *op. cit.*, p. 35. Italics mine.

76 "We might think . . . historic wrong."
Ibid., p. 36.

76 "Freedom . . . are unpracticed."
Ibid., p. 170.

77 "Freedom . . . in each act."
Ibid., p. 197.

77 "Those who profess . . . *it never will.*"
Ibid., p. 73.

78 Eastern societies and Marxism
The Marxist concept of the economic determinism of history is also a parallel to the Eastern veneration of tradition.

79 "It seems silly . . . a community."
Richard Tanner Pascale and Anthony G. Athos, *The Art of Japanese Management* (New York: Simon and Schuster, 1981), p. 50.

79 "Spiritual . . . is valued."
Ibid., p. 49.

80 "management . . . human resources."
Ibid., p. 50.

80 "You talk to me . . . *for freedom.*"
Translated by Lawrence Ferlinghetti with Anthony Kahn.

81 *"creative tranquility . . . to breathe."*
Rollo May, *The Courage to Create* (New York: Norton, 1975), p. 75. Italics mine.

page

81   "in order to be free . . . directly."
     Peter Stillman, "Freedom as Participation: The Revolutionary Theories of
     Hegel and Arendt," *American Behavioral Scientist* 20, no. 4 (March–April
     1977):482.

81   "For Hegel and Arendt . . . transforming the polity."
     Ibid., 489.

V. On Human Destiny

page

88   "A finite freedom . . . destiny."
     Paul Tillich, *Systematic Theology*, vol. 2 (Chicago: University of Chicago
     Press, 1957), pp. 31–32.

88   "That hour . . . Sisyphus happy."
     Albert Camus, *"The Myth of Sisyphus" and Other Essays* (New York: Vintage,
     1955), pp. 89–91.

90   "Freedom's great emotional potency . . . Destiny herself."
     Bronislaw Malinowski, *Freedom and Civilization* (New York: Roy, 1944), p.
     24.

91   "The destiny assigned . . . to himself."
     Marcus Aurelius, *Meditations*, 3:4.

92   "Oh, if I . . . a quiet life."
     J. W. N. Sullivan, *Beethoven: His Spiritual Development* (New York: Vintage,
     1960), pp. 72–73. Sullivan continues: "It is probable that every genius of the
     first order becomes aware of this curious relation towards his own genius.
     Even the most fully conscious type of genius, the scientific genius, as Clark
     Maxwell and Einstein, reveals this feeling of being possessed. A power seizes
     them of which they are not normally aware except by obscure premonitions.
     With Beethoven, so extraordinarily creative, a state of more or less uncon-
     scious tumult must have been constant. But only when the consciously
     defiant Beethoven had succumbed, only when his pride and strength had
     been so reduced that he was willing, even eager, to die and abandon the
     struggle, did he find that his creative power was indeed indestructible and
     that it was its deathless energy that made it impossible for him to die."

92   "No man . . . his destiny."
     Homer, *Iliad*, 6:488.

93   "Our will is . . . own creation."
     Cited by Rockwell Gray, "Ortega and the Concept of Destiny," *Review of
     Existential Psychology and Psychiatry* 15, nos. 2–3 (1977):178.

94   "The huge world . . . have it so!"

page

William James, *Principles of Psychology* (New York: Dover, 1950; reprint of 1890 ed.), II, p. 578.

94 "This design . . . *are in design.*"
Gray, *op. cit.*, 141. Italics mine.

94 Pressure to deny our destiny
A friend writes to me that women have suffered greatly in their attempts to affirm their vital design or destiny. She says, "I think of the anguish in many of my women friends now liberated."

94 Leaving behind the vital design
In extreme form, these are the kind of persons Ibsen describes in his last play *When We Dead Awaken*, who ask, "When we dead awaken, what shall we see?" The answer comes back to them in many different ways, all saying the same thing: "We shall see that we have never lived."

95 "fate-will," "destiny-will."
Cited by Gray, *op. cit.*, 178.

95 "So let there be . . . our being."
Ibid., 151.

96 "Each . . . destiny."
Virgil, *Aeneid*, 6:743.

96 "Thus freedom . . . to be."
Kurt F. Reinhardt, *The Existential Revolt* (Milwaukee: Bruce, 1952), pp. 183–84. The words are Reinhardt's interpretation of Jasper's views.

96 "We are doomed . . . born."
Quoted by J. Glenn Gray in Melvyn A. Hill, ed., *Hannah Arendt: The Recovery of the Public World* (New York: St. Martin, 1979), p. 231.

96 "Man is . . . freedom."
Cited by Gray, *op. cit.*, 16.

97 "Not I . . . its way."
Quoted by E. R. Dodds, *The Greeks and the Irrational* (Berkeley: University of California Press, 1968), p. 3.

99 "O alas . . . destined for them."
Ruth Nanda Anshen, *The Reality of the Devil: Evil in Man* (New York: Harper & Row, 1972), p. v.

VI. Destiny and Death

page
103 "Man is only . . . of morality."
Blaise Pascal, *Pascal's Pensées, or Thoughts on Religion*, ed. and trans. Gertrude Burford Rawlings (Mount Vernon, N.Y.: Peter Pauper Press, 1946), p. 35.

page

104 "She will use . . . you cannot hold."
Jean Giraudoux, *Amphitryon 38* (New York: Random House, 1938), pp. 97 ff.

104 "Son of Laertes . . . by each other."
Homer, *The Odyssey*, 5:192 ff. I am grateful to Michael Platt, "Would Human Life Be Better without Death?" *Soundings: An Interdisciplinary Journal* 63, no. 3 (Fall 1980):325.

106 "I will drink . . . not to yield."
Alfred Lord Tennyson, "Ulysses," in *Tennyson's Poetry*, ed. Robert W. Hill, Jr. (New York: Norton, 1971), pp. 52–54.

107 "a new appreciation . . . I am not immortal."
Cited in I. Yalom, *Existential Psychotherapy* (New York: Basic Books, 1981), p. 35. I am indebted to Dr. Yalom for valuable insights in this whole section.

107 "The good man . . . that serves death."
Erich Fromm, *The Heart of Man: Its Genius for Good or Evil* (New York: Harper & Row, 1964), p. 47.

109 Karl Pribram
Brain neurologist Karl Pribram maintains that almost all our mental content is projected on the world, and we achieve our sense of unity with others through the canons of our culture.

110 Pope Alexander IV and the Inquisition
Alan C. Kors and Edward Peters, *Witchcraft in Europe 1100–1700: A Documentary History* (Philadelphia: University of Pennsylvania Press, 1972), p. 77.

110 "no compact . . . and the like"
Ibid., pp. 119–20.

110 "Paul reckoneth . . . with the devil."
Ibid., p. 201.

110 "Put on the whole armour . . . darkness of the world."
Ibid., p. 202.

110 "The corpses . . . in any of the food."
Ibid., p. 96.

110 "continued sterility . . . the malice of the Devil."
Ibid., p. 217.

111 "Several men . . . makes the other shiver."
Ibid., p. 364.

111 "That is why . . . to foil the witch."
Ibid.

111 "The catholic faith . . . by their works."
Ibid., p. 72.

112 "the struggle . . . Satan was sure to triumph."
Ibid., p. 95.

page
112 "concerning the witches . . . who may be standing by."
     Ibid., pp. 114 ff.
114 "an illness has been given . . . too contemplative a life."
     Ibid., p. 365.
114 "you did not put . . . in their writings."
     Ibid., p. 364.
115 "Remove this cause . . . that will be his cure."
     Ibid.
115 "a prisoner . . . of madness than of crime."
     Ibid., p. 337.
115 Grand Inquisitor and self-delusion in the persecution of witches
     Ibid., p. 340.
115 "We justly fear . . . humbly beg forgiveness."
     Ibid., pp. 358–59.
116 "trifling philosophy . . . from our flesh."
     Ibid., p. 202. The book *The Reality of the Devil* is subtitled *The Evil in Man.*
     The devil does not have to be corporeal or a "thing" to have reality; the devil
     is taken by the author, Ruth Nanda Anshen, to be the evil in human beings.
117 "Experience has taught . . . the day of success."
     Frederick D. Losey, *Shakespeare* (Philadelphia and Chicago: Winston, 1926),
     p. 970.
127 "Events will take . . . the best account."
     Euripides, *Bellerophon*, Frag. 298.
127 "This day . . . we spin."
     John Greenleaf Whittier, "The Crisis," 10.
127 "What one individual . . . may fulfill it."
     J. W. N. Sullivan, *Beethoven: His Spiritual Development* (New York: Vintage,
     1960), pp. 165–66.
128 "I must die . . . not even Zeus can conquer that."
     Cited in Hannah Arendt, *The Life of the Mind*, vol. 2, *Willing* (New York:
     Harcourt Brace Jovanovich, 1978), p. 29.
128 "From the beginning . . . no freedom of choice."
     Carl G. Jung, *Memories, Dreams, Reflections*, ed. Aniela Jaffé, trans. Richard
     and Clara Winston (New York: Pantheon, 1961), p. 48.
128 "Goethe is the man . . . problematical task."
     José Ortega y Gasset, "In Search of Goethe from Within," in *The Dehuman-
     ization of Art* (New York: Doubleday, 1956), p. 146.
129 "However much . . . troubles him."
     Ibid., p. 150.
129 "goes wandering . . . *who* to be."
     Ibid.

page

129 "Am I poet . . . harmony with myself."
Ibid., p. 154.

129 Sense of abandon
When I was in my late teens, I picked up a phrase from some long-forgotten place: "Life is a thing of cavalry, to be dashingly used and cheerfully hazarded." That seems to me to be as relevant now as it was then. Buber speaks of "going forward to meet destiny."

130 "Was the man . . . his inner destiny?"
Ortega, *op. cit.*, p. 158.

130 Genius and the difficulty of life
Many students of Goethe would be more generous in their interpretation of his life than Ortega, possibly because they did not hold such high standards as those Ortega in his essay applies to Goethe. And one might think that if one were a poet of Goethe's caliber, one ought to be satisfied with that! For example, Ortega writes: "Living is precisely the inexorable necessity to make oneself determinate, to *enter into an exclusive destiny*, to accept it—that is, to resolve to *be it. We have*, whether we like it or not, to realize our personage, our vocation, our vital program, our entelechy—there is no lack of names for the terrible reality which is our authentic I" (p. 166).

130 Life for creative people
Only rarely does a highly gifted person, like J. S. Bach, find himself in an environment in which his creativity can be completely at home.

130 "troubles and disorients . . . its axis."
Ortega, *op. cit.*, p. 160.

131 James's books
His classic was the textbook *Psychology*, then *Varieties of Religious Experience, Pragmatism, The Will to Believe, Talks to Teachers*, etc.

VII. The New Narcissism

page

136 The 1960s
During that decade I attended a hippie wedding on a plateau in the mountains at Big Sur. It seemed a re-enactment of the gypsy scene in *Carmen*. Seventy-five to a hundred young people were dressed outlandishly but colorfully, all free from clock time since they had been up all the previous night and now slept on the ground whenever they felt like it, some dancing, some sitting dreamily looking out over the vast Pacific, some passing around bread

page

and wine. But a kind of sad obbligato surrounded the whole in the presence of unattached and bewildered small children drifting about as though they had no idea who in this group their parents were. Over the whole camp there seemed to hang a palpable cloud of pervasive and profound loneliness. Whenever one looked in the eyes of a celebrant, one felt this estrangement.

Everything in this conglomerate demonstration of "freedom" was without structure, without design, without a sense of destiny. The only element of structure was the expectation that the sun would rise in the morning, when they would perform some simple marriage ceremony.

136 "the individual . . . one's fate."
Peter Marin, "The New Narcissism," *Harper's Magazine* (October 1975), p. 48.

136 "Born often . . . all about him."
Quoted in George Wilson Pierson, *Tocqueville and Beaumont in America* (New York: Oxford University Press, 1938), p. 119.

138 "free men . . . to be involved."
Harry Brown, *How I Found Freedom in an Unfree World* (New York: Hearst, 1973), p. 128.

138 "Of what importance . . . happiness for it?"
Ibid., p. 163.

138 "Liberated . . . unsatisfied desire."
Christopher Lasch, *The Culture of Narcissism* (New York: Norton, 1979), p. xvi.

141 "How to set myself . . . self mutiny."
Quoted with permission. My friend informs me that she has written a later series about community and relationships, which means that she sees the area that is lacking in the quoted verses and moves to correct the situation.

141 "I do my thing . . . it can't be helped."
Clint Weyand, *Surviving Popular Psychology* (privately published).

142 "Nothing keeps . . . are free."
Frederick Franck, *The Book of Angelus Silesius* (New York: Knopf, 1976), p. 127.

142 "Reality has come . . . are shown by cameras."
Quoted by Lasch, *op. cit.*, p. 48.

145 "Let us come . . . lie with me!"
Robert Graves, *The Greek Myths: 1* (London: Penguin, 1972), pp. 286–87.

145 Narcissus and unrequited love
According to Graves, Narcissus did recognize himself. He did "know himself" in this sense. Is this the reason narcissism leads to death?

145 "At first he tried . . . as he expired."
Graves, *op. cit.*, pp. 287–88.

VIII. Is Sex without Intimacy Freedom?

page

153 "inability to feel . . . more animated outside."
Christopher Lasch, *The Culture of Narcissism* (New York: Norton, 1979), pp. 7–8.

154 "Brigitte Bardot . . . I like that."
Paul C. Vitz, *Psychology as Religion: The Cult of Self-Worship* (Grand Rapids, Mich.: Eerdmans, 1977), p. 122.

154 Sex-without-intimacy trend
See Rollo May, *Man's Search for Himself* (New York: Norton, 1953).

154 "out of a pervasive . . . in the first place."
Lasch, *op. cit.*, p. 27. Seymour B. Sarason has written similarly: " 'Stay loose,' 'keep your options open,' 'play it cool' are cautions that emerge from the feeling that society sets all kinds of booby traps that rob you of the freedom without which growth is impossible."

154 "Our society . . . pretend to cure."
Lasch, p. 30.

154 Gay Talese
Gay Talese, *Thy Neighbor's Wife* (New York: Doubleday, 1980).

155 "alone . . . sense of hope."
Ibid., p. 343.

156 "when a woman . . . nearly two months."
Ibid., p. 541.

156 Hugh Hefner
Ibid., pp. 475–76.

157 "In times . . . confer on it."
Sigmund Freud, "On the Universal Tendency to Debasement in the Sphere of Love" (1912), in vol. XI of the *Standard Edition of the Complete Psychological Works of Sigmund Freud*, ed. and trans. James Strachey (New York: Norton, 1976), pp. 187–88.

157 "the books . . . about sex."
Joseph Adelson, *New York Times Book Review* 10 August 1980, p. 13.

158 Benjamin De Mott and self-destruct
Such books as *The New Celibacy* by Gabrielle Brown are another indication of the self-destruct.

IX. The Significance of the Pause

page
164 "Freedom is . . . nothing."
John Lilly, personal conversation.

164 "this conception . . . the zero."
Dorothy Lee, *Freedom and Culture* (Englewood Cliffs, N.J.: Prentice-Hall, 1959), p. 55.

165 "We put thirty . . . makes it useful."
Lao Tzu, *Tao Teh Ching*, trans. John Wu (Jamaica, N.Y.: St. John's University Press, 1961).

165 Luther Standing Bear's and Modupe's childhood
Lee, *op. cit.*, p. 56.

166 Nō drama
Ibid.

173 "We poets . . . our knock."
Archibald MacLeish, *Poetry and Experience* (Boston: Houghton Mifflin, 1961), pp. 8–9. I have quoted this in *The Courage to Create* (New York: Norton, 1975), p. 79. I refer the reader to that book for a longer and more thorough discussion of creativity and the pause.

176 "Does this version . . . to creativity."
Lee, *op. cit.*, p. 58. Italics mine.

177 Psyche and ego
The nature of the self is crucial to any theory of personal freedom. No more persuasive demonstration of this is needed than the fact that writers on freedom, even when they are not psychologists, almost always conclude with a doctrine of the self. Mortimer Adler, in *The Idea of Freedom*, which he edited, ends the book with a discussion of the self. Christian Bay, in *The Structure of Freedom*, likewise spends a good deal of time on the self. Like the other two in that he is not a psychologist, Fritjof Bergmann, in *On Being Free*, is as aware as the others that there is no proper understanding of freedom that does not rest on the self.

178 "analysis does not . . . or the other."
Sigmund Freud, *The Ego and the Id*, Standard Ed., trans. Joan Riviere (New York: Norton, 1962), p. 40.

181 "No drives . . . *a free man.*"
Quoted in *Psychology Today* (March 1977), p. 88.

182 "The feeling . . . is the mystical."
Ludwig Wittgenstein, *Tractatus Logico-Philosophicus*, trans. D. F. Pears and B. F. McGuinness (London: Routledge & Kegan Paul, 1961), p. xxi.

182 "There are . . . what is mystical."
Ibid., p. 73.

page
183 "If we take . . . in the present."
   Ibid., p. 72.
183 "Sweet sounds . . . the world again."
   In Louis Untermeyer, *A Treasury of Great Poems* (New York: Simon and
   Schuster, 1955), p. 1166.
184 "What we cannot . . . in silence."
   Wittgenstein, *op. cit.*, p. 74.

X. The Dizziness of Freedom

page
185 Anxiety
   All of these emotions—wonder, awe, dread, fear—have anxiety within
   them.
193 "How terrible . . . sorrow."
   Sophocles, *Oedipus Tyrannus*, in *Dramas*, trans. Sir George Young (New
   York: Dutton).
194 "joy and woe."
   This is from a phrase in a poem by William Blake:
   Joy and woe
   Joy and woe
   If this we surely know
   Safely through the world we go.
195 "Consider . . . into human psychology."
   Irvin Child, *Humanistic Psychology and the Research Tradition: Their Several Vir-
   tues* (New York: Wiley, 1973), p. 176.
196 "will not solve . . . the environment."
   B. F. Skinner, *Beyond Freedom and Dignity* (New York: Knopf, 1971), p. 22.
   But how can "environment" be "responsible"? The logic is faulty.
196 "can be held . . . he does."
   Skinner, *op. cit.*, p. 17.
196 "A scientific analysis . . . to the environment."
   Ibid., p. 19.
196 "accept the fact . . . of better men."
   Ibid., p. 77.
197 "autonomous man . . . powers"
   Ibid., p. 86.
197 "A scientific analysis . . . by other men."
   Ibid., p. 196.

page
201 "there was nothing . . . the whole world."
Roger Urich, "Some Thoughts on Human Nature and Its Control," *Journal of Humanistic Psychology* 19 (1979):39.

XI. *Freedom and Destiny in Illness and Health*

page
205 "No improvement . . . well-being."
Quoted in Norman Cousins, *Anatomy of an Illness* (New York: Norton, 1979), p. 22.

205 "Recovery . . . resistance to disease."
Ibid., p. 16.

205 "*vis medicatrix naturae.*"
Ibid., p. 15.

205 The healing power of nature
When I was in bed for several years with tuberculosis, before there were any drugs for treating the disease, I made a similar and very important discovery. As long as I gave myself over to the physicians, trying only to follow their suggestions at every point in rest and exercise, I did not show any improvement. But when I realized that the bacilli were in *me*, not my doctors, and that the physicians knew very little about the disease (which they were the first to admit), I saw that I would have to take responsibility for my cure. This meant experiencing more personal anxiety and more guilt feelings since I had to acknowledge that my own previous style of life was a central cause of my coming down with the disease in the first place. But admitting this was surely a boon to my health. I then instituted a program for myself. I learned to listen to my body, to rest when I needed rest, to exercise when I felt the strength to do so. I learned to use, and rightly so, the active voice in the words about illness: we "cure" rather than "we are cured." I then began to get better. My engaging destiny directly increased my freedom to become healthy again.

205 "Feisty . . . women."
Leonard R. Derogatis, "Psychological Coping Mechanisms and Survival Time in Metastatic Breast Cancer," *JAMA* 242 (1979).

206 "They were going . . . fighting the disease."
Ibid.

206 "If negative emotions . . . have therapeutic value?"
Cousins, *op. cit.*, pp. 34–35.

207 "when I decided . . . beginning of the end."
Ibid., p. 160.

page
207   "Talk of enemies . . . than practical ones."
        Ibid., p. 123.
214   "Physicians must . . . abolish disease."
        R. R. Rynearson, "Touching People," *J. Clin. Psych.* 39 (1978):492.
215   "I was better . . . my life."
        Marguerite Yourcenar, *Memoirs of Hadrian* (New York: Farrar, Straus &
        Young, 1954), p. 252.

XII. *The Renewal of Life*

page
220   "Man is spirit . . . and necessity."
        Sören Kierkegaard, *"Fear and Trembling" and "Sickness unto Death"* (New
        York: Doubleday, 1954), p. 146. Where Kierkegaard says "necessity," I
        would use "destiny."
221   "Nature commands . . . soul is shown."
        Quoted by Noam Chomsky, *For Reasons of State* (New York: Vintage, 1973),
        p. 391.
221   "For fate . . . natural laws."
        Johann Wolfgang von Goethe, *Faust* (Baltimore: Penguin, 1949), p. 92.
222   "Mere purposive rationality . . . has an effective voice."
        Gregory Bateson, *Steps to an Ecology of Mind* (New York: Ballantine, 1972),
        pp. 146–47.
223   "the human spirit . . . grows and flourishes."
        Raymond Bernard Blakney, *Meister Ekhart* (New York: Harper & Bros.,
        1941), p. 192.
223   "the spirit . . . achieves unity and freedom."
        Ibid., pp. 192–93.
223   "Rather, he sets . . . true freedom itself."
        Ibid., p. 193.
223   "Your intentions . . . free."
        Ibid.
223   "For Boehme. . . . The fire is will."
        Nikolai Berdyayev, Introduction to Jacob Boehme, *Six Theosophic Points* (Ann
        Arbor: University of Michigan Press, 1958), p. xiv.
223   "According . . . all things."
        Ibid., p. xx.
223   "Freedom . . . all nature."
        Ibid., p. xxi.

223 "Boehme . . . than God himself."
Ibid., p. xxiii.

223 The wrath and love of God
Compare this to the Chinese concept that one must go through anger and
rage if one is to experience joy. (See p. 45).

224 "We must salute . . . true Christian philosophy."
Berdyayev, *op. cit.*, p. xxxii.

224 Placebos as tangible patterns
This reminds me of one lengthy reading I had of my astrological chart by a
Hindu astrologer. I have never been able to "believe" in astrology nor to
"disbelieve" in it. But this stranger, who apparently had not even known my
name or anything about me, came up with a number of amazing insights
that there seemed no rational way he could have discovered. Impressed, I
accused him of being a psychic. But he smilingly shook his head and said he
preferred to think of his insights as simply coming from a reading of the
stars.

225 "the tendency . . . one's self."
Quoted by Chomsky, *op. cit.*, p. xl.

228 "God allowed evil . . . in overcoming it."
Cited by Ruth Nanda Anshen, *The Reality of the Devil: Evil in Man* (New
York: Harper & Row, 1972), p. v.

228 "God is . . . an earthquake."
Frederick Franck, *The Book of Angelus Silesius* (New York: Knopf, 1976).

229 "A Dialogue of Self and Soul"
W. B. Yeats, *The Collected Poems of W. B. Yeats* (New York: Macmillan, 1956),
pp. 231–32.

230 Compassion
Donald N. Michael, "Industrial Society Today and Tomorrow," *World
Future Society Bulletin* 13 (1979).

232 "Unaided consciousness . . . plague the inventor."
Bateson, *op. cit.*, p. 146.

232 "pliable . . . error on that."
Blaise Pascal, *Pascal's Pensées, or Thoughts on Religion*, ed. and trans. Gertrude
Burford Rawlings (Mount Vernon, N.Y.: Peter Pauper Press, 1946), p. 38.

XIII. Despair and Joy

237 "There once was . . . 'I don't care.' "
Limerick by Tom Greening.

262   Notes

page

238   "despair . . . than himself."
Sören Kierkegaard, *Sickness unto Death*, trans. Walter Lowrie (New York: Doubleday, 1954), p. 186. This book is, in my judgment, the best psychological study of despair.

238   "Man when he . . . repeated by rote."
Sören Kierkegaard, *The Concept of Dread*, trans. Walter Lowrie (Princeton, N.J.: Princeton University Press, 1944), p. 85.

238   "Despair . . . as spirit."
Kierkegaard, *Sickness unto Death*, op. cit., p. 150. Italics mine.

238   "thing of despairing . . . could not despair."
Ibid., p. 149.

238   "a long time . . . deep-bosomed daughter."
Cited by Robert May, *Sex and Fantasy* (New York: Norton, 1980), pp. 7–13.

238   "But this small flaw . . . leaves and flowers."
Ibid., pp. 9–10.

238   "earth's period of barrenness . . . fruit and flowers."
Ibid., p. 13.

238   "pain followed by joy . . . winter followed by spring."
Ibid.

240   "Out of such abysses . . . has ever seen before."
Friedrich Nietzsche, *The Gay Science*, trans. W. Kaufman (New York: Random House, 1974), p. 37.

241   "endure the pains . . . hid in His joy."
Walter Hylton, cited by Frederick Spiegelberg, *The Religion of No Religion* (Stanford, Calif.: Delkin, 1953), p. 51.

Index

263